Developing Intercı
Perspectives on
Language Use

CW01011291

LANGUAGES FOR INTERCULTURAL COMMUNICATION AND EDUCATION

Series Editors: Michael Byram, *University of Durham, UK* and Anthony J. Liddicoat, *University of Warwick, UK*

The overall aim of this series is to publish books which will ultimately inform learning and teaching, but whose primary focus is on the analysis of intercultural relationships, whether in textual form or in people's experience. There will also be books which deal directly with pedagogy, with the relationships between language learning and cultural learning, between processes inside the classroom and beyond. They will all have in common a concern with the relationship between language and culture, and the development of intercultural communicative competence.

Full details of all the books in this series and of all our other publications can be found on http://www.multilingual-matters.com, or by writing to Multilingual Matters, St Nicholas House, 31–34 High Street, Bristol BS1 2AW, UK.

LANGUAGES FOR INTERCULTURAL COMMUNICATION
AND EDUCATION: 33

Developing Intercultural Perspectives on Language Use

Exploring Pragmatics and Culture in Foreign Language Learning

Troy McConachy

MULTILINGUAL MATTERS
Bristol • Blue Ridge Summit

DOI https://doi.org/10.21832/MCCONA9320

Library of Congress Cataloging in Publication Data
Names: McConachy, Troy, 1980- author.
Title: Developing Intercultural Perspectives on Language Use: Exploring
    Pragmatics and Culture in Foreign Language Learning/Troy McConachy.
Description: Bristol; Blue Ridge Summit: Multilingual Matters, [2018] |
    Series: Languages for Intercultural Communication and Education: 33 |
    Includes bibliographical references and index.
Identifiers: LCCN 2017035524| ISBN 9781783099320 (hbk : alk. paper) | ISBN
    9781783099313 (pbk : alk. paper) | ISBN 9781783099351 (Kindle)
Subjects: LCSH: Language and languages—Study and teaching. | Intercultural
    communication—Study and teaching. | Language and culture—Study and
    teaching. | Multicultural education.
Classification: LCC P53.45 .M395 2018 | DDC 418.0071—dc23 LC record available at
    https://lccn.loc.gov/2017035524

British Library Cataloguing in Publication Data
A catalogue entry for this book is available from the British Library.

ISBN-13: 978-1-78309-932-0 (hbk)
ISBN-13: 978-1-78309-931-3 (pbk)

Multilingual Matters
UK: St Nicholas House, 31–34 High Street, Bristol, BS1 2AW, UK.
USA: NBN, Blue Ridge Summit, PA, USA.

Website: www.multilingual-matters.com
Twitter: Multi_Ling_Mat
Facebook: https://www.facebook.com/multilingualmatters
Blog: www.channelviewpublications.wordpress.com

The policy of Multilingual Matters/Channel View Publications is to use papers that are
natural, renewable and recyclable products, made from wood grown in sustainable for-
ests. In the manufacturing process of our books, and to further support our policy, preference is given to printers that have FSC and PEFC Chain of Custody certification. The FSC
and/or PEFC logos will appear on those books where full certification has been granted
to the printer concerned.

Typeset by Nova Techset Private Limited, Bengaluru & Chennai, India. Printed and
bound in the UK by CPI Group (UK) Ltd, Croydon, CR0 4YY
Printed and bound in the US by Edwards Brothers Malloy, Inc.

Contents

Figures and Tables

Figures

Table

Acknowledgements

I've been fortunate to receive support and inspiration from many great people in the conceptualisation and production of this book.

First of all, I would like to thank Tony Liddicoat and Angela Scarino, who supported the original thesis from which this book derives. There aren't really words to express the thanks, respect, and admiration I have for you both.

I would also like to extend my thanks to colleagues in the Centre for Applied Linguistics at University of Warwick who offered encouragement or academic suggestions in the course of writing, particularly Helen Spencer-Oatey and Ema Ushioda. Thanks also to Annamaria Pinter for supporting my transition to work at Warwick after many years in Japan.

I'd like to express my gratitude to the series editors for allowing me to contribute this book to the series, and also to the friendly and efficient staff at Multilingual Matters for their professionalism.

A big thanks goes to my parents for their ceaseless encouragement, and also to my karate instructor in Japan – Shinji Adachi – who directly and indirectly taught me a lot about culture and life.

Any issues or errors with the book are my own responsibility.

Introduction

> Communication in today's world *requires* culture. Problems in communi-
> cation are rooted in *who you are*, in encounters with a *different mentality,
> different meanings*, a *different tie* between language and consciousness.
> Solving the problems inspired by such encounters inspires culture. (Agar,
> 1994: 23, italics in original)

As Agar (1994) intimated more than 20 years ago, we would be well advised
to recognize the complex ways in which culture is embedded in the fabric of
our communication and the implications that this has for interaction with
others in the current world. In recent years the popularization of tools for
online communication, the global spread of business activities and the surge
in interactions among people from around the world have spurred interest in
both academic and non-academic circles as to the nature of intercultural
communication and the consequences it has for our lives. Intercultural communication these days is an extremely vibrant and complex phenomenon.
Speakers from a wide variety of linguistic and cultural backgrounds use foreign languages to negotiate meanings and interpersonal relationships with
others, drawing on cultural assumptions and world knowledge sourced from
diverse contexts in the process. This means that the ways in which speakers
use language for communicative purposes are also diverse, contextually contingent and subject to change over time. For some, such a picture of intercultural communication conjures up images of insurmountable differences and
inevitable conflict. For others, it presents the possibility for individuals to
draw on their common humanity and goodwill to promote cooperative dialogue and deepen intercultural understanding.

   As one field which is particularly invested in (and responsible for) the
promotion of felicitous intercultural communication, foreign language teaching is faced with the question of how classroom learning experiences can be
designed to prepare learners for interacting with individuals from a wide
range of cultural backgrounds, including but not limited to native speakers
of the language. This book takes the position that developing the ability to
successfully manage interactions and relationships through the medium of a
foreign language goes far beyond the acquisition of linguistic skills. It requires
the cultivation of a perspective which recognizes the potential for diverse

norms, assumptions and values to influence the ways in which language is used and interpreted as a form of social action. This is not a matter of internalizing stereotypes about foreign 'communication styles', but rather requires a reflective and analytical engagement with how culture shapes meaning-making processes in interaction. This is something that can be fostered in the language classroom.

Intercultural Learning and the Role of Language

There have been many voices over the years emphasizing the importance of integrating language and culture study in the language classroom, often with the aim of developing learners' intercultural competence (e.g. Beacco, 2004; Byram, 1991, 1997; Damen, 1987; Díaz, 2013; Díaz & Dasli, 2017; Hinkel, 1999; Kramsch, 1993; Lange & Paige, 2003; Liddicoat & Scarino, 2013; Risager, 2007). However, despite the often-repeated notion that language and culture are inseparable, language learning curricula and materials predominantly present culture in terms of non-linguistic products and practices, such as popular foods, traditional clothing and unique festivals, as well as demographic facts and historical events of nations in which the target language is spoken. For language teachers, it can be difficult to see how attention to culture might fit in with the goal of developing learners' ability to use the target language. This can be traced to the fact that as a field we have generally struggled to articulate a view of language that conveys the centrality of culture to how linguistic meanings are constructed and interpreted (c.f. Díaz, 2013). Relatedly, we have also struggled to articulate a clear relationship between the development of communicative abilities in the target language and the development of intercultural competence. This kind of theoretical synthesis is challenging, given that the field of linguistics (which has primarily informed language teaching) has often excluded the concept of culture from its concerns, and theorizing on intercultural competence has generally failed to discuss the role of language effectively (Dervin & Liddicoat, 2013).

Most models of intercultural competence derive from the field of cross-cultural psychology and tend to give emphasis to psychological attributes such as mindfulness, anxiety management, empathy, perspective-taking, tolerance, and non-judgemental attitudes towards foreign cultures (see Deardorff, 2009; Spencer-Oatey & Franklin, 2009, for good overviews). In broad terms, what is most important from this perspective is the attributes that help individuals psychologically engage with and adapt to cultural difference, while gradually moving away from ethnocentric judgements of self and other (Bennett, 1993). However, any understanding of intercultural competence needs to be able to account not only for psychological attributes and attitudinal shift but also for the specific aspects of culture in relation to which these attributes should be applied. For instance, when theorists claim that individuals should aim to cultivate non-judgemental attitudes to cultural difference, do they mean that individuals should be non-judgemental about everything that might be called 'culture'? If not, what do they mean? If intercultural communicators should exercise 'mindfulness', what do they need to be mindful of specifically? In order to develop intercultural competence, whether in language teaching or intercultural training contexts, practitioners need an idea of the cultural phenomena in relation to which learners should hone their abilities. Without this, it is difficult to construct content for intercultural learning and foster learners' interpretive and reflective engagement with cultural and intercultural phenomena.

Due to disciplinary imperatives, models of intercultural competence developed in psychology have remained primarily within the mind. Consequently, they have had less to say about the nature of culture as an entity, especially the interrelationships between language and culture that become important in intercultural communication (Dervin & Liddicoat, 2013). Although some models do discuss the need to be aware of cultural differences in communication, as Spencer-Oatey (2010) points out, the object of awareness is typically limited to general tendencies towards directness or indirectness in communication which are purported to derive from high-context/low-context communication styles (Hall, 1974; Cardon, 2008, for a critical review). Such a framing remains abstract due to lack of reference 'to a theory of semiosis or, more specifically, a theory of language as a social-semiotic practice' (Warner, 2011: 13). In other words, the operationalization of communication in terms of communication style fails to capture the complex ways in which we use language to carry out a range of social acts and dynamically shape our messages in coordination with interlocutors based on ongoing consideration of contextual variables.

Meanwhile, in the field of language teaching there has been extensive conceptual and theoretical discussion around the notion of intercultural competence and how it might be developed in classrooms (e.g. Baker, 2009, 2011; Byram, 1997, 2008; Corbett, 2003; Dervin & Gross, 2016; Dervin & Liddicoat, 2013; Díaz, 2013; Hinkel, 1999; Kearney, 2016; Kramsch, 1993; Liddicoat & Scarino, 2013; O'Dowd, 2007; Risager, 2007). At present, Byram's (1997) model is the most well-known and influential attempt to theorize intercultural competence specifically for the purposes of language teaching and learning. This model recognizes that, although language learners aim to develop a communicative repertoire in the foreign language, this does not necessarily signify a desire or need to conform to second language (L2) norms at all times. Centred on the notion of the 'intercultural speaker', the emphasis is on developing the ability to 'manage interaction across cultural boundaries, to anticipate misunderstandings caused by difference in values, meanings and beliefs, and ... to cope with the affective as well as cognitive demands of engagement with otherness' (Byram, 1995: 25). Byram (1997) aims to bring together the notion of communicative competence and the notion of intercultural competence and place them within a single model for the development of what he calls intercultural communicative competence. Within the model, communicative competence is understood as consisting of linguistic competence, sociolinguistic competence and discourse competence. Meanwhile, intercultural competence is positioned as a separate construct consisting of cultural knowledge, skills of interaction and discovery, skills of interpreting and relating, attitudes of relativizing self and valuing others, and critical cultural awareness (principled evaluation).

One of the main strengths of this model is that it highlights the interactive and interpretive nature of intercultural competence – intercultural competence is instantiated in particular practices. Individuals utilize their cultural knowledge to engage in dialogue across cultural boundaries, drawing connections between behaviours and meanings situated in diverse cultural frameworks and developing their capacities for careful and reflective judgement. As has been critiqued by others (e.g. Byram, 2009; Díaz, 2013), the main limitation of the model is the theoretical separation between communicative competence and intercultural competence. Although a complementary relationship is implied, the question remains as to how the knowledge, skills and attitudes comprising intercultural competence might relate to the development of the learner's communicative ability in the target language. This may lead some to view intercultural competence as something to be developed after the learner's communicative competence has reached a certain level rather than being central to the language learning endeavour from the beginning.

More recently, Baker (2011, 2015) has articulated the notion of 'intercultural awareness' as a way of capturing the knowledge, skills and attitudes to be developed in language learning for intercultural communication. He defines intercultural awareness as follows:

> Intercultural awareness is a conscious understanding of the role culturally based forms, practices and frames of understanding can have in intercultural communication, and an ability to put these conceptions into practice in a flexible and context specific manner in real time communication. (Baker, 2011: 202)

This notion of understanding culturally based frames of understanding is not limited to awareness of L2 norms but is a more general awareness of the ways in which individuals inevitably draw on conscious and unconscious assumptions and expectations within the process of communication. This stems from the premise that when speakers from different cultural backgrounds interact with one another in a particular language, the norms and assumptions that shape that interaction are not only pre-existing but are also created dynamically within and across interactions among particular speakers. That is, speakers in intercultural communication necessarily accommodate to each other and, through a process of negotiation, come to establish consistent frames of reference and common ground that sustain communication (Kecskes, 2014). This represents an important shift away from static views of intercultural communication in which individuals instantiate culturally determined 'communication styles' (Dervin, 2011; Holliday, 2010; McConachy & Hata, 2013). In Baker's (2011) conception, it is important for language learners to develop awareness of specific cultural differences and also the ways in which the cultural knowledge of conversational participants is mobilized and negotiated in a dynamic sense-making process. In other words, the influences of culture should be viewed from both the perspectives of fixity and fluidity. It is valuable that this work draws attention to the fact that there is a variety of cultural frames of understanding at work in the process of intercultural communication and also in language learning. It is also valuable that it highlights the potential for individuals to construct norms for interaction and understanding within the process of communication. However, as in other models, further specification is required regarding the nature of the cultural frames of understanding that learners should become aware of and, in particular, how cultural frames of understanding influence the meanings and values that are ascribed to features of spoken communication.

In terms of making intercultural learning an integral part of the language learning process, the important issue for language teachers and researchers is not how culture relates to 'language' per se, but how culture relates to 'linguistic meaning-making' – to discourse (e.g. Dervin & Liddicoat, 2013; Kearney, 2016; Kramsch, 1993, 2009; Liddicoat & Scarino, 2013; Risager, 2007). Culture influences the ways in which individuals carry out specific communicative acts such as requests, apologies, compliments, invitations, etc., and also the ways in which individuals interpret the performance of these acts within interaction in terms of politeness, friendliness, arrogance, and a wide range of other interpersonal attributions (Liddicoat, 2006; Meier, 2003; Spencer-Oatey, 2008). How, then, can the learner's developing insight into the impact of culturally based frames of understanding on interpretation of such aspects of language constitute a form of intercultural awareness? How can we theorize the nature of intercultural learning that occurs as language learners begin to reflect on specific aspects of language use in context and view the interpretation of meaning from multiple perspectives? It will be argued in this book that reflection on language use provides opportunities for coming to see language not just as a code, but as a culturally interpreted form of social action. I, therefore, extensively illustrate and discuss the interpretive and reflective processes by which learners construct such a perspective on language use.

The Notion of Intercultural Perspective on Language Use

As one way of capturing the language learner's growing awareness of the various ways in which aspects of language use are interpreted and evaluated according to culturally constituted assumptions and values, in this book I develop the notion of 'intercultural perspective on language use'. This notion of intercultural perspective on language use starts from the premise that language is best viewed not primarily as a code but as a form of cultural behaviour which emerges out of, and is continually shaped by, humans' broader attempts to negotiate the structures, meanings and values of the social world within and across social groups (Duranti, 1997; Geertz, 1973). The communicative patterns within particular languages can be seen as a complex representation of the various pathways for meaning established by and for social groups to deal with everyday life and to attribute a sense of purpose to phenomena, people and events (D'Andrade, 1984; Fantini, 1995; Strauss & Quinn, 1997). Each language provides conventions for carrying out concrete social acts, such as requests, apologies, compliments, etc., and these acts are interpreted with reference to socioculturally constituted norms, frames of reference, assumptions and values (Hanks, 1996; Hymes, 1972). Speakers of a particular language interpret the social meanings and appropriateness of ways of carrying out linguistic behaviours by drawing on culturally derived assumptions about sociocultural factors such as interactional setting, age, gender and power, as well as more abstract norms which relate to the rights and responsibilities of individuals within social and interpersonal roles and relationships (Blum-Kulka et al., 1989; House-Edmonson, 1986; Kasper & Schmidt, 1996). Culture constitutes a resource which individuals use to interpret language use as socially meaningful. However, as people approach events and activities from different positions in the social structure and from a different background stock of knowledge and experiences, divergence in interpretation is an inevitable part of communication (Kramsch, 2009). Therefore, in this book, culture is not seen as a monolithic entity but as a semiotically encoded framework which individuals use for negotiating interpretations of social actions with others in an ongoing fashion (Geertz, 1973). This opens up scope for understanding the dynamic ways in which language learners utilize cultural understandings drawn from one language for interpreting language forms and meanings in another.

Indeed, language learning is a dynamic process by which learners come to interpret new linguistic forms and practices, while reflecting on how languages work to construct social meanings. The conventionalized patterns of use within the foreign language present to the learner the opportunity to explore new ways of viewing the world, and new ways of constructing the self and others while carrying out communicative acts which build and maintain interpersonal relationships (Kramsch, 2009). Such exploration requires engagement with potentially different assumptions about the nature of relationships and the ways in which perceptions of rights and obligations in particular relational and sociocultural contexts bear influence on how language is used and interpreted within communication (Spencer-Oatey, 2008). At the same time, as Byram (1991) rightly emphasizes, it is meaningless to pretend that the learner is *tabula rasa*. Language learners bring with them particular cultural schemas, assumptions about social relationships, and repertoires for interpreting interpersonal behaviour which have been developed through a history of life experiences in previously acquired languages (Kecskes, 2014). Importantly, learners will have (sometimes stereotypical) perceptions of L2 speakers and foreign cultures that mediate the attribution of meaning. The language learning process is thus one which is centred on complex processes of interpretation right from the beginning (Liddicoat & Scarino, 2013).

As an interpretive process, language learning involves exploring new ways of communicating while reflecting on one's own assumptions, testing out the extent to which they might work within contexts of L2 use, and then revising and reconstructing them as necessary. This does not mean that learners necessarily conform to the range of pre-established communicative patterns or frames of interpretation prevalent in the target language. Language learning is an inherently synergistic affair whereby new interactional patterns, new ways of communicating, new meanings, and new frames of interpretation are constructed by the learner as they learn and use the language for communicative purposes (Kramsch, 2009). Such a constructivist view of the intercultural in foreign language learning foregrounds the importance of the learner's ability to direct close attention to how language is used in context, to reflect on what one has observed and experienced within interactions, to compare what has been observed with what one already knows, and to develop the capacities for viewing the exchange of meanings from multiple perspectives (Liddicoat & Scarino, 2013). The notion of 'intercultural perspective on language use' is intended to capture a learner's emerging capacity for paying close attention to how language is used in context, reflecting on the construction of meaning from multiple (and conflicting) perspectives, and developing insight into the influence of cultural assumptions and frames of understanding on communication.

The development of an intercultural perspective on language use hinges very much on whether the learner is willing and able to suspend taken-for-granted perceptions and open up to other ways of seeing. An intercultural perspective on language use, therefore, necessarily embodies a strong reflexive orientation (Byram *et al.*, 2001; Dervin & Liddicoat, 2013; Díaz, 2013; Kramsch, 1993, 2009; Liddicoat & Scarino, 2013; Risager, 2007; Warner, 2009). It is not enough for learners to gaze at others. An intercultural perspective implies that an individual develops the ability to reflect on his or her own taken-for-granted assumptions about how language should be used, such as what is considered appropriate language use in particular situations and relationships, and then contextualize them against different assumptions applied to the same situation. The notion of 'perspective', therefore, does not imply a static way of seeing but a flexible lens for approaching the interpretation of language use which enables the individual to be mindful of the ever-present impact of cultural assumptions on how individuals interpret and evaluate each other in interaction.

From a teaching perspective, helping learners develop an intercultural perspective on language use is not primarily a matter of trying to present learners with a stereotypical body of knowledge about native speakers of the target language. It can be seen more as a process of socializing learners into the practice of looking at aspects of language use in the first language (L1) and L2 as a form of social action, interpreting the significance of linguistic choices from multiple perspectives, reflecting on interpretations with peers, and considering the nature of one's continually developing frames of interpretation and interactional repertoire as applied to a range of contexts and purposes. While this might sound like a daunting task for teachers, this book will aim to show that guiding learners in meaningful processes of reflection on language use can be achieved even with relatively conventional materials and questioning strategies that can be strategically deployed. Importantly, classroom learning activities aimed at developing intercultural perspectives on language use do not always need to involve explicit reference to other national cultures. For example, creating opportunities for learners to reflect on aspects of L1 communication in a range of contexts and to develop awareness of taken-for-granted assumptions in communication is a highly meaningful activity in terms of contributing to the development of intercultural perspectives. Not every aspect of learning needs to be about 'foreign' things in order to be conducive to the development of intercultural perspectives. This is a key point which will be illustrated in various ways throughout the book.

Pragmatics as a Resource for Developing Intercultural Perspectives

As a theoretical resource for articulating the notion of intercultural perspectives on language use in this book, I draw on work in the field of pragmatics and aim to fuse it with work from intercultural communication theory and social psychology. Pragmatics is chiefly concerned with the issue of meaning – how it is constructed and interpreted – and how individuals use language as a tool for managing their social relationships (Lo Castro, 2012; Spencer-Oatey, 2008). Research in this field has thus produced a range of insights into how individuals carry out social acts in their communication that have then informed foreign language teaching and learning. One of the significant ways in which pragmatics has influenced language teaching is that it has led language teachers to develop deeper awareness of the many different things that humans do with language in communication. This has translated into the teaching of common speech acts such as requests, apologies, compliments, complaints, etc., as well as many other pragmatic and discoursal features of language use (e.g. Alcón Soler & Martínez-Flor, 2008; Bardovi-Harlig *et al.*, 1991; Ishihara & Cohen, 2010; Kasper & Rose, 2001; Rose, 2005; Taguchi, 2015, and many more). Importantly, the presence of pragmatics in the communicative language curriculum has led to increased attention to notions of appropriate communication and some of the specific communicative norms that exist in particular languages.

However, despite increased emphasis on language use as a form of social action within communicatively oriented language teaching, the influence of culture on language use has been somewhat neglected. Awareness of pragmatic norms, typically expressed through the notion of pragmatic awareness, has been treated as a matter of whether learners are able to effectively recognize conventional mappings of form, function and context in the target language (Schmidt, 1993). That is, the emphasis has been on whether learners know which forms to select in order to carry out a particular speech act depending on to whom one is talking. Such a framing has led to relative lack of attention to how culture informs judgements about the appropriateness of linguistic forms when used in particular sociocultural and relational contexts. Meier (1999, 2003, 2010, 2015) is one author who has consistently advocated the need to more clearly bring together pragmatics and culture in pedagogy, but implementation has been hampered due to the difficulty in making the relationship between language and culture accessible to learners. Culture is clearly not an easy notion to deal with, particularly if it is seen as something that needs to be 'taught' in terms of rules or formulae.

In this book I offer a reconceptualization of the notion of pragmatic awareness and explain its relevance to the development of intercultural perspectives on language use in the language classroom. A core part of this reconceptualization involves renewed emphasis on the learner's awareness of their L1 (and any other previously acquired languages) and how culturally based assumptions about language use drawn from multiple languages influence the process of learning. It is important to point out that this book does not purport to offer a new 'method' or 'bag of tricks' for teaching pragmatics. In fact, one of the main aims of this book is to show that, although many teachers might feel overwhelmed by the idea of dealing with culture, it is possible to create opportunities for meaningful learning even with conventional materials such as coursebooks and by guiding language learners to analyze and reflect on their own interactional experiences inside and outside the classroom. In order to achieve this aim, I present data from a case study of the intercultural language learning of four learners of English taught by the author during a 10-week communicative English course at a study-abroad preparation institute in Tokyo, Japan. I show how making language use an object of analysis and reflection within collaborative activities leads learners to interpret and evaluate aspects of language use in insightful ways, exploring multiple ways of construing individual utterances and multiple-turn discourse while developing awareness of the (often unacknowledged) influence of cultural assumptions on one's own perceptions. The emphasis in this book, thus, is on how taking an interpretive orientation to commonplace resources for learning can create opportunities for intercultural learning.

Outline of the Book

In order to lay the theoretical groundwork for the analysis of learning through reflection on pragmatics, Chapter 1 of this book examines important issues related to the conceptualization and treatment of the links between spoken language and culture within communicative language teaching (CLT). This includes an analysis of how culture has come to be sidelined in CLT despite the fact that the cornerstone notion of CLT – communicative competence – is theoretically predicated on a strong relationship between communication and culture. This chapter will then go on to look at how the narrow approach to pragmatic awareness within language teaching has created barriers to facilitating intercultural learning through pragmatics in the classroom. Chapter 2 synthesizes concepts and theories from the fields of meta-pragmatics, interpersonal and intercultural pragmatics, and social psychology to develop a renewed notion of pragmatic awareness useful for the teaching of languages for intercultural communication. It also situates the development of pragmatic awareness within an intercultural orientation to language learning and explains the methodological approach taken in this study. Chapter 3 focuses on how language learners engage with scripted interactions from commercial textbooks and teacher-constructed dialogues to analyze aspects of language use with reference to sociocultural context and to justify their own interpretations with increasing specificity. Chapter 4 examines the role of reflection on interactional experiences outside the classroom and the role of what I call 'experience talk' in collaborative reflection on these interactional experiences. I show how the use of classroom talk to construct accounts of previous interactional experiences generates opportunities for learners to interrogate interpretation of events and pay renewed attention to the foundation of their evaluations of interlocutors. Chapter 5 then looks at how observation and reflection based on role-play activities provide opportunities for exploring meaning-making processes and reflects on options for constructing meanings and impressions in the L2. Chapter 6 pulls together the discussion of the main points raised throughout the book and articulates the broader implications of this study for the development of intercultural perspectives on language use within foreign language learning.

1 Pragmatics and Culture in Communicative Language Teaching

Introduction

Since the communicative turn in foreign language teaching, one of the biggest classroom aims (and difficulties) has been to teach language as a dynamic system of meaning potential rather than simply as a structural system. To teach 'meaning' is an incredibly complex affair in many respects. Within the context of communication, meaning is something which must ultimately be constructed by individuals as they pay close attention to each other's verbal and non-verbal cues and mobilize background knowledge and assumptions to interpret utterances within the flow of discourse. Moreover, such interpretation must take into account the sociocultural context in which utterances are exchanged, including the relationships between participants and what is being conveyed, not simply in terms of information but also in terms of the identities of the speakers and their social positioning vis-à-vis one another (Kramsch, 2009). The situation is even more complex in the case of intercultural communication, as ways of reading sociocultural context and the weighting given to particular aspects of context can be interpreted very differently, as can ideas about how speakers are expected to behave in view of their social and interpersonal roles (Spencer Oatey, 2008). Language learners, too, are actively engaged in interpretative processes right from the beginning of learning. Learners engage with the foreign language on the basis of existing assumptions about the nature of the social world, the way individuals interact in a range of social and interpersonal contexts, and what communicative behaviours are considered preferable over others. Within the foreign language classroom there is much potential for promoting intercultural learning by drawing attention to the ways in which participants in interaction, including learners themselves, construct and interpret meanings. However, whether this potential is realized or not is ultimately dependent on how the links between language and culture, as well as the learners' awareness of these links, are conceptualized. This chapter will focus on the conceptualization of these links within communicative language teaching (CLT) and discuss the ways in which views of pragmatic awareness dominant in the field have constrained the potential for intercultural learning.

The Place of Culture in the Communicative Turn

CLT has been strongly predicated on the existence of a close relationship between language and culture since its inception, although this relationship has not necessarily been well articulated within classroom practice. The influential work done on the ethnography of speaking in anthropology (Hymes, 1972), as well as the work by the natural language philosophers (Austin, 1962; Searle, 1969; Wittgenstein, 1958) helped to highlight the nature of language as a form of social action and the centrality of cultural knowledge and assumptions to how communicative acts are structured and understood. Particularly influential to language teaching was Hymes (1972), whose notion of 'communicative competence' inspired applied linguistics to see the goals and methods of language teaching in new ways. Hymes (1972) argued that cultural knowledge is essential to any speaker's communicative competence, shaping judgements as to the significance of particular utterances and communicative sequences within larger speech events.

> This competence … is integral with attitudes, values and motivations concerning language, its features and uses, and integral with competence for, and attitudes toward, the interrelation of language with the other codes of communicative conduct. (Hymes, 1972: 60)

Culture helps individuals recognize the speech events which help constitute social life and the implicit and explicit norms which relate to these events and the individuals who take part in them. As such, it shapes the interpretive frameworks through which members of a speech community locate particular phrases, adjacency pairs, speech act sequences, conversational routines and other linguistic phenomena within the social activities that they help constitute (Atkinson & Heritage, 1984). Importantly, culture gives individuals a sense of what is expected behaviour given the sociocultural context in which language is used. This understanding of language as a tool for negotiating social life resonated with many applied linguists, and subsequently led to the operationalization of communicative competence for the purposes of language teaching by Canale and Swain (1980), Bachman (1990), and others. Most models see the interface between language and culture in terms of two types of linguistic mapping – the mapping between linguistic forms and functions and the mapping between linguistic functions and features of sociocultural context. For instance, in Canale and Swain's (1980) work, culture is most closely related to 'sociolinguistic competence', which encompasses 'rules of use' and 'rules of discourse' for spoken interaction in context. 'Rules of use' concerns both the appropriateness of particular utterances for achieving particular functions, and the appropriateness of choice of communicative function in a given sociocultural context. 'Rules of discourse', on the other hand, concerns the appropriateness of the sequencing of utterances within a specific speech event. Culture is thus seen in terms of knowledge of how to linguistically formulate utterances and situate them appropriately given the nature of the speech event and other contextual variables at play.

Viewing appropriateness from the dual perspective of form-function mappings and function-context mappings resonates with the distinction between pragmalinguistics and sociopragmatics (Leech, 1983; Thomas, 1983). Pragmalinguistic knowledge allows the individual to select appropriate forms for carrying out particular communicative functions, while sociopragmatic knowledge guides the individual in making judgements regarding the appropriateness of language use in view of sociocultural context and the roles and relationships relevant to a situation. This is why Leech (1983: 10) famously remarked that 'sociopragmatics is the sociological interface of pragmatics'. Whenever language is used in its social context, its meaning is only interpretable through 'social values and expectations' that fill out a particular context of use (Coupland & Jaworski, 2004: 19). Essentially, cultural assumptions about social roles, relationships, gender, age, locations, genres of communication, and many other variables influence communicative choices and the ways in which individuals make sense of communicative acts within larger social activities. Cultural knowledge, therefore, is fundamental to communicative competence.

The fact that CLT builds on notions of communicative competence (Hymes, 1972), and thus aims to develop learners' ability to communicate 'appropriately' in the target language, naturally implies an engagement with culture. However, although the communicative turn in language teaching was largely successful, the role of culture in communication has often been minimized within language learning curricula, materials, and pedagogy. The shift towards communicative competence as goal of language teaching was reflected in the functional-notional syllabi that emerged out of the Council of Europe (van Ek & Alexander, 1975) and the work done by Wilkins (1976). This work gave important consideration to how languages are for real communicative purposes, how 'authentic' language use could be captured in textbooks, and how 'authentic' contexts for use could be simulated in classroom settings. Although this is a sound direction for language teaching to take, what became problematic as CLT was popularized was that too much attention was devoted to linguistic realization patterns and not enough attention to the cultural norms of appropriateness that underlie the social activities within which linguistic patterns manifest. This is closely related to a reductionist view of communication that came to characterize CLT.

Discourses on CLT have frequently treated communication as a primarily transactional process involving the bridging of an 'information gap'. The bridging of an information gap is essentially the process of transferring the information in the mind of one speaker to the mind of another speaker, also referred to as the telementation model of communication (Eisenchlas, 2009). Much discussion of pedagogy has been concerned with how information gaps can be created in the classroom so that students can use the linguistic resources at their disposal to 'negotiate meaning' and bridge the gap. This process of 'negotiation of meaning' is in turn purported to promote language acquisition (Long, 1983; Varonis & Gass, 1985). However, the nature of the 'meaning' being negotiated tends to be seen in terms of information exchange, which can be achieved by the application of an inventory of strategies for getting one's meaning across (Magnan, 2008; Savignon, 1990). This is not to imply that indexical aspects of language such as speech acts (most commonly referred to as 'functions') have not received attention in CLT. However, for the most part, the ability to use these aspects of language has been equated with the 'capacity to fit appropriate language to specific transactions' (Byram, 1991: 18). What this has meant is that the role that culture plays in constituting a framework for the negotiation of meaning in a true sense has been obscured. Scarino (2007) explains:

> Communication was reduced to the process of developing 'skills', without developing students' understanding of the way that language and culture are integral to personal interpretation and meaning making with others in social interaction. In practice, with some forms of CLT, classroom interactive activities or tasks became no more than 'display' monologues', pseudo-communication activities designed to 'make students talk', rather than talk as the joint realization of potential meanings in conversation. (Scarino, 2007: 7)

The reductionist view of communication is particularly evident in the way that speech acts have been treated in many 'communicative' coursebooks. One problem observable in many textbooks is that speech acts are not treated as contextualized social acts, but as things that can be achieved by correctly selecting the appropriate phrase from a list of phrases in a box (Ren & Han, 2016). For instance, textbooks frequently present the speech act of requesting as a matter of choosing among phrases listed in a box such as 'Would you mind ... ¿', 'Could you ... ¿' or 'Can you ... ¿'. Phrases are often simply listed without further guidance. The problem here is thus one of decontextualization (Dewaele, 2008).

One of the ways in which textbooks do aim to contextualize language for carrying out speech acts is by situating them within short dialogues constructed by textbook writers. This is certainly preferable to simply having a list of phrases in that there is more potential for learners to consider how speech acts might be utilized in connection with larger communicative goals in a given interaction. However, the dialogues themselves are often absent of information describing the sociocultural context of the interaction, such as the speakers' gender, age, relationship, location, and more. The message that comes across from such dialogues is that what is actually important is that the learners simply scan through the dialogue to identify where the target phrases are being used, and that the larger communicative and relational concerns are peripheral (Martínez-Flor & Usó-Juan, 2006; McConachy, 2009; Cohen & Ishihara, 2013). This orientation to communication is reinforced by the fact that comprehension questions following dialogues tend to focus almost exclusively on the retrieval of factual information. Conversely, analytical questions that prompt learners to reflect on the significance of linguistic choices observable in the dialogue, to consider their naturalness or appropriateness, or to compare strategies with the L1, are largely absent (McConachy, 2009).

These tendencies reflect the broader orientation towards a 'transactional' view of communication and the tendency in CLT to underplay 'the symbolic link between language and culture, i.e., the use of language in discourse as *enacting* social roles and *representing* cultural perceptions and misperceptions' (Kramsch, 2003: 21, emphasis in original). Of course, some might question the usefulness of promoting reflection on interaction represented in textbook dialogues, given that dialogues are often constructed for showcasing target utterances rather than being accurate representations of interaction. This is a point worth considering, because it is true that textbook dialogues have been criticized for presenting unrealistic examples of language use (Gilmore, 2007; Wolfson, 1981). However, one could counter that this is precisely why it is necessary to treat language in textbooks and any other learning resource as something to be examined, whether it can be defined as 'authentic' or not. Particularly given the global spread of languages and the concomitant diversification of speakership, learners will frequently encounter instances of language use that might not necessarily conform to narrow conceptions of 'authentic' language based on idealized native-speaker centred norms. It is important that learners are able to analytically engage with the language that they do encounter. From this perspective, the structural features discussed above are counterproductive in that they contribute to socializing language learners into a view of language as code rather than sociocultural resource.

One way in which communicative language textbooks have tried to make more explicit links between language and culture is through descriptions of communication styles associated with various national cultures drawn from early work in the field of intercultural communication studies (e.g. Hall, 1976; Hofstede, 1980). Within this work, national cultures are categorized as 'low-context' or 'high-context' according to highly general preferences for explicitness or implicitness in communication. Nations classified as low-context are typically regarded as displaying preference for 'directness', often tied to culture-level individualism. Contrastively, nations classified as high-context are suggested to value 'indirectness' in communication, usually as a reflection of culture-level collectivism (Gudykunst & Nishida, 1999; Gudykunst & Ting-Toomey, 1988). Based on such work, English language textbooks designed for the international market might advise learners that Japanese people value an 'indirect' or 'polite' communication style stemming from a cultural preference for 'harmony' in social relations (see McConachy & Hata, 2013, for a specific example of this).

The high degree of abstraction involved in such formulations results in an essentialist characterization of cultures not only because it presents cultures as uniform but because it obscures the context-dependency of actions and understandings of actions (Angouri, 2010; Holliday, 2009). Within such a framing, the indexical relationship between language (communication style) and culture (values) is positioned as static and uni-directional – that is, language simply *represents* culture (Kramsch, 2003). This obscures the reality that the specific ways in which communicative strategies such as indirectness are utilized depend very much on contextual assessments made by participants in any given encounter. Naturally, indirectness is not something that will be a salient feature of every communicative encounter, nor is it something that is inherent to a particular cultural group. Teaching the link between language and culture as primarily a matter of communication styles minimizes the role of speakers in constructing interactional responses to communicative needs and can thus inadvertently lead to the creation or reinforcement of stereotypical views of cultural groups.

As above, the overemphasis on decontextualized language patterns is problematic because it is too 'micro', whereas the emphasis on national-level communication styles is problematic because it is too 'macro'. The former starts from language but fails to get to culture. The latter starts with culture, but essentializes the relationship between language and culture by not accounting for the dynamism which underlies how language is used and interpreted within the context of concrete social activity. If the place of cultural knowledge in the interpretation of spoken interaction remains obscure, learners may arrive at the misconception that the interactional conventions and associated cultural assumptions from one language can be unproblematically transferred across languages. It is therefore essential to make the link between culture and communication more transparent as it specifically relates to the interpretation of meanings in face-to-face interaction in specific settings. This is something which has been the goal of more explicit approaches to teaching aspects of pragmatics.

Pragmatics Teaching and the Notion of Pragmatic Awareness

Over the last few decades there has been increased recognition of the importance of more explicitly conceptualizing the norms associated with spoken interaction and finding ways to make them accessible to language learners (e.g. Alcón Soler, 2005; Bardovi-Harlig, 2001; Bardovi-Harlig & Dörnyei, 1998; Ifantidou, 2014; Kasper & Rose, 2002; Kondo, 2008; Martínez-Flor & Usó-Juan, 2010; Padilla Cruz, 2015; Rose, 2005; Schmidt, 1993; Taguchi, 2015; Takahashi, 2005; Takimoto, 2012; Usó-Juan & Martínez-Flor, 2008; van Compernolle, 2014). Theoretically, this would imply an engagement with the cultural assumptions surrounding pragmatic acts in various contexts of use. In practice, the potential for intercultural learning within instructional pragmatics has been constrained by the narrow ways in which pragmatic awareness (or meta-pragmatic awareness) has been operationalized and the disproportionate attention that has been given to pragmalinguistics over sociopragmatics within teaching and research.

The notion of pragmatic awareness has generally been conceptualized within the interlanguage perspective on language development. This perspective sees the learner's L2 linguistic system as progressively moving along a developmental continuum towards a native-speaker norm (Selinker, 1972). The extent of linguistic transfer – understood as the unintentional application of L1 patterns and frames of understanding to the L2 – is seen as indicating how far the individual has progressed along the interlanguage continuum (Kasper & Dahl, 1991). Within the subdiscipline of interlanguage pragmatics, L2 pragmatic development is seen as a matter of reducing negative pragmalinguistic and sociopragmatic transfer from the learner's L1 while gradually incorporating more native-like pragmatic features into the learner's developing linguistic system, thus becoming able to use and interpret the L2 appropriately according to native-speaker norms (Kasper, 1992). The primary aim of developing pragmatic awareness, therefore, is situated in reference to these interrelated goals. Arguments for the need to specifically develop learners' pragmatic awareness stemmed from Schmidt's (1990, 1993, 1995, 2010) influential 'noticing hypothesis', which posited that a certain degree of conscious attention to correlations between forms, meanings and contexts was necessary for acquisition (Kasper & Rose, 2001). This hypothesis theorizes awareness from the perspective of two related cognitive constructs: 'noticing' and 'understanding'. Noticing is seen as the allocation of focal attention to features of input in specific instances of exposure, whereas understanding is a higher order form of awareness characterized by explicit knowledge of linguistic rules. In the case of acquisition of L2 morphosyntax, noticing requires that learners are able to detect form-meaning mappings in input, whereas understanding implies that learners are able to explain the mappings in terms of linguistic rules or principles. In the case of pragmatics, it is suggested that for learning to take place learners need to notice features of the input that allow them to infer consistent associations between linguistic forms, the functions they realize, and the aspects of context they tend to correlate with (Bialystok, 1993; Schmidt, 1993). Schmidt (1995) provides the illustration below:

> In pragmatics, awareness that on a particular occasion someone says to their interlocutor something like, 'I'm terribly sorry to bother you, but if you have time could you look at this problem?' is a matter of noticing. Relating the various forms used to their strategic deployment in the service of politeness and recognizing the co-occurrence with elements of context such as social distance, power, level of imposition and so on, are all matters of understanding. (Schmidt, 1995: 30)

As can be gleaned from this description, the notion of pragmatic awareness within the interlanguage paradigm is built on a view of language as a pre-existing system of conventionalized mappings between forms, functions and features of sociocultural context. Within such a perspective, the development of L2 pragmatic awareness is therefore primarily a matter of gradually becoming familiar with the pragmalinguistic options for achieving illocutions and contextualizing them against broader norms of communicative appropriateness based on relatively static contextual variables. This would imply that pragmatic awareness helps learners develop new cognitive representations which incorporate understanding of the different ways that L2 speakers index aspects of context and their relationships through language.

Bialystok (1993) sees the process of pragmatic development as closely related to the gradual construction of three levels of cognitive representation in the mind: the conceptual, the formal and the symbolic. Conceptual representation is a stage of development in which the individual can select forms to accomplish speech acts, but does not necessarily have a high degree of awareness of the forms – attention remains focused primarily on getting meaning across. Formal representations represent a more developed form of knowledge in which individuals have greater awareness of the multiple linguistic realizations available for a given act. For instance, learners might know that if they want to make an invitation in the target language, there are several conventionalized phrases that could be used for doing this. Symbolic representation builds on the first two, but is constituted by more explicit understanding of the relative impact of particular linguistic choices within the contexts in which they are used. It is thus not simply knowing how forms and functions fit together, but adding to this a higher-order awareness which relates forms to contexts and is able to consider how mitigation strategies and other politeness markers influence the meanings which come across. According to Bialystok's (1993) theory, as adult L2 learners bring with them conceptual representations from their L1, the primary task in L2 learning is gaining processing control over these existing representations while adding to their cognitive system the new representations required by the second language. At the level of pragmalinguistics, this involves creating representations for the linguistic encoding of aspects of social relationships not marked in the L1 (such as the T/V distinction in French for speakers of English), as well as differences in semantic formulae used for achieving speech acts. At the level of sociopragmatics, this involves creating new representations for the cultural logic that underlies the norms of interaction within particular role relationships. The gradual construction of new symbolic representations leads to higher order pragmatic awareness, manifested in the learners' ability to reflect on the nature of their own knowledge and articulate it. In other words, the development of symbolic representations links to the learner's ability to objectify and explain to others elements of his or her own knowledge.

As above, the development of pragmatic awareness within the interlanguage paradigm has primarily been theorized as a process of noticing and understanding L2 pragmatic norms, while at the same time becoming aware of and controlling L1-based pragmatic knowledge which might interfere with the language acquisition process. Based on this theoretical imperative, and based on a view of language as a system of rule-relations, the object of pragmatic awareness – what learners are actually supposed to be aware of – has often been treated in highly normative and restrictive terms in teaching and research (Ifantidou, 2014; Meier, 1999; Murray, 2012; van Compernolle, 2014). Meier (1999) has been particularly critical of the tendency to present the notion of pragmatically appropriate language use to language learners in terms of simplistic mappings:

> Speech act sets or sociopragmatic sets expressed in pedagogically transferable terms would have a form something like, 'say X if you are in a context embodying properties A, B, C and your relationship with your interlocutor has the characteristics of D and E, and you want to be appropriate'. (Meier, 1999: 118)

As also vehemently criticized by van Compernolle (2014), such prescriptions treat the norms of interaction as inherently rigid and 'appropriate' language use as a matter of calculations. Kasper (2006: 296) sees such a tendency as a reflection of the 'convention view of meaning' imported from the speech act paradigm, in which meaning is seen as instantiated by relatively fixed relations between semantic formulae and the speech act sets they are thought to comprise. Aside from the issue of to what extent strict norm-based prescriptions of language behaviour are even possible or accurate (Thomas, 1983), there are several problems with presenting language in this way to learners.

The first is that such formulations of pragmatic norms treat context as a collection of individual variables such as power distance (i.e. institutionally defined hierarchy), social distance (i.e. degree of interpersonal closeness), etc., which reside primarily outside language (Spencer-Oatey, 1996). This would imply that the meaning-making process is constructed around the identification of static variables based on which speakers can draw on computational type knowledge to produce appropriate linguistic output. In reality, context is not a transcendental entity with an uncontroversial nature based on which speakers of a language simply calculate their linguistic utterances. From a sociocultural perspective, context is constituted by a wide variety of social categories and positionings, including gender, age and social class, as well as diverse institutional and interpersonal roles and relationships (Spencer-Oatey, 2008). Context also relates to specific physical settings and the social activities usually associated with those settings, as well as to the ways in which actions and information tend to be organized within activities (Hymes, 1972; Malinowski, 1923). Context is thus a complex, multi-layered construct which binds the linguistic and the social by shaping the ways in which individuals coordinate their turns of talk and the kinds of meanings that are derived from particular ways of speaking. Importantly, individual contextual variables and the impact that they have (or do not have) in interaction are ultimately dependent on cultural conceptualization – what 'social distance' actually means, for example – rooted in a wide range of assumptions about the nature of social reality. As Meier (2003) points out:

> Context, however, does not constitute the bottom line of pragmatics. Rather, one must look farther to the interpretations of the context and its variables, interpretations which are conditioned by the user's underlying cultural values and beliefs. (Meier, 2003: 190)

Judgements concerning what counts as context, as what is most relevant in a given interactional moment and why, are formed on the basis of 'values and beliefs about the world, held by the members of a speech community, in effect, the substratum underlying all assumptions of daily life' (Lo Castro, 2003: 228). This is not to suggest adherence to a uniform cultural fabric within a particular speech community or discourse community. Rather, it is to acknowledge that speakers' judgements about the relative appropriateness or inappropriateness of pragmatic realizations within the flow of communication do not start from context, but from a deeper realm of culturally derived assumptions which individuals' selectively draw on for the purposes of interpretation. This resonates with Malinowski's (1923) distinction between 'context of situation' and 'context of culture'. Culture and language become linked in pragmatics by virtue of the fact that knowledge of linguistic structures is filtered through complex associations of knowledge and assumptions, thus constituting the framework of assumed shared knowledge which constitutes the foundation for the inferential work that allows individuals to interpret the intentions of other speakers in context (Lo Castro, 2003; Meier, 2010; Thomas, 1983).

The second major problem with treating pragmatic norms as a matter of linear rational calculation is that 'appropriateness' of language use is not black and white, nor is it necessarily the most important criterion of language use in all situations. Within communication, there are certainly many rituals and situation-specific conventions that are highly normative in character. These are most observable in ceremonial discourse such as weddings, funerals, award conferment, certain conversational routines (such as 'How are you?' interactions in English), and speech acts such as apologies (Goffman, 1981; Kádár & Bax, 2013; Kecskes, 2014). However, much social interaction, particularly conversation, is not constrained according to a very rigid system of norms, deviation from which will immediately render one socially and communicatively 'inappropriate'. Individuals do approach social interactions with a complex range of expectations and assumptions as to what kind of communicative behaviour is usual or unusual in a particular physical or social context, but these assumptions are merely a starting point for the meaning-making process (e.g. Arundale, 2006; Haugh, 2010; Kasper, 2006). What comes to be regarded as effective or appropriate communication (among other potential attributions) depends significantly on how participants negotiate meaning within the flow of discourse while interpreting and mutually coordinating their actions (Arundale, 2006; Kasper, 2006). In other words, judgements related to appropriateness ultimately depend on 'interactionally-grounded evaluations occurring at the level of individual cognition' (Haugh, 2010: 142).

One indicative area is that of politeness. While textbooks often rank linguistic realization patterns for a given speech act according to degree of politeness, the attribution of politeness (as well as impoliteness) by speakers in interaction is a highly context dependent and interpretative process. That is, whether language use is judged as polite or impolite depends on the dynamics of the interactional context, including how the participants perceive the nature of their relationship and the respective rights and obligations that derive from this relationship (Kádár & Haugh, 2013; Spencer-Oatey, 2008). It is perfectly possible for a particular speech act realization pattern (such as to achieve a request, for instance) to be 'appropriate' in the sense of conventional politeness, but undesirable for a particular speaker in a particular relationship. A 'polite' request form, for example, could be interpreted as decidedly impolite or sarcastic within the context of an argument with a close friend. 'Polite forms' thus do not always create 'politeness' (Haugh & Chang, 2015). This is not to suggest that the notion of pragmatic norms can be abandoned and that the sense making of individuals in interaction is random. What is important is that face-to-face communication is seen as an interpretive activity where individuals draw on their knowledge of broadly established understandings of social situations, relationships and notions of appropriate communication and use these as a resource for interpretation and negotiation within an interactive process. Meanings, pragmatic judgements and interpersonal impressions are managed within frames of understanding that are both socioculturally situated and contextually emergent (Haugh, 2012; Kecskes, 2014).

In terms of developing intercultural perspectives on language use, presenting pragmatic meanings as a matter of calculations and pragmatic learning as a matter of becoming able to carry out 'correct selection' is problematic because it engenders a view of language in which all instances of language in use can be judged in terms of their 'appropriateness' on the basis of a priori specifications. In other words, pragmatic awareness comes to be primarily understood as a matter of knowing what the rules are, according to a narrowly defined system, not only by researchers but also teachers and learners. This conceptualization constrains opportunities for deeper reflection on the situated judgements that speakers make in interaction and the culturally shaped knowledge and assumptions they draw on in the process. This has particularly important implications for intercultural communication in an L2 as there is obviously much more scope for variable interpretations of what constitutes appropriate language use, and it is important that learners are able to look at the dynamics of meaning-making in relation to context, while continually evaluating what in fact constitutes relevant context in a given interaction and how participants show their orientation to it. What this suggests for language learning is the need to place emphasis on the development of the learners' capacity for insightfully interpreting language use in context and considering potential judgements of appropriateness or inappropriateness from multiple perspectives. This necessitates a shift from pragmatic awareness to meta-pragmatic awareness.

From Pragmatic Awareness to Meta-pragmatic Awareness

Within the field of foreign language learning, the terms 'pragmatic awareness' and 'meta-pragmatic awareness' are often used inconsistently or interchangeably. For instance, Kinginger and Farrell (2004: 20) utilize the term meta-pragmatic awareness to refer to 'knowledge of the social meaning of variable second language forms and awareness of the ways in which these forms mark different aspects of social contexts … '. Safont Jordá (2003: 48) also defines meta-pragmatic awareness as 'the acknowledgement of those contextual features that determine the extent to which a given linguistic routine may be appropriate for a particular situation'. Such formulations do not appear to diverge significantly from Schmidt's notion of pragmatic awareness. It is therefore not clear how the 'meta' level is being conceptualized. As one way of making a distinction, Nikula (2002) suggests that the term pragmatic awareness is best used to refer to the knowledge that one needs to be able to use the language to accomplish particular pragmatic acts, but that does not necessarily presuppose the reflexive ability to articulate in detail the nature of one's knowledge. This understanding seems to be in line with others such as Ifantidou (2014) and Verschueren (2004), for whom meta-pragmatic awareness is a higher-order awareness in which the basis of linguistic judgements can be reflected on and articulated. Such awareness is characterized by a growing ability to describe, evaluate and explore one's own and others' interpretations of features of language in use. It can be said that meta-pragmatic awareness is rooted in an individual's capacity for analyzing and reflecting on language use within a range of contexts, while being attuned to the potential for diverse frames of understanding to be operative in the negotiation of meaning (McConachy, 2013). In this sense, the development of meta-pragmatic awareness is essential to the development of an intercultural perspective on language use over time.

In view of the need to develop language learners' capacity for reflecting on language use in context, some authors have taken an approach to meta-pragmatic awareness (although not all authors use this term) which is useful for considering the potential for intercultural learning through pragmatics (e.g. Barraja-Rohan, 2003, 2011; Cheng, 2016; Cohen & Sykes, 2013; Crozet, 2003; Huth & Taleghani-Nikazm, 2006; McConachy & Hata, 2013; Murray, 2010; van Compernolle, 2014; Wang & Rendle-Short, 2013). One strand of this work advocates the use of conversation analytical data to develop learners' awareness of mechanical features of verbal interaction which are prone to differ across cultures, such as conversational openings and closings, adjacency pairs, feedback tokens, speech acts, and more. Beyond awareness of specific pragmatic features, this can help make salient to learners the fact that interaction is based around certain expectancies and that speakers in interaction draw on and signal these expectancies to each other on a turn-by-turn basis (Haugh & Chang, 2015). It can also foreground the ways in which individuals draw on their respective base of knowledge and experience to create common ground. Thus, learners can develop insight into the fact that interaction is characterized by both structural regularities as well as negotiation and contingency (van Lier, 1996).

Recent work conducted within the framework of sociocultural theory (SCT) also adds complexity to the conceptualization of meta-pragmatic awareness in a way that is useful for foreign language teaching. The sociocultural theoretic perspective on learning emphasizes the process of appropriating tools for mediating one's own cognitive and social functioning (Vygotsky, 1978). Specifically, learning is not only about acquiring propositional knowledge, but appropriating from more competent others sociocognitive resources that mediate decision-making within concrete social activity, including cognitive representations such as schemas, scripts, concepts and assumptions (Lantolf & Thorne, 2007). Such a perspective gives further impetus to the move away from teaching and learning aspects of L2 pragmatics as a restrictive form of rule-based knowledge – what van Compernolle (2014) criticizes as pragmatic rules of thumb. From the perspective of SCT, any form of rule-based knowledge is ultimately constructed with reference to particular concepts, which are themselves culturally defined. For example, a language textbook might instruct a learner to choose a particular pragmalinguistic form (such as a request form) over another in order to be 'polite' when there is more 'social distance', but neither of these concepts is necessarily transparent or culturally neutral (McConachy & Hata, 2013; van Compernolle, 2014). In the realm of pragmatics, learners' ability to carry out goal-directed social actions is mediated both by pragmalinguistic and sociopragmatic knowledge resources, including each individual learner's conceptual understanding of notions such as 'friendliness', 'politeness', 'social distance', and more (van Compernolle, 2014). Therefore, in order to develop the ability to use the L2 effectively for communicative purposes, learners need to develop insight into the ways in which such notions are conceptualized.

Rather than encouraging language learners to see linguistic choices as a matter of simple norm-following, work on L2 pragmatics rooted in SCT advocates starting with sociopragmatic notions such as politeness, power and social distance, and then encouraging learners to see how L2 linguistic forms are used to construct these features of interpersonal relationships (van Compernolle & Kinginger, 2013). Such a reversal in building understanding means that learners examine assumptions about what social distance is (among other important aspects of context), and how individuals signal particular orientations to social distance within and across instances of interaction and within a wide range of contexts. This instigates a shift in perspective in the learner from seeing language as a code to seeing language as an interpersonal resource (van Compernolle, 2014). In terms of meta-pragmatic awareness, learners develop a conceptual understanding of features of sociocultural context and use this to mediate their understanding of how individuals use particular ways of speaking to construct meanings and interpersonal impressions (such as formality, for instance), not in a prescriptive way, but in a dynamic way depending on broader issues such as what is going on in an interaction (such as the nature of the speech event), and the respective agendas of the participants in the interaction, among a range of variables. Concept-based meta-pragmatic awareness, as articulated in the SCT perspective, is suggested to evolve into a broader understanding of 'contingency' as a principle of interaction (van Compernolle & Williams, 2012). In other words, when learners' meta-pragmatic awareness is characterized by heightened awareness of sociopragmatic meaning potential, they are able to see interactional options as more complex than simply a matter of acting out pragmatic prescriptions. van Compernolle and Williams (2012: 237) suggest that awareness of contingency forms a central part of what they refer to as 'meta-sociolinguistic awareness', which they suggest is fundamental to sociolinguistic agency – the ability to agentively exploit language variation to index one's identity.

The slight difference in terminology notwithstanding, the idea that meta-pragmatic awareness is central to agency is an important one. To have agency within any realm of activity, including communication, is not simply a matter of being able to carry out actions according to the pre-existing rules of a particular system. The essence of agency is the ability to draw on the structural resources provided by a particular system (such as prescribed rules for behaviour, symbols, conventional meanings, etc.) in a considered way to craft a course of action that can be interpreted as socially meaningful, even if the meaningfulness that results from that action needs to be established as a result of negotiation with others (Giddens, 1991; Kramsch, 2009). From this perspective, it is difficult for language learners to develop a true sense of agency in their use of L2 pragmatics if they are socialized into a view of language as a highly constrained rule system. Conversely, if learners are to develop a view of language as a dynamic system of interactional resources adopted and adapted by groups and individuals for their interpersonal needs, then there is more scope for the learner to reflect on how they might want to adopt the L2 for their own ends and to index aspects of their own subjectivities (Kramsch, 2009). As van Compernolle and Williams (2012) suggest, developing awareness of variation in pragmatic features (such as personal pronouns, speech act realizations, etc.) and how speakers exploit variation for a range of interpersonal ends is an important part of constructing a more dynamic perspective on language as a whole. In sociocultural theoretic terms, conceptual understanding plays a role in mediating the development of meta-pragmatic awareness (van Compernolle, 2014).

One limitation of the current theorizing on pragmatic awareness in SCT is that it does not give enough attention to the ways in which knowledge and assumptions drawn from the learner's L1 shape processes of interpretation and the consequences this has for the development of agency in the L2. It is important to point out that language learners are emerging multilinguals who necessarily draw on interpretive and linguistic resources embedded in multiple languages in order to assess situations, interpret linguistic actions and manage the negotiation of meaning (Cook, 2003; Kecskes, 2014; McConachy & Spencer-Oatey, forthcoming). Throughout the learning process, language learners mobilize a wide range of cultural assumptions drawn from their history of interactions in the L1 and use these to mediate their initial understanding of the foreign language and how it can be put to use for communicative purposes. The development of meta-pragmatic awareness in the L2 thus is not a unidirectional phenomenon, but a dynamic and synergistic engagement between knowledge and assumptions drawn from multiple languages and cultural contexts (McConachy & Spencer-Oatey, forthcoming). Although the learner's agency is certainly enhanced by L2 meta-pragmatic awareness developed according to the SCT perspective, it is difficult to understand the phenomenon of agency without reference to the dynamic engagement between assumptions and pragmatic knowledge drawn from multiple languages and how the learner draws on this knowledge to formulate plans for communicative action.

One phenomenon that is particularly germane to this discussion of agency is the experience of resistance to adopting certain features of

L2 pragmatics which emerges for many learners at different points during the learning process. The pragmatics of another language marks orientations to relationships (such as egalitarianism or hierarchy) and ways of looking at the world which can challenge a learner's sense of normalcy and deep-seated assumptions about proper social behaviour. This can manifest in the form of pragmatic resistance – a resistance to adopting certain pragmatic norms within the L2 (Ishihara & Tarone, 2009). The occurrence of such a phenomenon has been documented in relation to the learning of pragmatic features such as honorifics (Ishihara, 2010; Ishihara & Tarone, 2009), obligatory humble language in workplace contexts, expressions of gratitude (Siegal, 1996), conversational routines (Davis, 2007), and others. The experience of pragmatic resistance directly links with the issue of agency because learners need to manage their cognitive and affective reactions while finding a way to interact without necessarily forcing themselves to follow L2 pragmatic norms in their entirety (Crozet & Liddicoat, 1999). For the learner, this necessitates a reflective engagement with their own perceptions and exploration of the assumptions that lie behind resistance. In other words, the decision as to how to interact and position oneself as a person within the target language is a complex cognitive and affective process which requires recognizing and reflecting on starting-point assumptions about L1 and L2 pragmatics as a way of gradually developing a sense of agency (McConachy & Liddicoat, 2016).

Many researchers and language teachers recognize that it is unreasonable to force learners to adopt L2 pragmatic features they are uncomfortable with and therefore see the comparison of L1 and L2 pragmatics as a way of helping learners determine their own language use (e.g. Bardovi-Harlig, 1996; Crozet, 1996; Dewaele, 2008; Dufon, 2008; Eslami-Rasekh, 2005; Ishihara & Tarone, 2009; Iwasaki, 2008; Judd, 1999; Kasper & Rose, 1999; Lo Castro, 2003; van Compernolle & Williams, 2012; Yashima, 2009). For instance, Ishihara and Cohen (2010: 87) suggest that for language teachers it is important 'to ensure that learners recognize the shared interpretation of their utterances in the community and potential consequences of their pragmatic behavior'. What is being advocated is not ignorance of L2 pragmatic norms, but an awareness of two dimensions: (1) what the norms themselves are; and (2) what the potential consequences could be for diverging from them. This is illustrated by Eslami-Rasekh (2005) as follows:

> Through awareness-raising activities, students acquire information about pragmatic aspects of language – for instance, what strategies are used for apologizing in their first language (L1) and second language (L2), what is considered an offence in their culture compared to the target culture, what are different degrees of offence for different situations in the two languages, and how the nature of the relationship between the participants affects the use of apologies. (Eslami-Rasekh, 2005: 200)

From a comparative perspective, development of pragmatic awareness is minimally understood as the growing acknowledgement of differences between the pragmatics of the L1 and L2, which will help the learner avoid unintended pragmatic transfer (Bardovi-Harlig, 1996; Eslami-Rasekh, 2005; Ishihara & Cohen, 2010; Kasper & Rose, 2001; Martínez-Flor & Usó-Juan, 2006; Thomas, 1983). At a more general level, pragmatic awareness enhances the learner's ability to consider the interactional consequences of particular linguistic strategies in interaction. In other words, it assists learners to 'listen to interactions, to watch for reactions, to consider what may result from one choice of words over another' (Bardovi-Harlig, 1996: 29). In this way, meta-pragmatic awareness development can be seen as the cultivation of sensitivity to the nature of communication which then empowers the learners to experiment with language and encode their own values into a 'clear, unambiguous message' (Bardovi-Harlig, 2001: 31). Over time, this feeds into the development of an analytical ability that learners can utilize for pragmatic learning beyond the classroom (Bardovi-Harlig, 1996; Eslami-Rasekh, 2005; Thomas, 1983). This notion of meta-pragmatic awareness development within a broadly 'analytical' orientation to learning is important as it signals that awareness is more than knowledge. When the scope of 'pragmatic' awareness goes beyond knowledge of specific pragmatic norms and develops into a broader capacity for reflection on pragmatic decision making and interactional effects, the nature of the awareness can be viewed as developing towards the 'meta-pragmatic'.

In practical terms, the notion that teachers should be sensitive to the fact that learners may not wish to adhere to the norms of the L2 in certain instances of language production is certainly a valid notion. However, it raises the issue: What is the alternative to following L2 norms? Is the intercultural dimension simply seen in terms of learners having the agency to decide how to interact? Developing awareness of L2 pragmatic norms under the proviso that one need not follow the norms does not constitute a satisfactory resolution to the dilemma of how language learners should interact in the target language. It also does not provide the theoretical resources for understanding the dynamic ways in which learners draw on cultural frames of reference and move between languages through the learning process (c.f. Liddicoat & Scarino, 2013). If the intercultural dimension is theorized primarily as a matter of the learner being left with the agency to make their own interactional decisions on the basis of L2 pragmatic knowledge, then this presents problems for theorizing the more complex ways in which individuals make use of culturally derived assumptions and frameworks for meaning drawn from multiple languages to construct decisions not simply about how to orient to L2 pragmatic norms but how to position oneself as a 'person' in the L2. Cohen and Sykes (2013) approach this issue in terms of helping learners adopt pragmatic 'strategies' for making informed linguistic decisions, but they do not theorize the role of awareness or the ways in which learners move between cultural frames of understanding in their decision making. Therefore, at present there is still a lack of theoretical development regarding the intercultural dimensions of meta-pragmatic awareness and the role that development of such awareness plays in the language learning process.

Chapter Conclusion

Although the teaching of communication has come to be an important goal in language teaching contexts in many places around the world, the ways in which aspects of communication – especially aspects of pragmatics – have been conceptualized and approached have tended to emphasize the learner's acquisition of linguistic patterns without a strong emphasis on culture or the development of intercultural abilities. The focus has primarily remained on the nature of the input – the linguistic rules constituting the system – and how awareness of the rules of the system, combined with classroom practice, can help learners more effectively develop their abilities to map forms, functions and contexts in their comprehension and use of the L2. It is important to be cognizant of the fact that the way we present language to learners not only provides input for acquisition, but it also shapes their perspectives on what language is and how it works. Presenting pragmatic norms in a prescriptive way based on a narrow concept of appropriateness tells learners that communication is a process of acting out predetermined and rigidly constrained linguistic behaviour. Whether intended or not, this is clearly a disadvantageous message to impart to learners when considering the cultural variability in language use that they will inevitably be exposed to when engaging in intercultural communication in the target language.

If learners are to develop the capacities to engage in intercultural communication and successfully negotiate their own and others' identities through the medium of the foreign language, beyond knowledge of L2 conventions, learners need to develop meta-pragmatic awareness that is conducive to the long-term development of an intercultural perspective on language use. This means that meta-pragmatic awareness needs to be redefined in a way that takes account of the nature of learners' L1-based knowledge resources and how reflection works to help learners more explicitly link knowledge and assumptions drawn from separate languages that directly influence the ways aspects of pragmatics are interpreted and used. In the next chapter, I offer a way of reconceptualizing the notion of meta-pragmatic awareness within an overtly intercultural orientation to language learning.

2 Linking Pragmatics and Intercultural Language Learning

Introduction

Intercultural language learning represents an orientation to languages education that places intercultural learning and the development of intercultural competencies at the core of learning, using and teaching the target language (Byram, 1997; Corbett, 2003; Crozet & Liddicoat, 1999; Kohler, 2015; Kramsch, 1993; Liddicoat & Scarino, 2013; Risager, 2007). This involves seeing the language learning process as characterized by ongoing exploration of the ways that cultural and individual assumptions influence the ways in which aspects of language use are understood and evaluated within and across linguistic and cultural boundaries (Liddicoat & Scarino, 2013). As represented by Byram's (1997) notion of the intercultural speaker, it is not assumed that learners will necessarily wish to wholeheartedly adopt all of the norms of the target language in all cases, but rather that learners will develop the knowledge, awareness, skills and attitudes necessary for understanding linguistic and non-linguistic phenomena from a variety of perspectives and develop an interactional repertoire that enables them to communicate comfortably and effectively. As an important part of this development, learners (and teachers) decentre from their taken-for-granted perceptions on language and culture to engage with multiple ways of representing and interpreting reality through language (Byram et al., 2001; Liddicoat & Scarino, 2013). Interculturality, therefore, is not understood in terms of a process of comparing essentialized cultural differences but as a process of interpretation in which learners interpret and critique a range of perspectives on cultural phenomena while reflexively engaging with their own assumptions and cultural positioning. In this chapter, I draw on concepts and theories from fields including meta-pragmatics, intercultural communication, social psychology and intercultural learning to reconceptualize the notion of meta-pragmatic awareness and suggest its role in the development of an intercultural perspective on language use throughout the process of language learning.

Language Teaching within an Intercultural Orientation

Situating language teaching within an intercultural orientation does not represent an attempt to negate the importance of grammar, vocabulary or communication within the language classroom. What is does represent is an attempt to more explicitly tease out the ways in which assumptions about the nature of the social world influence the ways in which we imbue various aspects of language with meaning (Kramsch, 1993). If we are to teach learners language as a form of communication, particularly for use with speakers from diverse cultural backgrounds, then we ultimately need to engage learners in reflection on how meanings become constituted in communication and how particular linguistic actions can be variably interpreted in context depending on the assumptions that different speakers bring to any instance of communication. This, in turn, works to support learners in the development of their communicative abilities, as they are able to more consciously reflect on the nature of their own language use and the meanings and impressions that they hope to construct. From this perspective, culture is not something which we 'add on' to language learning – culture has always been there as an essential constituent of learning how to make meaning in the L2, but the ways we have conceptualized the notion of culture and its role in the language classroom have sometimes limited the ways in which we have attended to it.

Within an intercultural orientation to language teaching and learning, culture is not seen primarily as a static body of knowledge, but as a dynamic meaning system embodying knowledge, assumptions and values which shapes, and is again shaped by, individuals' use of symbolic resources – particularly language (Hall, 1993; Kecskes, 2014; Liddicoat & Scarino, 2013). Although culture is often seen within language teaching in terms of national culture, this should not imply that culture within a given nation is a static, monolithic entity, but rather a system that contains varying degrees of coherence and differentiation in terms of thought, behaviour and meaning-making practices across discourse communities, as well as gender-based, socio-economic and political structures (Hansen, 2000). This means that, although all individuals within a nation can be viewed as culturally situated, the meanings and practices within a particular national culture are not equally adhered to by all members. A corollary of this is that 'no person represents a whole culture, and cultural patterns are not shared by all members of a cultural group in the same way' (Damen, 1987: 43). Culture is instead understood as a framework from which individuals selectively structure their social worlds (Geertz, 1973). As a fundamental framework, culture shapes and is shaped by the behavioural practices engaged in by individuals within a given collectivity. Linguistic practices can be understood as reflecting broadly shared cultural ideas and, at the same time, creating a context for cultural ideas to be reconfirmed, contested and reconstructed (Duranti, 1997). For Hansen (2000), it is the interplay between similarity and difference within a culture that creates affordances for the formation of individual identity. This means that, through utilizing culture as a framework, individuals are able to express and negotiate meanings, and also to appropriate ways of speaking as a means of achieving both solidarity and differentiation from others. Individuals also draw on ideologically constructed images of their own national culture as a resource for interpreting actions and creating intersubjectivity with others (Anderson, 1991; Billig, 1995).

Such a view of language and culture allows for a move away from a view of one nation having one all-encompassing coherent culture which is equally shared by all members of a given nation. Moreover, as many authors have pointed out, the global spread of information technologies and movement of people across the world as part of globalization have brought about cultural flows which extend across multiple nations (Pennycook, 2007; Risager, 2006, 2007). In the current world, the nation is only one possible framework for looking at culture, and there is a need for awareness of the fact that 'variation and variability exist in linguistic practice and, correspondingly, that many local linguistic norms exist' (Risager, 2007: 196). In the teaching of foreign languages, thus, there is an impetus for seeing culture as discursively constructed in various localities and communities within and beyond the nation (Abdallah-Pretceille, 2006; Baker, 2011; Pennycook, 2007; Risager, 2007). This is not to deny that relationships between language and culture can still be abstracted to some degree at the national level; however, this should not be presented as the only frame through which language and culture operate. The relationship between language and culture is inherently complex, and it is important that learners engage with this complexity by considering the ways in which cultural behaviours and meanings are defined and negotiated in a range of contexts.

Adopting a non-essentialist view of culture has important consequences for how we see intercultural language learning. Specifically, if culture is treated as a dynamic phenomenon which is contingent upon the meaning-making actions of individuals and groups in a range of contexts (c.f. Geertz, 1973), then culture is something which can only be understood through gradually participating in these meaning-making practices and increasing one's capacity for meaningfully interpreting them (Liddicoat & Scarino, 2013; Risager, 2007). The notion of 'hermeneutic' recognizes the interpretive nature of learning and the fact that the development of understanding depends on the individual learner's interpretive starting point – their existing knowledge, perspectives, assumptions, values and history. Understandings of language and culture are constructed through an interplay between newly encountered cultural information and existing knowledge and perspectives. Put differently, learning depends on the construction of meaning and relevance from the structured standpoint of the learner (Ashworth, 2004). Learners draw on their pre-existing knowledge, assumptions and values as a framework for making sense of foreign meanings, and gradually develop the capacity for recognizing and moving between different interpretations of behaviours drawn from different cultures (Byram, 2003; Kramsch, 1993; Liddicoat & Scarino, 2013). The act of learning about other languages and cultures is therefore positioned as an intercultural endeavour from the beginning.

Two important points to emphasize here are that learners who come from a particular national background are not necessarily culturally situated in the same way, and that intercultural learning is not simply a matter of comparing and understanding one essentialized culture in relation to another (Holliday, 2010). Rather, an integral part of learning involves reflecting on one's own cultural positioning and generating awareness of the kinds of knowledge resources that one has developed from a range of sources, including various social groups and discourse communities within and beyond the nation in accordance with one's historical biography (Kramsch, 2009; Risager, 2007). Similarly, one's engagement with the L2 is also conducted with a view to observing, exploring and understanding various levels of coherence and differentiation in linguistic practices which exist in particular contexts where the language is spoken, including lingua franca contexts (Crozet, 2015; Rathje, 2007). Learners engage with L2 linguistic practices while reflecting on what they themselves take for granted, actively interpreting new information and reinterpreting existing knowledge. This hermeneutic perspective on learning particularly foregrounds the importance of discovering and problematizing one's own assumptions, especially those that are likely to lead to ethnocentric judgements of foreign linguistic practices (Byram, 1997).

It is within such a view of culture and intercultural learning that I wish to situate the notion of 'intercultural perspective on language use'. As discussed in the Introduction, this notion relates to the language learner's ability to view aspects of language use (both in L1 and L2) as a form of social action – to develop insight into the various social acts that individuals perform with language and the kinds of assumptions about interpersonal relationships, sociocultural context and communication itself that enter into our interpretation and use of language. As discussed in Chapter 1, the notion of meta-pragmatic awareness has been used within language teaching to primarily denote the learner's awareness of how choice of particular pragmatic realization patterns (such as speech acts, honorifics, etc.) tends to be influenced by particular features of context. However, due to primarily relying on a view of language as code, the ways in which cultural assumptions underlie perception of context itself and the ways individuals construct meanings within multiple-turn discourse have not received systematic attention. Moreover, the ways in which assumptions drawn from experience in multiple languages enter into the learner's interpretation processes, and how this shapes their perspective on their own and others' language use has been neglected.

Therefore, the notion of intercultural perspective embodies the learner's growing awareness of links between language use and culture in various national and regional contexts in which the L2 is spoken. It also embodies the learner's growing reflexive awareness of how he/she interprets aspects of the L1 and L2, including the dynamic application of frames of reference from one language when understanding another. Such awareness provides scope for the learner to view linguistic behaviours from a variety of perspectives within and across cultures, learning to decentre from one's own assumptions and open up to diversity and complexity (Crozet, 2015; Liddicoat & Scarino, 2013). In this way, the development of an intercultural perspective on language use is a long-term process contingent upon sustained interpretive engagement with aspects of language use and the development of meta-pragmatic awareness. In order to elaborate this notion further, in the sections following I will articulate an enlarged theoretical view of pragmatics and the nature of meta-pragmatic awareness as it functions within the language learning process.

Engaging with Pragmatics as Social and Moral Practice

From the viewpoint of teaching and learning, the development of intercultural perspectives on language use requires moving away from a view of pragmatics as the instantiation of a rule system to adopt a view of pragmatics as a social and moral practice. Since people put language to use to achieve concrete social goals and negotiate their relationships, language use functions as an important form of cultural behaviour. The norms and conventions of spoken language use within each language are not simply a neutral overlay for a universal social reality but are constitutive of that reality, helping people construct features of interpersonal relations such as hierarchy, politeness, aspects of social identity, and more (Goodwin & Duranti, 1992; Spencer-Oatey & Kádár, 2016). To interpret an aspect of language use in context is not simply to identify what the act is in linguistic terms, but to recognize it as a form of social action which can be evaluated in relation to broader cultural norms, expectations and assumptions. In this sense, the interpretation and production of linguistic meanings constitutes a form of social action.

At the same time, our observations and evaluations of others' interpersonal behaviour leads us to construct impressions of them as likeable or potentially problematic people (Hinton, 2015). As an important aspect of behaviour, language use is no exception. It can be said that the interpretation of language use also contains a moral dimension in that we derive from the way people speak particular evaluations of them as particular types of people. For instance, when we interpret a suggestion from another person as 'too direct' or an apology as 'insincere', we make a judgement not simply about the linguistic action but about the person performing the action. That is, we often slip from a judgement about language use to a judgement about the speaker in moral terms – 'impolite language' can easily be construed as evidence of an 'impolite individual' (Gumperz et al., 1979; Sarangi, 1994). In our interpretation of daily communication, we constantly interpret linguistic actions and the people performing those actions in terms of evaluative adjectives such as 'polite', 'impolite', 'friendly', 'kind', 'selfish', 'arrogant', and more. It is through such a process that we create, maintain or revise interpersonal impressions of others. In the sense that such adjectives represent categories that carry positive or negative valence, they can be viewed as value judgements (Houghton, 2012). In more technical terms, such adjectives function as meta-pragmatic frames through which social behaviour, and hence the individuals who engage in such behaviour, are judged (McConachy & Hata, 2013).

Naturally, the ways in which individuals derive such judgements are not arbitrary. At the same time, interpersonal evaluation is not simply a matter of judging individuals according to narrow rule-based notions of 'appropriateness' or 'inappropriateness' in particular contexts. The social and moral dimensions of pragmatics are inextricably intertwined with deeper underlying assumptions concerning the rights and responsibilities of people in particular roles and relationships (Spencer-Oatey & Kádár, 2016). Within our relationships, even among strangers, we have (frequently unconscious) expectations relating to others' obligations towards us and our entitlements to particular kinds of behaviour and attitudes from them. Similarly, we have a sense of our own obligations towards others and their entitlements from us. We have expectations for doctors, teachers, parents, children, friends, and others not simply about the kinds of activities that individuals might perform in these roles, but about their obligations towards us relating to care, kindness, fairness, loyalty, and a range of other moral foundations (see Haidt & Kesebir, 2010). For instance, we might expect a doctor to be 'friendly but professional', or we might expect a good friend to be 'caring and reliable'. But where do such expectations come from? Moreover, how do we recognize the instantiation of such characteristics within communication? One might say that 'friendliness' is an interpersonal resource instantiated within communication whose value is interpreted not simply with reference to concrete interactional context of the moment, but more fundamentally with reference to the relationship at play and the sense of rights and obligations associated with that relationship.

To interpret an aspect of language use in context is not simply to identify what the act is in linguistic terms, but to treat it as form of social action which is inevitably contextualized within broader expectations in the realm of interpersonal relationships. These notions as to what we can reasonably expect from others and what others can expect from us imbue aspects of pragmatics with a moral nature. Naturally, this is not a static conception. Interpersonal expectations and the evaluation of communicative acts are influenced by prevalent attitudes towards forms of social organization in a given society, including attitudes towards authority, gender, family, in-group versus out-group distinctions, and many more (Haidt & Joseph, 2007; Spencer-Oatey & Kádár, 2016). In other words, the wide range of judgements that speakers make about language use in social and moral terms are filtered through a complex architecture of assumptions about larger social activities and relations (Kádár & Haugh, 2013). Pragmatics interfaces with culture primarily through the ways in which individuals draw on culturally derived frames of reference and assumptions to interpret particular linguistic actions as socially meaningful, generate interpersonal impressions of other speakers, and strategically construct their own impressions in interaction.

Obviously, this is not to imply that one language has one pragmatics. All pragmatic phenomena – whether it is greeting routines, small talk, ways of making a request to a superior in the workplace, apologizing for a serious offence, or any other communicative act – manifest national, regional, institutional and context-specific variation in regard to how acts are performed, interpreted and evaluated (Schneider & Barron, 2008). Kádár and Haugh (2013: 94) suggest that these frames of reference are 'dispersed to varying degrees across various kinds of relational networks, ranging from a group of families and friends, to a localized community of practice, through to larger, much more diffuse societal or cultural groups'. These authors posit that the expectancies can be viewed in terms of multiple layers within a given society. First-order expectancies are the probabilistic conventions used to evaluate social actions which are formed on the basis of each individual's experience as a language user. Second-order expectancies are those which are more broadly shared and conventionalized within particular communities of practice and larger social groups. Third-order expectations are those which are typically understood as societal-level norms (Kádár & Haugh, 2013). It is important to note that these are reflexively layered, which essentially means that first- and second-order expectancies necessarily draw on third-order expectancies. This notion of reflexive layering allows for recognition of the fact that the particular meta-pragmatic judgements made by individuals within a given culture are not wholly determined by the third-order (societal/cultural) expectations. Culturally derived expectancies constitute an overarching framework of reference and a resource for locally constructed judgements by individuals. It is not always a matter of having identical knowledge to other speakers, but sharing the broad frames of reference within which claims to meaningfulness and judgements of appropriate social action can be mediated within interaction. Viewing meta-pragmatic frameworks as layered in this way is highly congruent with a non-essentialist view of culture, in which culture informs but does not 'determine' the sense-making of each individual.

The fact that individuals form impressions of others based on largely unacknowledged assumptions is a troubling one for intercultural communication. It means that when individuals encounter pragmatic strategies which diverge from their expectations, there is the risk of making negative snap judgements and constructing stereotypes or fortifying existing ones (Roberts, 1998). However, such a process is not limited to intercultural communication. The process of foreign language learning itself presents learners with unfamiliar linguistic practices rooted in particular ways of looking at the world, which can similarly lead to ethnocentric judgements (Ishihara, 2010). To a certain degree, communicative language teaching (CLT) has introduced into learners' consciousness the idea that we need to be aware of judgements of 'appropriateness' or 'inappropriateness' and, more recently, 'politeness' (e.g. Bou-Franch & Garcés-Conejos, 2003; Haugh & Chang, 2015). However, less attention has been given to the ways in which pragmatic aspects of language use can function to generate other interpersonal impressions.

The notion of intercultural perspective on language use is centred on recognition that speech acts and other aspects of pragmatics are not simply a form of social action but are also a tool for interpersonal evaluation (Spencer-Oatey, 2008). This has consequences for the conceptualization of meta-pragmatic awareness and its role in the development of an intercultural perspective. Specifically, an intercultural perspective on language use is constructed over time by the development of meta-pragmatic awareness at multiple levels. As per traditional conceptions of meta-pragmatic awareness (e.g. Safont-Jorda, 2003; Schmidt, 1993, etc.), learners need to develop understanding of the pragmalinguistic patterns for achieving speech acts in the target language, the common sequences involved in interactional routines, and how these tend to correlate with aspects of context such as the setting of communication, the relationship between the participants, and others. In line with the work on pragmatics learning within sociocultural theory (SCT) (e.g. van Compernolle, 2014), learners need to move beyond reliance on pragmatic rules of thumb to develop insight into the conceptualization of context and how individuals use language to create impressions such as familiarity, authority, friendliness, etc. Beyond this, learners need to develop insight into the ways in which cultural assumptions influence the interpretation of language use in context and lead to a wide range of interpersonal evaluations. Meta-pragmatic awareness is not simply a rule-based awareness, but awareness of the multiple and complex ways in which culture enters into the interpretation of language use and language users (McConachy, 2013). Such awareness is developed not only in relation to the L2 but to the L1 as well. It therefore necessitates an account of learning that encompasses the intercultural dimensions of an interpretive engagement with language.

Intercultural Dimensions of Meta-pragmatic Awareness in Learning

Based on the hermeneutic perspective on language learning articulated earlier, in this section I will discuss more specifically the intercultural dimensions of meta-pragmatic awareness in learning. The starting point for this discussion is the hermeneutic understanding that all learning starts from a process of interpretation based on the individual's existing knowledge, perspectives and experiences, primarily embodied in language (Gadamer, 2004; Liddicoat & Scarino, 2013). This pre-existing knowledge – what Gadamer (2004: 269) refers to as 'fore-understandings' – both enables and constrains the interpretation of new information and experience. Similarly, language learners come to the act of learning with a wide range of assumptions about the nature of the social world, embedded in a complex architecture of knowledge and assumptions that have been constructed through exposure to culturally circulated normative ideas and the individual's interpretation and adaptation of these ideas over time. This architecture of knowledge consists of cognitive resources such as cultural schema, cultural scripts, stereotypes, knowledge of behavioural norms (including pragmatic norms), and a wide range of deeper (often unconscious) assumptions about what is right and fair in social interactions, which are sanctioned by values dominant in society and smaller subgroups within society (Kecskes, 2014; Wilson & Sperber, 2004). I refer to this complex amalgam of cognitive resources through the metaphor of 'interpretive architecture'. This notion resonates with what Fairclough (2015) calls 'members' resources'. He sees these as resources which individuals 'have in their heads and draw upon when they produce or interpret texts – including their knowledge of language, representations of the natural and social worlds they inhabit, values, beliefs, assumptions, and so on' (Fairclough, 2015: 57).

However, whereas the notion of 'resources' can give the impression that items within the mind are more or less autonomous and arbitrarily assembled for a particular purpose, the notion of 'architecture' aims to represent the idea that the constituent knowledge and assumptions which underlie the interpretation of social behaviour – in this case, aspects of pragmatics – are often structured in the form of conventionalized associations. Within interaction individuals are very quick at attributing meanings and making evaluative judgements about behaviour in context, including linguistic behaviour. For instance, within interaction one speaker might interpret a compliment as 'too personal' or an apology as 'insincere' very quickly. Such interpretations often take the form of a snap judgement as frames of understanding are mobilized on the basis of conventionalized pathways for interpretation (Hinton, 2015). The interpretation of self, others, activity and action draws on knowledge, assumptions and values which are 'assembled' on the basis of an individual's conventionalized interpretive pathways. I suggest that this notion of interpretive architecture is, therefore, useful for discussing in more specific terms the nature of the learner's knowledge and how learners draw on aspects of knowledge embedded in multiple languages as they go through the process of language learning.

In the early stages of language learning, learners' understanding of L2 patterns and meanings is largely filtered through L1-embedded knowledge (and also previously acquired languages in the case of multilinguals). Over time, learners come to see the L2 not as an epiphenomenon of the L1, but as a meaning system in its own right which is interpreted according to the norms of established users of that language, often within a particular geographical locality (Byram, 1991; Ochs & Schieffelin, 1984). In other words, language learners come to see the L2 as a system with its own logic, not simply in terms of having different linguistic rules to the L1, but in terms of encoding a variety of different meanings and perspectives. It could be said that a learner's L1-based interpretive architecture shapes the construction of initial understandings of the L2 and, as more advanced understanding of the L2 develops, the learner is then able to more systematically compare languages and notice differences (Kramsch, 1993). In other words, learners begin to consciously and unconsciously bring cultural frames of understanding drawn from separate languages into relationship with each other. Such a process can be understood in terms of the notion of intercultural mediation (Byram, 1991; Liddicoat, 2014; McConachy & Liddicoat, 2016).

As McConachy and Liddicoat (2016) have suggested, the process of mediation begins from the learner's own perception of cultural difference across languages and becomes more sophisticated as they attempt to interpret that difference. At a superficial level, mediation might manifest as stereotypical comparison of pragmatic norms in the L1 and L2, expressed in formulations such as, 'If you want give a compliment in the L2 you say this, but in the L1 you say this'. Such a characterization indicates pragmalinguistic awareness, but remains unanalyzed. A shift in perspective occurs when language learners develop awareness of the fact that pragmatic realization patterns in different languages contain the potential for indexing different cultural meanings. Liddicoat's (2006) study on Australian learners of L2 French showed that in learning how to use the pronouns *tu* and *vous* (both meaning 'you' in English), learners progressed from a stage of not being able to differentiate the two (such as the former is informal and the latter is formal/polite), to then relying on the kinds of pragmatic rules of thumb often contained in textbooks, to finally developing a more sophisticated understanding of the various ways in which these pronouns can be used to index distance, familiarity and formality which are not available in English. This could be understood in terms of the sociopragmatic dimension of awareness. Beyond this, Liddicoat's data show that learners also developed awareness of how the word 'you' is used in an undifferentiated way in Australian English and how this links to particular assumptions about equality and informality. The learners gradually opened up to alternative ways of constructing meanings and thus decentred from their taken-for-granted assumptions. What this suggests is that, at a more sophisticated level of mediation, learners are not simply comparing linguistic forms, but developing awareness of what particular forms signify in terms of social relationships, how meanings can be culturally variable, and how they themselves interpret the L2 on the basis of cultural assumptions. In contrast to the interlanguage view of learning, languages are seen as working in complementary and synergistic ways rather than competing ways for learning (Scarino & Liddicoat, 2016).

Within a view of pragmatics as social and moral practice, a particularly important dimension of meta-pragmatic awareness is constituted by the learner's awareness of cultural assumptions which influence evaluations of linguistic behaviour and the concepts used for evaluating language use in interpersonal terms. These concepts typically manifest as terms which express communicative effects such as 'politeness', terms which reflect aspects of context such as 'social distance', or other culturally defined notions such as 'respect', 'responsibility', 'sincerity', etc. While the work on meta-pragmatic awareness in SCT (e.g. van Compernolle, 2014) also emphasizes the importance of attention to the construal of these meta-pragmatic notions, the focus generally remains language internal. Research in ethnopragmatics (e.g. Goddard, 2012; Wierzbicka, 1985, 2006, etc.) and meta-pragmatics (e.g. Haugh, 2004, 2007; Spencer-Oatey, 1993; Spencer-Oatey & Kadar, 2016) has helped us understand that many of the terms used for meta-pragmatic evaluation contain culture-specific meanings. The notion of 'politeness' is a classic example. Not only can the conceptual domain of individual politeness terms differ across languages, but politeness terms themselves are embedded in a network of related terms, sometimes referred to as a 'semantic field' (Haugh & Hinze, 2003). For example, the English notion of politeness not only has multiple meanings, but these meanings can only be understood relative to other terms such as 'deference' or 'courtesy', which have obtained salience in the language based on their history of cultural meaning (Haugh, 2004). These individual concepts and their relationally defined meanings cannot be assumed to be the same across languages. In the Japanese language, the notion of *teinei* (polite) can be viewed as existing in a semantic field along with related notions such as *reigi tadashii* (well-mannered), which is again related to notions such as *keii* (deference) and more (Haugh, 2004).

These notions enter into speakers' evaluation of linguistic behaviour and can thus be said to function as meta-pragmatic frames for evaluation. Each language provides such terms as a resource for evaluating linguistic and non-linguistic behaviour, but such terms are necessarily nested in a complex semantic and meta-pragmatic architecture. In the language learning process, learners are likely to start from the assumption that the evaluative terms in the L1 will mean the same thing in the L2. As learners develop meta-pragmatic awareness they start to develop insight into the fact that what differs across languages is not simply the ways in which politeness is shown, but that the actual conception of politeness is different. In other words, emerging awareness of the variety of ways in which different languages instantiate and evaluate politeness can lead to insight into the relativity of the conceptual architecture around politeness. This has important implications for the development of an intercultural perspective on language use, as awareness of the culturally variable nature of the categories used for evaluating language use can provide a resource for making more considered evaluations of individuals from different cultural backgrounds, even when ways of communicating diverge from one's expectations.

Mediation is the attempt to consciously bring languages and cultures in relation to each other in the act of interpretation, and the meta-pragmatic awareness that develops from such a process encompasses elements of foreign cultural frames of understanding and also elements of one's own interpretive architecture. In this sense, the ability to effectively mediate depends on the learner's capacity for bringing implicit knowledge and assumptions into awareness through reflection. This is a challenge given that the specific architecture of knowledge and assumptions which underlies pragmatic interpretation is tied up with an individual's entire worldview. Giddens (1984) suggests that, of the amalgam of tacit knowledge that underlies our ability to give meaning to events, our reflexive capacities generally only operate in relation to a relatively small proportion of knowledge. While individuals who come from similar cultural backgrounds are likely to draw on broadly shared assumptions in their meta-pragmatic judgements, it is often more problematic to cogently articulate a rationale for such judgements. In the case of more highly formalized pragmatic norms in institutional discourse it may not be difficult for individuals to regurgitate specific norms such as 'In this context you should say X not Y'. However, it is inherently more problematic to comment on the broader cultural notions and values which allow such a rule to exist in the first place. This means that the systemic arrangement of cultural assumptions which the individual has internalized, shaped by the dominant ideological frameworks which provide the conditions for normativity, are likely to remain resistant to conscious identification. In fact, there is often a discrepancy between what people say they do in interaction and what they actually do (Deutscher, 1973). As Jaworski et al. (2004) explain:

> Metalinguistic representations may enter public consciousness and come to constitute structured understandings, perhaps even 'common sense' understandings – of how language works, what it is usually like, what certain ways of speaking connote and imply, what they ought to be like. (Jaworski et al., 2004: 3)

This means that there is a tendency to reproduce the more explicit third-order understandings of language use which are commonly articulated among language users in a given society, even when these notions may be may be incongruent with actual experience (Matsumoto, 2006). In Japan, for instance, the explanation might be offered that in Japanese it is often possible to omit the grammatical subject from the sentence in communication because 'Japanese people don't like to emphasize the self too much'. Or the tired old notion that 'Japanese people are shy' might be used to explain a perceived failure to acquire foreign languages well enough (Seargeant, 2009). Here, thus, aspects of language use are explicitly tied to a group's preferred way of seeing itself, and simultaneously given legitimacy in the process (Hirose & Hasegawa, 2010). In this way, individuals draw on social representations to form conventionalized explanations for behaviour, constituting what social psychologists call 'interpretive repertoires' (Wetherell & Potter, 1988). Interpretive repertoires are largely shaped by dominant discourses within a society and take the form of judgements accompanied by conventionalized justifications for these judgements. In terms of Kádár and Haugh's (2013) notion of layered expectancies, it is important to recognize the impact of ideology, particularly articulated through the prism of national identity or national characteristics, on an individual's justifications for meta-pragmatic evaluations. In the same vein, the individual's interpretive architecture ultimately needs to be seen as under the influence of dominant cultural narratives and ideological frameworks which are propagated within society (Agha, 1998).

Similarly, the way that learners relate to (or fail to relate to) the pragmatics of the foreign language can depend on the stereotypes they have of target language speakers. It is hard to overlook the fact that value judgement is intrinsic to intercultural communication and also to language learning, particularly when it comes to aspects of pragmatics (Littlewood, 2001). Exposure to different interactional practices can make learners uncomfortable at certain points and also generate ethnocentric (and sometimes quite negative) value judgements of aspects of the target language and its speakers (Liddicoat, 2014). At the cognitive level, one of the reasons why this occurs is that many individuals are simply not aware that their own assumptions exert such an influence on their own perception, or that they are even making judgements on the basis of assumptions at all (Hinton, 2015). The difficulty seems to be that many speakers 'cannot perceive that they are making culturally bound meta-pragmatic judgments and simply assess the speaker on the basis of simple ethnic stereotypes or more negative evaluations of unreasonableness, incompetence, and so on' (Roberts, 1998: 121).

One explanation for this is provided by construal-level theory in social psychology, which posits that we tend to 'construe psychologically near people (such as friends) in terms of concrete and detailed representations, but as the distance increases (to strangers) the construal becomes more abstract and generalized' (Hinton, 2015: 53). Thus, when interpreting behaviours of an outgroup population there is a tendency to come up with simplistic interpretations of observed phenomena. As pragmatic acts are essentially an instantiation of a particular view of social relations and individuals, any positive or negative stereotypes which learners possess about L2 speakers can colour their perceptions of the interactional features of the language and the interpersonal attributions they make. Importantly, stereotypes can decidedly affect the degree to which the learner wishes to appropriate the pragmatic features of the language (Ishihara & Tarone, 2009). Views of foreign others or of 'foreignness' in general cannot be separated from views of one's own cultural group and are thus necessarily ideological in nature (Holliday, 2010; Piller, 2011).

The ideological dimension of meta-pragmatic awareness has important implications for learning, particularly in understanding the difficulties and resistance that individuals can have in viewing pragmatic phenomena from alternate cultural perspectives. As discussed by Ishihara and Tarone (2009), for individuals coming from a background in which egalitarian ideologies are dominant, it can be very confronting to learn a language in which hierarchical distinctions are more salient and in which the assumption that 'we are all equal' fails to apply. When ideologically sanctioned assumptions drawn from one's own culture appear not to work, the common response is to denigrate the other. This incites a rationalization process whereby stereotypes of the target group are activated – such as the idea that 'they have no individuality' – or formulated in order to ease one's own cognitive dissonance (Hinton, 2015). Thus, pragmatic differences can trigger emotional reactions which lead to ethnocentric reasoning based on stereotypes. The problem is not so much a matter of being unable to recognize different ways of seeing things but being attached to a particular version of how things *should be*. The learners' interpretive architecture thus will potentially contain unacknowledged stereotypes of self and other at multiple levels. Attempts at developing meta-pragmatic awareness within the classroom will therefore involve engaging with stereotypical representations of cultural groups and teachers' and learners' perceptions of how these influence communication patterns. To the extent that learners' preconceptions and stereotypes about foreign languages and their speakers enter into the act of meta-pragmatic interpretation, they constitute important elements of interpretive architecture which deserve interrogation in the language classroom. As Warner (2011: 14) suggests, time needs to be spent in the classroom to 'complicate their presuppositions about what a language is and what it means to use it, and to question the very categories through which we understand cultures and what it means to analyze or participate within them'.

As above, the development of meta-pragmatic awareness requires engaging not simply with knowledge of pragmatic norms, but with fundamental assumptions about the nature of social reality and ideologically constructed stereotypes of cultural groups. This necessarily involves stepping outside one's usual frames of reference to look at others and oneself (within and across cultures) in new ways, making an effort to go beyond simplistic intercultural comparisons to interrogate the layers of assumptions that lead to meaning and value attributions (Byram, 1997; Liddicoat & Scarino, 2013). In the intercultural field, this process of distancing oneself from existing assumptions is referred to as 'decentering' (Byram *et al.*, 2001), and is often assumed to be part of the process of moving from an ethnocentric to an ethnorelative perspective on a foreign culture (Bennett, 1993). Applied to the process of language learning, this kind of relativistic stance does not mean that the language learner needs to abandon his or her own values, but rather needs the willingness and ability to engage reflexively with his or her own assumptions about language and how it functions as a cultural tool (Crozet & Liddicoat, 1999). It means being aware of the ways that assumptions about ways of communicating lead to interpersonal evaluations and that this has consequences for how one evaluates and is evaluated by others.

Such a process is not necessarily easy. It can be a confronting experience to disconnect from one's conventional ways of seeing the world and many people experience resistance in their attempts to do so (Haidt & Joseph, 2007; Hinton, 2015). In the realm of pragmatics, learners' ability to decentre from existing assumptions and see foreign interactional practices as legitimate is very contextual, as is their ability to objectify L1 practices (McConachy & Liddicoat, 2016). For instance, a learner of Japanese as a foreign language may accept the need to use honorifics to those whose superior status is institutionally sanctioned (such as a teacher or supervisor), but not see why it is necessary to use honorifics in informal contexts simply for reasons such as the interlocutor being a little older than them (Siegal, 1996). Or there may be initial acceptance, which later turns to scepticism and then rejection of the target language norms. The learners' reaction to aspects of target language pragmatics can oscillate from suspicion and discomfort to acceptance and back again depending on the context of the interaction. Importantly, the learners' perceptions of L2 pragmatic norms, and how they react to them at a cognitive and affective level, influences how they choose to use the L2 inside and outside the classroom. In this sense, meta-pragmatic awareness as articulated in this section is a resource which links interpretation and performance. This will be discussed further below.

Intercultural mediation and the construction of second language performance

Any behavioural trajectory that we take vis-à-vis others has the potential to be viewed as indexing who we are, not simply at that particular moment but who we are in a broader sense as a social and moral human being. Therefore, as a key social behaviour, the issue of how to use language in face-to-face communication is simultaneously a question of meaning, as well as impression management and identity. It is through our interactional decisions that we stake a claim to particular roles, identities and positions, depending on how see ourselves and how we imagine others see us (Goffman, 1959; Harre

& van Langenhove, 1999). In this sense, the individual speech acts that we carry out and the ways we negotiate discourse come to constitute identity resources (Bucholtz & Hall, 2010). The task in coming to use the target language is indeed learning how to 'do things with words', but the things that are done with words go beyond an exchange of information or the simple performance of a linguistic act. Moreover, the development of the ability to put the L2 to use in a productive capacity involves mediating between existing understandings of the social world and relating these to the L2 input which is encountered in the learning process. This is an ongoing creative activity. As Kramsch (2009) has highlighted by her notion of symbolic competence, the task of the learner is an exploratory one which involves creatively utilizing aspects of the target language to construct social meanings and impressions, and find new ways of being in relation to others. The conventional meanings of target language forms are a resource for the learner, but the learner will necessarily bring his or her own meanings to them and put them to use in ways that may diverge from convention (Canagarajah, 2007). The construction of agency in the L2 – the ability to make informed decisions about how to interact – is a process which involves conscious reflection on cultural understandings drawn from multiple sources and the ability to direct attention to the context of interaction, the interpersonal relationships that are at play, and the kinds of impressions that one wants to convey through the interaction. The development of meta-pragmatic awareness, as conceptualized in the previous section, is an important foundation for exercising agency in an L2.

One way of looking at the link between meta-pragmatic awareness and agency more concretely is by considering the ways in which individuals might want to manage the interpersonal impressions they convey. As discussed at various points so far, interpersonal evaluation is an important concern for language learners, especially when they begin to engage in intercultural communication in the L2 outside the classroom. If a learner has as a part of his or her self-concept the perception of him-/herself as a 'kind' person, for instance, this is likely to be an impression that the learner will want to construct when interacting with L2 speakers. The question, then, would be how the impression of 'kindness' might be constructed through the medium of the target language, given that this will need to take into account local interpersonal and interactional norms and expectations. This can be applied to almost any key attribute that an individual might hope to convey for the purposes of impression formation and management, such as how to be 'competent', 'assertive', 'tolerant', 'respectful', and more. When the pragmatic aspects of the L1 and L2 are quite similar, constructing one's intended impressions can be relatively unproblematic. However, when the conventions for interacting in the L2 significantly diverge from the L1 and are rooted in very different cultural norms and conceptions, the possibilities for using L2 linguistic resources for coming across as a 'polite', 'serious', etc. can be hard to identify. In this sense, a learner's agency in the L2 is enhanced by meta-pragmatic awareness of a wide range of L2 conventions and how they can be used to convey particular attributes (van Compernolle, 2014).

However, any attempt to exercise agency in communication in the L2 is also dependent on the context of communication, whose norms are dominant within that context, and the various roles that the individual is able to take up in the L2 community (such as employee, friend, boss, etc.). It is also dependent on power relationships and the extent to which members of an L2 community are willing to grant the learner the right to articulate their own voice (McKay & Wong, 1996; Norton, 2013). In the case of lingua franca interactions that take place outside a clearly defined speech community, the dynamics will be different as it may not be clear what norms and expectations might be at play. Crucially, a learner's construction of performance in the L2 will depend on perceptions of contexts, roles and relationships drawn from L1-embedded interpretive architecture (Liu, 1995). Additionally, the construction of performance depends on how comfortable learners are with wholeheartedly adopting the pragmatic conventions of the target language. This is a complex matter, as there will be learners who may wish to emulate native speakers and those who may not, or those who may wish to do so in some instances and not in others. Decisions about which interactional features of the target language to adopt and when to adopt them are contextually formulated on the basis of mediation between the cultural assumptions and sense of self established in the first language/s and that of the target language. In terms of interactional agency, thus, it is a much more complex affair than simply knowing the conventional options for interacting in the target language. Considered decision making vis-à-vis how to position oneself through interactional choices additionally requires reflexive awareness of the ways that one's culturally shaped assumptions influence the ways the options for interaction are understood (Byram & Zarate, 1997). In this sense, meta-pragmatic awareness developed on the basis of ongoing intercultural mediation is inherent to the ability to exercise agency.

In terms of how mediation manifests in language performance, the metaphor of the 'third place' has often been invoked to highlight the fact that rather than conforming to existing cultural norms, the intercultural speaker uses language to construct intermediary positions (Crozet & Liddicoat, 1999; Kramsch, 1993; Liddicoat, 2005). In early work, authors such as Kramsch (1993) and House (2008) emphasized what they regard as the inevitable distinctiveness of the ways individuals use a foreign language. They described the third place as a linguistic and cultural standpoint characterized by hybridity in language use – language use which appears to conform to neither L1 nor target language norms. Such hybridity has been construed positively as evidence of speakers generating creative solutions to the issue of self-presentation based on mediation of the cultural systems at play. However, one problem with the notion of the third place is that it has been accompanied by a tendency to uncritically value hybridity in language use. In fact, in many instances, intercultural language use is considered synonymous with hybrid-ity (Block, 2007; Zotzmann, 2017). In intercultural communication, speakers may draw on aspects of their first language, or aspects of L2 norms, or in lingua franca contexts they may accommodate to the interlocutor's norms. It is necessarily fluid and dynamic, based on the various contingencies in a given interactional context and desire for indexing particular aspects of a speaker's identity, his or her relationship to the interlocutor and other sociolinguistic variables (Baker, 2011; Kramsch, 2009). Regardless of whether actual language performance conforms to L1 norms, L2 norms or is a hybrid accommodation, what is fundamentally important is that the choices that led to the perfor-mance were considered ones (Liddicoat, 2005). In other words, language use is not considered 'intercultural' simply based on its surface features; intercul-turality is constituted by the mediation of languages and cultures to arrive at a suitable outcome given the learner's contextual assessment. From this per-spective, language use which conforms to target language norms can be con-sidered intercultural if it is what the speaker determines as the most suitable course of action considering the cultural variables at play. Conversely, hybrid-ity in language use is not by itself evidence of intercultural mediation because the nature of the individuals' intercultural understanding cannot automati-cally be inferred from it (Sewell, 2013).

Throughout the language learning process, learners have opportunities to put the target language to use for a range of communicative purposes. However, in communicatively oriented classrooms, there is often emphasis on getting the message across rather than reflecting on the nature of the message and what the selection of linguistic strategies might symbolize in terms of social identities or generation of interpersonal impressions (Scarino, 2007). If learners are to develop agency to put the target language to use for their own purposes – which are not just linguistic but also social – then the development of meta-pragmatic awareness is an important tool for helping develop that agency. As has been discussed in this section, this is equally a matter of know-ing the norms for interaction in the L2 as it is of being aware of one's own assumptions about appropriate and effective ways of communicating in par-ticular roles and relationships, as well as the kinds of impressions one wants to convey to others. Meta-pragmatic awareness is a necessary resource for considering the options for interaction and this awareness is sustained and enhanced by interpretation and reflection on the basis of ongoing interac-tional experiences (Gohard-Radenkovic *et al.*, 2004; Liddicoat & Scarino, 2013).

Layers of meta-pragmatic awareness in intercultural language learning: A synthesis

As has been articulated throughout the previous sections, meta-pragmatic awareness is awareness of the various layers of meaning which are brought to bear for the purposes of interpreting and using language as a form of social action. Meta-pragmatic awareness is a layered phenomenon which links awareness of linguistic forms to use in contexts, interpersonal roles and relationships, and also to ideologically constructed views of cultural in-groups and out-groups. The conceptualization of meta-pragmatic awareness development in intercultural language learning builds on understandings from earlier work on noticing (Schmidt, 1993) and conceptual understanding (van Compernolle, 2014), but contains two main conceptual expansions. First, it expands the scope of meta-pragmatic awareness to include learners' awareness of the ways in which interpersonal impressions derive from the interpretation of other people's ways of speaking. In this sense, it foregrounds the fact that pragmatic judgements are value judgements and that awareness of the ways in which we slip from interpretation of language to interpretation of others is important in learning an L2 for intercultural communication. Seeing pragmatics from the perspective of value judgement allows for a move away from exclusive focus on 'appropriateness' as the single criterion for evaluating language use and opens up room for exploration of the basis of a wider range of interpersonal evaluations shaped by cultural assumptions, stereotypes and ideologies. The second expansion is the addition of the notion of interpretive architecture and the idea that development of awareness of that architecture is essential to considered interpretation of L1 and L2 pragmatics and also to exercising agency in one's own use of the L2.

In intercultural language learning, meta-pragmatic awareness is developed in relation to multiple languages and includes reflective understanding of how cultural assumptions drawn from the pragmatics of individual languages influence learners' own perceptions of language use throughout the learning process. It thus provides one potential resource for developing insight into various connections between language and culture, enhancing the learners' capacities for insightful interpretation, and gradually contributing to the development of an intercultural perspective on language use over time. Learners draw on and reflect on their pre-existing knowledge, assumptions and values as a framework for making sense of foreign language meanings, and move between cultural frameworks through ongoing interpretation in order to establish a sense for the meaning potential at one's disposal (Byram, 2003). This leads to an expansion and reorganization of the individual's interpretive architecture as the learner engages in a process of discovering and interpreting the cultural frameworks within which L2 pragmatic forms are embedded and attempting to reconcile these with one's own assumptions derived from the L1. Throughout the learning process, the learner's interpretive architecture is in a constantly emerging synergistic state whereby the individual brings culturally derived frameworks from separate languages into relationship (Kecskes, 2014).

Intercultural Learning Practices in Classroom Interaction

From both a teaching and a learning perspective, the development of an intercultural perspective on language use is a long-term process which is driven by a consistent interpretive engagement with aspects of language use and the development of meta-pragmatic awareness. For the language teacher, an immediate question is what might constitute such an interpretive engagement in more concrete terms. One way of looking at this is in terms of specific practices that constitute interpretation. Liddicoat and Scarino (2013) suggest that intercultural language learning can be seen as occurring through a cycle of learning practices (Figure 2.1), encompassing interacting, noticing, comparing and reflecting on aspects of language and culture.

In a language classroom which aims to teach communication, learners will have various exposure to samples of communication (written, audio, computer mediated, etc.), and opportunities for discussion and trying out new expressions, new speech acts and new tasks. Learning occurs as learners engage with a range of linguistic input, alone or in conjunction with other learners, in order to actively understand what they are being exposed to. As a potential entry point into the cycle, *noticing* functions as a metaphor for the development of awareness into features of the target language such as vocabulary, rhetorical patterns, norms for interaction, etc. (Liddicoat & Scarino, 2013). Noticing can be seen in terms of Schmidt's (1990) conception of consciously registered input and is considered an important part of developing awareness of linguistic regularities and potential differences across languages.

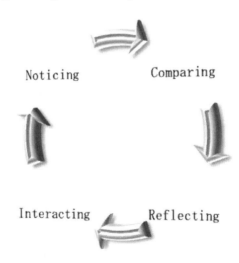

Noticing   Comparing

Interacting   Reflecting

Figure 2.1 Practices of intercultural learning
Source: Liddicoat and Scarino (2013: 60).

Comparing means that learners attempt to reconcile and explain what they have noticed about the target language in relation to their existing L2 knowledge and also what they know about other languages. This is theorized to help develop further clarity of awareness about what has been noticed and how it may or may not differ across cultures. *Reflecting* involves learners in a process of considering the meaning of what is being observed, including how aspects of language embody and presuppose particular ways of viewing the world. Reflection encompasses both a cognitive and affective dimension, as learners consider how they position themselves in relation to aspects of language and the consequences that this has for identity management. All of these processes are supported by *interacting*. The concept of interacting here highlights that the abovementioned aspects of interpretation are not only cognitive and affective but also discursive. That is, noticing, comparison and reflection are manifested in the ways learners talk about language, both with teachers and with one another. In other words, interaction is chiefly characterized by performance tasks and languaging – talk in which language itself is made the object of discussion (Swain, 2006).

Languaging occurs both as an individual and a collaborative activity within the classroom to serve the dual function expressing learners' perspectives on the material to which they are exposed, helping them develop insight into their own thoughts, and also by scaffolding the collective development of insightful interpretations into aspects of language and culture (Liddicoat & Scarino, 2013; Phipps & Gonzalez, 2004). In theoretical terms, this is supported by the dialectical relationship between speaking and thinking posited in SCT, whereby the act of articulating one's thoughts simultaneously helps to develop it (Vygotsky, 1978). Intercultural language learning thus draws on SCT as a theoretical resource for understanding the role of talk in shaping how language and culture are interpreted within classroom interaction.

The individual practices of intercultural learning combine to constitute the interpretive engagement with aspects of language and culture that leads to learning. Applied to pragmatics, it means that learners relate to input about target language pragmatics, individually and collaboratively reflect on what they have encountered, and compare aspects of interaction across cultures. Through such a process, learners develop sensitivity to the contingency of meaning across languages and cultures and explore the cultural assumptions that influence how meaning and impressions are constructed. Although many assumptions underlying perception of the social world and expectations regarding language use in context remain unarticulated, it is significant that as humans we are capable of bringing underlying assumptions into awareness through reflection, particularly through talk about talk (Kramsch, 1993). The classroom can be used for engaging in a range of metapragmatic commentary, such as commenting on language use, requesting clarification of meanings, explaining meanings, criticizing ways of using language, and more (Verschueren, 2004). Such activities support the important function of helping learners specify their expectations regarding linguistic meanings and also how they think something should be expressed for a particular purpose in a particular interpersonal context. Explicit talk about the conditions of language use and the reflection on meaning that is facilitated by this talk means that meta-pragmatics is 'a critical instrument of fundamental importance in digging up and highlighting presuppositions as well as the different kinds of the unsaid' (Caffi, 1994: 2465). This provides a clear link between explicit talk about language and the development of meta-pragmatic awareness which can be exploited in the language classroom, particularly in the form of collaborative dialogue for comparing interpretations of language and culture among learners (Swain & Lapkin, 1995).

Within the classroom, the intercultural learning practices are not simply a vehicle for developing meta-pragmatic awareness but for developing the interpretive capacities learners need for intercultural communication in the L2. Learners are helped to become analytical and reflective users of the L2 who are able to use their skills for ongoing learning (Liddicoat & Scarino, 2013). It is the development of the learners' capacities for interpretation and the ability to develop meta-pragmatic awareness through experience that is essential to the development of an intercultural perspective on language use over time. The teacher plays a key role in helping learners meaningfully engage in the learning practices. In the intercultural classroom, the teacher's role is complex as teachers themselves come with their own perspectives on language use shaped out of their own experiences. In this sense, teachers are also mediators of language and culture (Kohler, 2015). The ways in which teachers express their own perspectives, as well as the ways in which they present input to students and prompt them to engage with it have a large effect on the learning affordances that can be derived. This is something that will be discussed and illustrated in great detail in the chapters following.

The Current Study: A Classroom-based Study of English as a Foreign Language Learning in Japan

In the previous sections, I have reconceptualized the notion of meta-pragmatic awareness and discussed its role in the development of a learner's intercultural perspective on language use throughout the learning process. The argument that I am putting forward is that an intercultural perspective on language use is constructed over time by the development of meta-pragmatic awareness. However, the development of meta-pragmatic awareness is highly dependent on learners' interpretive engagement with aspects of language use. As suggested by Liddicoat and Scarino (2013), this interpretive engagement can be seen in terms of processes of noticing, reflecting, comparing and interacting. Liddicoat's (2006) study on the learning of L2 French by Australian learners presents individual learners' commentary elicited at several points during a semester to show how noticing, comparison and reflection led learners to decentre from L1-based perspectives and develop more nuanced understandings of target language pragmatics. What this study does not show is how such an interpretive engagement might actually unfold in the classroom as learners interact with one another and the teacher. In fact, in the field of foreign language teaching, there has been very little research looking at the various ways that learners analytically engage with aspects of language use and how meta-pragmatic awareness is developed within the context of classroom interactions. van Compernolle's (2014) study on learners of L2 French in the United States remedies this to a certain extent through the close attention it pays to the construction of conceptual understanding of pragmatic features within teacher – student interactions during tutoring sessions. However, it does not adopt an intercultural perspective or show how learning is constructed within interactions among learners themselves.

The study here does not aim to show the development of learners' intercultural perspectives on language use from a longitudinal perspective. What it aims to show primarily is the nature of learners' interpretive engagement with aspects of pragmatics and how the process of interaction shapes the learners' engagement in the practices of noticing, reflection and comparison. It looks at how meta-pragmatic awareness is developed through these practices in a variety of classroom learning activities which are engineered towards helping learners look at meaning-making processes from multiple perspectives. As such, the notion of 'development' essentially refers to the construction of meta-pragmatic awareness within particular analytical activities, evidenced by the emergence within classroom talk of more complex interpretations of pragmatic aspects of language in use and insight into learners' own interpretive architecture.

Course design, stance towards materials, and implementation

As mentioned in the Introduction, the data come from a case study on intercultural language learning within a 10-week communicative EFL course taught by the author at a study-abroad preparation institute in Tokyo, Japan. The course consisted of four hours of classroom-based learning per week, amounting to 40 hours overall. Due to the institute's mandate to prepare students for study-abroad (at that time, mostly in the UK and Australia), the course was intended by the institution to have dual aims: (1) the development of the learners' communicative ability in the four skills to an 'upper-intermediate' level; and (2) to impart the kind of cultural knowledge useful for daily life when studying abroad in the UK. To achieve these goals, the institution had specified use of *New Headway: Pre-Intermediate* (written by Soars & Soars, 2002, published by Oxford University Press) as a general coursebook for developing overall communication skills.

As many teachers know, the specification of an international coursebook for use in classes presents both opportunities and constraints, particularly when hoping to implement interculturally oriented language teaching. For those who take the position that intercultural language teaching can only be implemented with the use of 'authentic materials' or ample direct contact with L2 speakers, the specification of a coursebook for use might appear to eliminate the possibility of focusing on language and culture in a meaningful way. After all, textbooks are frequently criticized for the overly simplistic ways in which they present L2 communication and aspects of culture (e.g. Liddicoat, 2002; McConachy & Hata, 2013; Nguyen, 2011). However, the stance I adopted in this course was that, in the same way that the use of authentic materials does not guarantee authentic learning, the use of inauthentic materials cannot be equated with inauthentic learning (Breen, 1985). The development of an intercultural perspective on language use over time is predicated on the acquisition of a certain amount of knowledge of L2 norms derived from authentic materials or from direct experience of using the language in contexts outside the classroom. However, the main source of authenticity derives from the nature of the learners' interpretive engagement with language and the ways in which learners are socialized into the practice of looking at language use in analytical ways, reflecting on how meanings are understood and exploring their own assumptions (Liddicoat & Scarino, 2013). This does not exclude the use of authentic materials, but it does not always necessitate them. An additional dimension of my stance was the understanding that, in a world in which languages are used by speakers from a wide range of linguistic and cultural backgrounds, language learners need the ability to reflect on the significance of the language they encounter whether it conforms to conventional notions of authenticity or not. From this perspective, treating coursebook content as an artefact to be examined opens up the possibility for meaningful engagement and learning. Given the reliance on coursebooks in many communicatively oriented language classrooms around the world, it is important to work creatively with the resources available, while treating the resources themselves as things to be examined by learners within the process of learning (McConachy, 2009).

Based on the stance articulated above, two specific goals I established for the course were: (1) to develop awareness of the role of cultural knowledge and assumptions in the interpretation and evaluation of language use; and (2) to develop the ability to decentre from one's existing interpretations and perspectives. In order to achieve these goals, I identified units within the coursebook which contained a pragmatic focus and constructed a 10-week plan (Table 2.1).

One aspect of pragmatics was focused on each week, with a particular emphasis on speech acts. In designing the content for this course, the aim was to spend several weeks focusing on familiar conversational routines, then move on to common speech acts, and finally move on to more complex

Table 2.1 Outline of course content

Week 1	Greeting routines
Week 2	Interactional routines about the weekend
Week 3	Common customer service interactions
Week 4	Requesting
Week 5	Apologizing
Week 6	Complimenting
Week 7	Inviting
Week 8	Role-plays based on Week 1–7 speech acts and routines
Week 9	Dialogue analysis based on 'SPEAKING' (Hymes, 1974)
Week 10	Exploring cultural generalizations

analytical tasks which aimed to synthesize knowledge and understandings generated in earlier lessons. At the planning stage, it was determined that one lesson (110 minutes) would provide enough time for a range of both analytical and performance-based activities based on a given pragmatic focus, meaning that each lesson would be relatively self-contained. Classroom activities consisted mainly of brainstorming, cloze activities, contextual analysis, reading tasks, dialogue performance, role-plays and reflective discussions. In addition to classwork, students were asked to keep a learning journal, in order to consolidate their own learning and to provide a valuable data source for this study.

Principles for teaching

In order to create a suitable environment for interpretive engagement with pragmatics-based ideas and texts, the following pedagogical principles were outlined for planning purposes prior to the course and thus constituted a framework for teaching and learning.

(1) Learners are encouraged to use both English and Japanese as a resource for discussion in the classroom.
(2) Learners are encouraged to reflect on their experiences of communicating in Japanese and English.
(3) Learners are encouraged to explore both cognitive and affective dimensions of language use.
(4) Learners are encouraged to build abilities for reflecting on language use in relation to context.
(5) The teacher is flexible in terms of introducing new activities and content depending on how learning unfolds each week.

The assumption behind such principles was that engaging in reflection on aspects of pragmatics would necessitate a large amount of language analysis by learners, characterized by explicit discussion of interactional features and meaning in relation to context and culture. To promote intercultural mediation, such discussion would require reference to both Japanese and English for examples, and also as a medium for discussion. Learning activities were thus structured on a view of interaction as central to learning and of all available languages existing as potential resources (Swain & Lapkin, 1995). The orientation to pedagogy can be understood as aiming to promote the active construction of meanings across languages and cultures (Liddicoat & Scarino, 2013).

Participants

There were four participants in the study, aged between 20 and 25. Although none of the students had spent extended periods of time living overseas, all of them had travelled internationally and were looking forward to living and studying in the UK in the near future. Names indicated below are pseudonyms. The students and teacher were not acquainted prior to commencement of the course.

Tai: 20-year-old male student majoring in tourism at a university in Tokyo. He hoped to attend graduate school in the UK.

Seiji: 20-year-old male student majoring in French literature at a university in Tokyo. He hoped to study intercultural communication at a university overseas in the future.

Misato: 23-year-old female graduate student studying gender studies at a university in Tokyo. She hoped to complete an MA or a PhD in the UK. She subsequently hoped to return to Japan to become a professor of English at a university.

Hikari: 25-year-old female company employee who was hoping to study fashion in the UK in the future.

Data collection and analysis

The study utilized multiple methods for data collection, including audio-recordings of the classes in their entirety, researcher notes, student learning journals and post-course interviews. In order to tap into the learners' interpretations and the ways in which interaction shaped the development of ideas, it is advantageous to have such multiple data sources so that themes can be cross-referenced and a more revealing picture of the sense-making process of all participants constructed (Miles & Hubermann, 1994). Although I approached the data by looking for the expression of particular perspectives on language and culture, I did not generate coding categories in advance. Rather, once the audio data had been transcribed in their entirety, content analysis was conducted on the transcribed interactional data from the first three lessons. Content analysis was understood as 'a careful, detailed, systematic examination and interpretation of a particular body of material in an effort to identify patterns, themes, biases, and meanings' (Neuendorf, 2002). The preliminary analysis of the first three lessons was done in order to generate preliminary coding categories. Examples of early codes that came up were 'language as scripted' and 'language as action', which were chosen to represent the view of language that learners appeared to reveal through their commentary. These initial categories constituted a lens for the analysis of the next several lessons, after which categories were revised to reflect the increasing complexity revealed by the emerging analysis. In this way, there was a high amount of self-reflexivity in the coding process, which allowed the categories to be further refined (Hammersely & Atkinson, 1995). Another technique which was used at this point was the writing of research memos (Miles & Hubermann, 1994), which eventuated in several publications (McConachy, 2008, 2013). Once content analysis had been conducted on each lesson contained within the audio data, I looked across the entire sequence of lessons in order to examine the salience of the coding categories and draw connections regarding the nature of learner perspectives. This was combined with content analysis of the learning journals, researcher notes, and finally the interview data.

Chapter Conclusion

This chapter has reconceptualized the notion of meta-pragmatic awareness within an intercultural orientation to language teaching and suggested the role of meta-pragmatic awareness in the learners' development of an intercultural perspective on language use. It has further outlined the stance taken to teaching and learning in the course which constitutes the foundation for discussion of classroom learning in the next chapters.

3 Developing a View of Language Use as Social Action

Introduction

The development of an intercultural perspective on language use depends greatly on the learner's ability to begin to view language use as a form of social action and reflect on the ways in which meanings and impressions are constructed and negotiated among speakers. This in turn requires that language learners are encouraged to move beyond pragmatic prescriptions and develop the ability to explicitly consider the role of sociocultural context in language use (van Compernolle, 2014). This chapter looks at a specific learning activity that I refer to as contextual analysis. Resonating with Crystal's (1997) view of pragmatics, contextual analysis engages learners in processes of collaborative reflection on constructed conversational dialogues, primarily from the perspective of the linguistic choices made by speakers, the sociocultural factors that might have influenced their choices, and the effects that choices appear to have on the interlocutor within the negotiation of meanings and impressions (McConachy, 2009). In concrete terms, learners are guided to pay close attention to specific utterances used by dialogue characters within sequential interaction, and then construct interpretations regarding the feelings and communicative intentions of the speakers which they justify with explicit reference to the setting of the communication, the relationship between the interlocutors and a host of other sociocultural variables. This, however, does not necessarily mean that learners are expected to come up with deterministic explanations for language use in view of context. Rather, it means that learners engage in perspective-taking and explore the potential significance of language choices within unfolding interaction. In other words, contextual analysis requires not so much a 'matching' of language forms to context, but a relating of language forms to context. Such a process mobilizes the learner's interpretive architecture and provides a route to closer reflection on learners' own assumptions about language use in context (Meier, 2010). The chapter is structured around sequences of classroom discussions based on particular dialogues

57

which show how a range of analytical foci are constructed within the classroom talk and how processes of reflection, noticing and comparison support the development of meta-pragmatic awareness.

Interpreting and Evaluating Language Use from a Strategic Perspective

In order to be able to gradually develop insight into the fact that language use is interpreted with reference to culturally shaped expectations, language learners first of all need to gradually develop a view of language as a dynamic resource that speakers utilize for a range of social ends (Liddicoat, 2006). One of the ways in which contextual analysis is conducive to the development of such a view is when learners collaboratively reflect on motivations behind linguistic choices, both in relation to individual utterances and to sequences of utterances. Such reflection generates an analytical frame within which learners begin to examine how social intentions (such as the intention to have one's request met) are strategically encoded by a speaker, interpreted by a hearer, and then negotiated over multiple turns. Through analysis and reflection within classroom interaction, learners begin to attend to language use as a strategic, context-dependent and interactionally negotiated phenomenon (Haugh, 2012).

Language input: Requesting

Face-threatening acts such as requests are particularly valuable for contextual analysis, in that those who make a request generally need to balance their need to have the request met with the need to attend to the face needs of the interlocutor (Brown & Levinson, 1978). Whereas textbooks often present requests as achieved primarily by single phrases, dialogues present request forms within an interactional context which can be taken up to engage learners' interpretive processes. Most dialogues constructed by teachers or found in textbooks will necessarily be simplified to a certain degree in comparison to the messiness of real-world face-to-face interaction. When the aim of learning is to enhance learners' interpretive abilities, particularly of beginner and intermediate learners, this simplified structure is highly advantageous. As below (Figure 3.1), when dialogues contain multiple interactional moves such as a pre-request, a rejection and further negotiation moves, attention can be directed to these features to help learners construct a view of language use as a negotiated accomplishment.

One issue that emerges immediately when learners engage with a dialogue is what they will pay attention to (i.e. 'notice') and whether or not they will consider the sociocultural context of interaction at all. If learners see the dialogue simply as one way of putting sentence-level discourse (phrases for requesting, for example) into a situation, then they are less likely

Aiko and Julia work at a busy Western-style restaurant in Tokyo. They have worked together here for 6 months.

Aiko: Hi, Julia. Are you busy?

Julia: Not really. What's up?

Aiko: Actually I was wondering if I could ask you a big favor.

Julia: Oh yeah? What's that?

Aiko: I know it's a bit sudden, but I was wondering if you could do my shift for me this Saturday.

Julia: Ahh…actually I have plans to go shopping with a few friends on Saturday…

Aiko: Oh, ok. It's just that my son has a big swimming competition on Saturday and I'd really like to go and watch him compete. I had completely forgotten about it until this morning.

Julia: Oh, no. Sorry to hear that. Well, what time does the competition finish?

Aiko: Um, it starts at 6:00 in the morning, so it should be finished by around 10:30. Would you mind covering for me just until then? I promise I'll get here as soon as I can.

Julia: All right. If it finishes around that time it shouldn't be a problem. I'm not meeting the girls until lunch time anyway.

Aiko: Oh, that's fantastic! Thanks, I really appreciate it!

Figure 3.1 Aiko and Julia dialogue
Source: McConachy (unpublished resource).

to give close examination to the nature of the situation itself and how the interactional choices within reflect the communicative needs of the respective participants. The extract below represents a teacher-led reflective discussion based on a comparison of Tai and Seiji's performance of the dialogue and the teacher's performance of the dialogue (in the role of Aiko) together with Misato. The opportunity to compare performance leads learners to notice the strategic use of paralinguistics (tone) in performing the request, which then leads to reflection on the logic underlying such a strategy.

Extract 3.1

1 **Teacher:** So did anything feel different to when you read it?
2 **Tai:** Um, Aiko as you played, Aiko showed that she has a bad feeling about this question.
3 **Teacher:** Right, right. That's one very important thing I think. It's a kind of big request and it's very sudden. So, I guess if she doesn't show that she feels bad about making the request, it's kind of rude. Did you have any other feelings about that?

4 **Tai:**   Julia, um, wasn't think it's okay.
5 **Teacher:** At first? Yeah.
6 **Tai:**   Actually, Julia accepted her request because Aiko sounded
              kind.
7 **Teacher:** Good.

As can be seen above, the teacher prompts comparison immediately following his performance, to which Tai responds quickly (Line 2) that he interprets something strategic about the way the head act is performed. The teacher takes up this noticing in his next turn and interprets it with reference to the size and timing of the request, presenting them as important sociocultural variables which may become linked to judgements of (im)politeness (Brown & Levinson, 1978). He then prompts the students for further comment, in response to which Tai interprets (in Lines 4 and 6) the character Julia as being initially unwilling to comply with the request, only eventually agreeing to do so as a result of Aiko's use of intonation modelled by the teacher or, as Tai puts it, sounding 'kind'. The nature of Tai's commentary reveals that in examining the interaction he is taking up the perspective of both speakers: on the one hand considering how the use of paralinguistics was tied up with the speaker's intent, and on the other hand considering the effect that this had on the interlocutor in the interaction (Crystal, 1997).

Comparison between student and teacher performance can be seen to provide a context for reflection, which is in turn facilitative in Tai's noticing of the strategic use of paralinguistics. In other words, reflection provides a catalyst for noticing based on comparison. The teacher works with Tai's interpretations by relating them to sociocultural context and prompting further reflection, helping him to articulate a perspective on the speech act as involving strategic language use and negotiated between the speakers over multiple turns of talk. From a structural perspective, Lines 1–3 of this interaction can be viewed as a type of initiation-response-feedback (IRF) sequence (Cazden, 2001), although here the teacher does more than just provide feedback with Line 3. The teacher's commentary has clear scaffolding functions in terms of developing the analysis. The teacher's meta-pragmatic commentary that, '... *if she doesn't show that she feels bad about making the request, it's kind of rude*', contains an approximation of Tai's language in Line 2 ('*show she has a bad feeling*'). This linguistic approximation within the reformulation functions to create more obvious coherence across the two turns and makes it clear that the teacher is building on Tai's interpretation. This strategy can thus be seen as scaffolding the development of his interpretation and contributing to the emerging analysis by making important aspects of context available for further reflection. The nature of the meta-pragmatic awareness here can be seen in terms of the emergence of a lens for the examination of language use as social action negotiated among participants. Even within a short interaction, language in a dialogue is repositioned as something to be analyzed rather than simply repeated and memorized. This then also opens up a space for looking more closely at the request sequence itself, as below.

Here, Hikari and Misato are working together to construct an answer to the question, 'How many parts does Aiko's request have?' Although the idea of a request having 'parts' appears to be initially confusing, the students bring up the different ways in which the request has been formulated in the dialogue in response to the need to obtain Julia's agreement. Through their interaction below, Hikari and Misato take a perspective on requests as 'unfolding' in discourse, rather than as achieved by isolated phrases (Kasper, 2006; Lo Castro, 2003).

Extract 3.2

1 **Hikari:**   I still haven't understood this meaning: 'How many parts does Aiko's request have?' How did she proceed?
2 **Misato:**   Ah, so I thought that means how many times did she try. Maybe Aiko tried to ask Julia by changing her form of request.
3 **Hikari:**   Yeah, yeah, she just try and try.
4 **Misato:**   Yes, I think she is trying by changing her form of request.
5 **Hikari:**   Yeah, yeah, yeah. So in the beginning part, she just wanted to change for the day, but after that she asked about Julia's condition and she changed a little bit.
6 **Misato:**   This and this is question, but this sentence is not. She tells only what she to do but enter kind of indirect request I think.

In the first two lines Hikari and Misato are trying to understand the questions they have been asked to discuss and answer. For Hikari it seems that the idea of a request having parts seems to be causing confusion. Conversely, Misato seems to interpret the idea of parts in terms of the varying forms which Aiko uses in the dialogue to make her request. On the surface it may appear that in Lines 1 and 2 the students are engaging in a kind of pre-task opening (Hellermann, 2007), where they try to make sense of the task, and therefore the analysis has not yet begun. From a different perspective, as the implicit purpose of this task was to develop in the students a view of requesting as achieved over multiple turns, this kind of talk can be viewed as mediating the students' control over the task, and thus helping achieve the aim of the task (Brooks & Donato, 1994). Misato's idea from Line 2 about variation in request forms constituting 'parts' seems to lead Hikari to recognize the variation as strategic (Line 3), which Misato aligns with in Line 4. In Line 5 Hikari begins to articulate in more detail how Aiko's strategic use of language was manifested in social terms. Alternatively, Misato looks at how Aiko's request was realized from a linguistic perspective (Line 6). While this might appear to be a grammatical analysis on the surface, Misato is using this talk about sentence structure to highlight the issue of illocutionary force and how this ties in with the interactional strategies taken by Aiko. What is important throughout this discussion is that the students develop a view of Aiko's request as consisting of multiple utterances, which are strategically utilized and contingent upon Julia's reactions to each part. In other words, although the components of the speech act set are being viewed as internally connected and strategic, the emergence of these components is being viewed as contingent upon the responses of the interlocutor. In this way, students are viewing speech acts as fundamentally situated in sequential discourse (Kasper, 2006) – in other words, from a discourse perspective.

An analytical engagement with language from a discourse perspective helps students develop insight into how language functions as a tool for social action because it encourages them to pay attention to speaker intentions and the perceived effect of turns at talk on next turns (Liddicoat, 2007). Reflection also allows students to relate sequences of talk to broader interactional goals, essentially linking the linguistic and the sociocultural through multiple layers of interpretation. Although the talk in the extract above is mostly descriptive, the extract below shows how the awareness developed through this description can be then built upon in further talk which takes a more evaluative focus. When the focus of classroom talk turns towards explicit consideration of the social significance and appropriateness of ways of achieving pragmatic acts, learners begin to externalize more of their assumptions about interaction. This can be observed in Extract 3.3 below, where learners are working in pairs to discuss the question: 'Do you think Aiko's request is reasonable?'

Extract 3.3

1 **Tai:**   I thought that she emphasized a lot about her reason. I thought she kind of pushed. Do you think it is a reasonable request?

2 **Seiji:**   Reasonable? ... hmm ... Aiko was just selfish. And Julia was kind, but she was not going to change at first. She was not willing to do Aiko's shift.

3 **Tai:**   Maybe no-one wanted to. Yeah but I think Aiko will do something for Julia if she is Japanese.

4 **Teacher:**   What do you mean by that Tai?

5 **Tai:**   Um, in Japan, in my part-time job we often does someone's shift. And if I did, he or she do something for me. Yeah, sometimes she gave me a chocolate or some other snack.

6 **Teacher:**   Ha ha.

In the above, Tai initiates the discussion with a focus on the way in which Aiko explained the circumstances surrounding her request to Julia in the dialogue. He seems to negatively evaluate the extent to which Aiko explained the circumstances behind her request, particularly that she did this persistently over multiple turns. Seiji, in relation to this aspect of the request, goes so far as to characterize Aiko as selfish (Line 2). It is important to note here that it is the focus on the request from a discourse perspective which constitutes the frame for the construction of evaluative accounts within the talk here. An additional issue of potential relevance is that the students are essentially making judgements about the requesting behaviour of a Japanese person speaking English. In fact, there is some evidence within the talk that some students are drawing on Japanese cultural frames of understanding in their evaluation of Aiko's language use. In Lines 1 and 2 the relevance of Aiko's Japaneseness is not made explicit; however, Tai's comment in Line 3 constitutes a prediction regarding the action that Aiko will be likely to take based on her status as a Japanese person. In other words, Tai explicitly invokes his perception of a Japanese cultural norm that workplace favours such as this would warrant some kind of token of reciprocity. Therefore, Tai is using reflection on his perception of Japanese cultural norms, and his own experiences specifically, as a resource for commenting on the mutual expectations that would arise in the context under examination. The evaluative dimension of this discussion and the fact that one of the dialogue characters is Japanese provides a context for the referencing of the learners' perceptions of Japanese cultural norms, which is then brought to bear on the analysis. One thing that is missing in this analysis is consideration of the fact that Aiko's requesting behaviour in this dialogue may actually be preferred from the perspective of English pragmatic norms. In other words, the students have not explored the possibility that Aiko is attempting to accommodate to L2 communicative norms – that her choice of strategy here may be the outcome of intercultural mediation (McConachy & Liddicoat, 2016).

Viewed together, the three extracts discussed above present the potential of contextual analysis of a simple teacher-constructed dialogue to promote meaningful reflection on linguistic choices from a strategic perspective. Through engaging in collaborative reflection, learners have heightened their awareness of requesting as a delicate social act which is negotiated by participants in interaction and have come to evaluate the strategic use of language in relation to a particular interpersonal context. Students have not explicitly considered the sociocultural dimensions of social distance, power distance, age, etc., but have been primarily focused on the nature of the interactional negotiation. Culturally derived assumptions about rights and obligations in a Japanese workplace context have been brought to bear on this analysis, but at this point it has been a matter of 'referencing' these assumptions rather than problematizing them. Learners' interpretive architecture is being mobilized and articulated within collaborative reflection for the purposes of interpretation, but there is not yet evidence of the kind of reflexivity that would allow learners to step outside their own assumptions.

Viewing Language Use as a Tool for Relationship Management

In social interaction, the apology is perhaps one of the most important acts in terms of maintaining interpersonal relationships (Ogiermann, 2009). While foreign language textbooks often deal with the pragmalinguistics of apologizing – what to say in order to apologize – they rarely contain activities which encourage learners to reflect on the sociopragmatics of apologizing. That is, they rarely prompt learners to consider the logic underlying why an apology is deemed by one or more of the participants as necessary on a given occasion and how this ties in with expectations about the relationships the people are in. Many textbook writers may assume that the logic behind such acts is culturally universal and thus immediately transparent to learners (McConachy, 2009). This section focuses on the role of contextual analysis in creating opportunities for examination of the social expectations surrounding apologies and the culturally variable notion of 'responsibility'. The process begins with analysis of a textbook dialogue and a focus on how speakers index emotions through talk.

Language input: Apologizing

Students are working with a dialogue taken from a collection of materials that had been written earlier by the teacher and a colleague to exhibit elements of English apology discourse identified in the research literature. Olshtain and Cohen (1983) identified English apologies as frequently constituted by: expression of apology (head act); acknowledgement of responsibility; an explanation; an offer of repair; and a promise of non-recurrence. The dialogue with which the students engage below (Figure 3.2) contains all but the last element and is utilized to prompt reflection on how the speakers negotiate the apology situation, how assumptions about the interpersonal context might influence their choices and how responsibility for the problem is negotiated.

As apologies are particularly important for repairing relationships following perceived breaches of interpersonal rights or obligations, the affective states of dialogue characters at various points in the dialogue are effective starting points for reflection. To interpret affective states requires that learners pay attention to language use within an interactional frame and closely consider the logic according to which the apology is carried out given the interpersonal context and particular problem that has occurred. In the class discussion below, the analysis of the dialogue begins from discussion of the students' perceptions of the dialogue characters' emotional states and intentions, as indexed by what is said. Students consider the kinds of inferences that the speakers are making through the interaction in order to negotiate the

> Gary and Kevin are good friends living in a retirement community. Last night there was a dance for residents, and everyone had a good time – except now Gary has something to tell Kevin. They are chatting at breakfast.
>
> +
>
> Kevin: That sure was a fun dance last night, wasn't it?
>
> Garry: It sure was, but listen, I have to tell you something.
>
> Kevin: Oh? What is it?
>
> Garry: Remember I borrowed your favorite yellow tie for the dance last night? Well, uh, I spilled some red wine on it.
>
> Kevin: What? You ruined my favorite tie?
>
> Garry: I'm so sorry that it happened, Kevin. It was my mistake. I was dancing and someone knocked my glass. I should have put it down somewhere.
>
> Kevin: But it was my favorite tie!
>
> Garry: I know. Please let me buy you a new one.
>
> Kevin: Oh, don't worry about it Garry. It wasn't that expensive. I'm just happy that you were honest about it.

Figure 3.2 Garry and Kevin dialogue
Source: McConachy and Meldahl (2007).

potentially face-threatening situation. Through the analysis, students can be observed to draw on specific language from the dialogue to represent and justify their understandings of the interaction. This strategy allows for more focused reflection and comparison of similar utterances in the students' L1.

Extract 3.4

1	**Teacher:**	So, how do you think the speakers are feeling?
2	**Seiji:**	Kevin might abandon to charge him for the tie. Actually he is thinking Garry is bad, but *'shikata nai'* (It can't be helped).
3	**Teacher:**	So you think he's really angry but he's just forgiving his friend?
4	**Seiji:**	Yes, because he said twice 'My favourite tie'. So he really like it.
5	**Teacher:**	Yeah, possibly. Any other comments?
6	**Hikari:**	'But it was my favourite tie' means he got angry?
7	**Teacher:**	What do you think?
8	**Hikari:**	Hmm, I don't know.
9	**Teacher:**	Okay, how would you say it in Japanese?
10	**Hikari:**	*'Boku no suki na tai darou'?* (It was my favourite tie you know)
11	**Teacher:**	*'datta no ni'* (It was unfortunately)
12	**Hikari:**	Ah, disappointed.
13	**Teacher:**	And so after that Garry says, 'I know'.

14 **Tai:**   So I think if I were Kevin I didn't lend my favourite tie.
15 **Teacher:**   Oh, so you think it is his fault? He was stupid for lending
                   the tie, so it's his responsibility?
16 **Tai:**   So, then what happened is possible. I mean anything is
                   possible.
17 **Teacher:**   Oh right? So he has responsibility?
18 **Tai:**   Yeah.

It can be seen that the task framing, as an exploration of the perceived feelings of the dialogue characters, led the students to notice particular aspects of language use and to consider the speakers' intentions through them. In other words, framing the task as interpretation of a cognitive phenomenon (emotions) led the students to pay attention to the capacity of language to index emotion and intention (Duranti, 1997). In Seiji's comment in Line 2, interpretation of the speaker's emotional state and intentional state are brought together as Seiji considers the action that Garry might take in response to Kevin's action. In this way, language use is being viewed as a form of social action within an explicitly interpersonal lens. Although Seiji formulates a relatively detailed interpretation, at this point in the talk it is not clear exactly what led him to think in this way. It is the teacher reformulation in Line 3 which seems to prompt him to justify his interpretation in Line 4, here quoting Kevin's utterance, *'but it was my favourite tie'* from the dialogue as evidence of his anger. Reference to the dialogue is used to mediate the construction of an 'evidence-based' account which demonstrates what Seiji has noticed and how he perceives its significance. Both the task framing and the teacher's scaffolding moves in Lines 1–4 provide a context for more elaborated interpretation.

It can also be seen that as this elaboration by Seiji becomes more explicit, it then stimulates Hikari to reflect on and re-evaluate her own understanding of the dialogue. In Lines 6 and 8 what becomes clear is that Hikari is unsure as to the nuance expressed by *'but it was my favourite tie'*. This highlights an important aspect of collective scaffolding in the sense that the voiced interpretation of one student has led another student to notice a gap in knowledge or uncertainty about how to interpret something. The notion of 'noticing the gap' as one element on noticing has been taken up in second language acquisition (SLA) research mainly in cases where learners notice problematic aspects of their own language use (Swain, 1995). The noticing of the gap here is somewhat different. Hikari obviously understands the literal meaning of this language but is not yet sure how to interpret its implication and how it is functioning as a form of social action in this context. This is worked on in the discussion as the teacher encourages Hikari to translate this language into Japanese. In Line 10 Hikari offers *'boku no suki na tai darou'* (*That was my favourite tie, you know*), to which the teacher (Line 11) offers an alternative *'[boku no suki na tai] datta no ni'* (*But that <u>was</u> my favourite tie*). In

Japanese, although *'darou'* is used to appeal to as aspect of shared knowledge and could also express imply disappointment here, *'datta no ni'* could be regarded as perhaps capturing the nuance of disappointment more clearly. First, *'datta'* as the past tense of the copula emphasizes that the tie was his favourite. Secondly, *'no ni'* is typically used to express regret or disappointment, and thus combined with *'datta'* may emphasize this emotion. In fact, the offering of this L1 equivalent by the teacher can be seen to immediately lead to Hiker's recognition of this emotion in Line 12. Thus, the act of prompting reflection on L1 equivalents can be seen to have acted as a scaffold for the development of understanding of the nuance conveyed by the utterance (Swain & Lapkin, 2010). Within this process of examining nuance, it can also be seen from Line 13 onward that the teacher facilitated a discourse perspective by prompting attention to Garry's uptake of what Kevin had said. This thus helps socialize the students into the practice of focusing on the ways in which particular utterances are attended to and taken up in subsequent lines of talk. In other words, such scaffolding work functions to make students aware of the importance of looking at the co-text when determining the social action achieved by a particular utterance (Lo Castro, 2003).

Also important is the movement of the frame of the analysis from language use per se to the broader sociocultural context, which was generated by Tai's contribution in Line 14. Here he shifts the focus of the analysis from the speakers' feelings and intentions to the social act of lending someone one's favourite tie. This should not be interpreted as going 'off topic'. In fact, it was the explicit focus on Kevin's disappointment in Lines 6–13 which appears to have led Tai to reflect on whether Kevin himself had any responsibility for what happened. The shifting of the lens in Line 14 therefore can be viewed as driven by reflection and functioning to establish a frame within the talk for evaluation of the social act per se. In Line 15 the teacher offers a reformulation of Tai's comment and invites him to take a position on the issue of responsibility more explicitly. This concept is repeated by the teacher in Line 17 in order to scaffold the articulation of Tai's stance. Tai's response in Line 16 implies that he does see Kevin as sharing the responsibility for the incident. Thus the mode of analysis within the discussion has shifted from interpretation of language in context to interpretation of the context of situation (Malinowski, 1923), allowing Tai to voice the assumptions which underlie his evaluation. In short, the students' interpretive work with regard to speaker feelings (disappointment) and intentions as indexed by language use can be seen to lead to reflection on the onus of responsibility for the incident, thus functioning to create a bridge between language and culture in the analysis. Although the cultural assumptions which underlie the students' interpretations of responsibility do not come out in detail here, they do come out in a more interculturally oriented follow-up discussion (see Extract 3.6).

As a further scaffolding strategy, the teacher's use of reformulation helps the students develop their evaluation of the situation. Reformulation can be understood as the rephrasing of a previous comment for confirmation (Heritage, 1985). An example of this can be seen in Line 2, where the teacher's reformulation of Tai's Line 1 utterance can be seen to directly lead him to elaborate on his interpretation by quoting from the dialogue. A second example can be seen in Line 15, in which the teacher's reformulation of Tai's commentary from Line 14 leads to elaboration on this commentary by him in Line 16. The introduction of specific mediational tools within reformulations is also significant. The teacher's reformulation in Line 3 contains the language 'forgive', which provides a resource for conceptualizing an outcome of the interaction as indexed by language in the dialogue. Furthermore, in Lines 15 and 17 the teacher introduces the concept of 'responsibility' to help Tai to articulate the reason for his opinion. What is important in the case of developing meta-pragmatic awareness is that reformulations go beyond their role as confirmations and promote elaboration on previous commentary. Although in these cases the students do not actually incorporate these concepts into their own commentary, they clearly orient to the teacher's use of them in their responses. It can be said thus that these concepts provide a resource for conceptualizing the interaction being interpreted; in other words, they mediate the development of meta-pragmatic awareness (van Compernolle, 2014).

Constructing a discourse perspective on the apology

After initial reflection on the various communicative intentions of the speakers in the dialogue, the focus of reflection turns to the realization of the speech act set of apology itself. The teacher can be observed to actively scaffold the construction of a discourse perspective on the apology, first through the use of the following questions as a discussion springboard: (1) Where does he apologize? (2) Where does it start and where does it finish? This can be seen to actively prompt learners to look at speech act realization as a form of multiple-turn discourse.

Extract 3.5

1 **Teacher:** Okay, let me ask you some more questions. Where does he apologise? Where does it start and where does it finish?
2 **Hikari:** 'I'm so sorry'.
3 **Teacher:** 'I'm so sorry that it happened'? Where does it finish?
4 **Tai:** 'Please let me buy you a new one'.
5 **Teacher:** Okay, so let's say this is the first step. The saying 'I'm sorry'. What's the second step?
6 **Hikari:** 'It was my mistake'.
7 **Teacher:** Right. So what is this? What is he doing here?
8 **Hikari:** *Mitomeru* (Admit)。
9 **Teacher:** Yeah, but *nani wo mitometeiru*? (What is he admitting?)

10 **Hikari:**   His fault.
11 **Teacher:** Okay. So *sekinin* (responsibility)? He's accepting
                  responsibility. Okay, then what happens after that?
12 **Misato:**   So he is explaining what happened.
13 **Teacher:** Yep. Then what's next?
14 **Misato:**   So he explains what he should have done.
15 **Teacher:** Right. So we'll call this the 'point of regret'. So this is
                  almost like one set, isn't it? It kind of flows. It's all
                  necessary. But what is the next thing that happens?
16 **Tai:**   Um, suggesting the solution?
17 **Teacher:** Good. Good. So basically, offer to do something. But what
                  happened before this?
18 **Seiji:**   Like introduction?
19 **Teacher:** Good. So it was the same last week when we studied the
                  requests. We don't just say, 'Oh, can I borrow your watch?'
                  or suddenly 'I'm sorry I spilled wine on your tie'. We need
                  to introduce the topic. So did you notice how he said,
                  'Remember I borrowed your yellow tie for the dance last
                  night? Well, ah, I spilled some red wine on it'. Why does he
                  say 'Ah'?
20 **Seiji:**   It's hard to say directly?
21 **Teacher:** Good. Maybe it is really hard to say. Or maybe he wants to
                  show that it is hard to say.

A first point of importance in terms of teaching is that the initial questions used by the teacher in this task, '*Where does it start and where does it finish?*', create a context in which the students can notice that the act of apologizing is not always something achieved by a simple set phrase such as 'I'm sorry'. Instead, this question requires that the learners focus on the speech act of apologizing as something that is achieved over multiple turns in connected sequences, each part constituting a part of the whole which meets the interactional needs of the speaker. In contrast to Extract 3.2, which also focused on a speech act in discourse, this task consists of a teacher-led whole-group discussion rather than a pair discussion. In addition, the interactional sequences are characterized by heavy elicitation by the teacher, which may be viewed as IRF sequences (Cazden, 2001). These kinds of sequences have tended to be viewed negatively within SLA research due to the fact that they appear to severely limit the output of the learners (Wells, 1993). However, this extract has features which suggest that teacher-fronted sequences can be an effective type of interaction for helping learners to present their understandings while simultaneously developing their languaging abilities.

Lines 1–4 show the teacher eliciting the parameters of the speech act sequence by having the students quote from the dialogue the phrases that would constitute the first and last steps. From this juncture, the teacher returns to the first step in Line 5 and, through the rest of the discussion, pro-ceeds to fill out the rest of the steps with the assistance of the students as he encourages them to quote from the dialogue. Through referring students back to the dialogue he helps them jointly articulate the basis of their interpreta-tion, while also drawing in meta-pragmatic labels to represent the interac-tional functions for the semantic formula the students take up. For instance, in Line 5 he labels *'I'm so sorry that it happened'* from the dialogue as *'The saying I'm sorry'* rather than the 'apology', to avoid promoting an utterance-level view of apologies (Olshtain & Cohen, 1983). In regard to the second step, Hikari in Line 6 quotes *'It was my mistake'* from the dialogue. Instead of labelling this one for the students, the teacher in Line 8 asks the important question, *'What is he doing here?'*, which leads to Hikari offering the Japanese term *'mitomeru'*, meaning 'admit'. Thus, we can see that the teacher's question is not simply eliciting something from Hikari; it is prompting her to create meta-pragmatic labels to represent her understandings of speech act structure. In other words, his question functions to scaffold the construction of meta-pragmatic tools that Hikari can use for her own learning. As further evidence of this aspect of teaching and learning, the teacher does not make efforts to translate Hikari's *'mitomeru'* into English. He instead orients to her use of the L1 and scaffolds the development of the meta-pragmatic labelling within the L1 through a reformulation in Line 10 to elicit elaboration, and through introduc-ing the concept of *'sekinin'* (responsibility). Through this scaffolding process in Lines 7–11 the third stage of the apology is eventually labelled by the teacher in Line 11 as 'accepting responsibility'.

The creation of meta-pragmatic labels for elements of the speech act sequence can be considered an important scaffolding process due to the fact that it provides a resource which students can use to represent their under-standings of the nature of interaction, and thus plays a constitutive role in the development of meta-pragmatic awareness. The ability to identify utterances as being connected to particular speech acts is one of the key elements in tra-ditional understandings of meta-pragmatic awareness (Kinginger & Farrell, 2004; Safont Jordá, 2003). However, the orientation to mapping of forms and functions in this task can be seen to facilitate a broader awareness of speech acts as having structures constituted by interrelated functional components which can emerge over multiple turns of talk. The acquisition of the ability to describe speech acts from a discourse perspective is particularly important for intercultural learning as it can help learners attend to and discuss the variable ways in which discourse is structured, within and across cultures, and what this structuring tends to symbolize for speakers of different languages.

Cross-cultural comparison of speech act structure

The facilitation of noticing of aspects of speech act structure and reflec-tion on how linguistic choices tie in with people's interpersonal intentions and assumptions builds up meta-pragmatic awareness which can then be utilized for the purposes of more focused cross-cultural comparison. Rather than attempts at abstract comparisons of 'Apologies in English' versus 'Apologies in Japanese', the use of a specific dialogue as a reference point allows the comparison to be anchored in a particular context. Extract 3.6 shows students reflecting on potential differences at the level of apology discourse that might manifest if this interaction had been in Japanese.

Extract 3.6

1	**Teacher:**	Okay, so do you think anything here would be different to apologizing in Japanese? For example if this situation involved two Japanese people.
2	**Tai:**	Point of regret?
3	**Teacher:**	You wouldn't say this bit?
4	**Tai:**	Maybe we wouldn't say it. It's obvious.
5	**Teacher:**	Oh yeah? Any other ideas? How about this one? Would you say, 'I was dancing and someone knocked my glass'.
6	**Hikari:**	I think I would explain.
7	**Seiji:**	I think it's not necessary in Japanese because it's kind of excuse.
8	**Tai:**	It sounds like an excuse?
9	**Seiji:**	Yes. I feel like that.
10	**Teacher:**	Even though he says, 'It was my mistake'?
11	**Seiji:**	Hmm, this sounds like to show sincerity.
12	**Teacher:**	Which part?
13	**Seiji:**	Where he says, 'It was my mistake'.
14	**Teacher:**	Oh yeah? So you think in Japanese it would be best if it didn't have this explanation, and just he says that he takes responsibility for it?
15	**Seiji:**	Yes, perhaps.
16	**Tai:**	I think he shouldn't have to say 'someone knocked my glass'.
17	**Teacher:**	Yeah, it does sound like a little bit of an excuse. I can understand why you would think that. But I think in English it is usually necessary to explain what happened. This is because you want to show the other person that you didn't intend to do something bad or that you had no control or just made a mistake. It's important to show that you understand your mistake to make the other person feel like you won't do it again. This is so that the other person can trust you again.

Within the talk it can be seen that initial cross-cultural comparison, first of all in relation to speech act structure, helps to bring out the students' interpretations of cultural ideas underlying apologizing in Japanese. In Line 2 of this extract Tai comments that a Japanese apology in this situation would not require mention of the 'point of regret', because such a matter is 'obvious' (Line 4), the implication being that in a comparable Japanese interaction stating the obvious would be unusual. In Line 5 the focus is shifted by the teacher to whether it would be necessary to explain the circumstances leading up to the fault. Regarding this issue, the talk sees contrasting opinions emerge from Hikari and Tai, respectively. Whereas Hikari suggests that she would explain (Line 6), Tai suggests in Line 8 that he would not explain as it could be construed as an excuse in Japanese interaction. The application of the word 'excuse' here is most likely a translation of the Japanese equivalent 'iiwake', which has a characteristically negative connotation. The implication in Japanese would be that explaining the circumstances in which a negative action occurred would often be seen as an attempt to alleviate one's responsibility for an action (Barnlund & Yoshioka, 1990).

We cannot infer whether Seiji sees Garry as trying to evade some responsibility for the action, but it is clear that he sees such explanatory behaviour as likely to be interpreted negatively within the context of Japanese interactional norms. In his meta-pragmatic explanation, the English word 'excuse' is invoked to express a meaning which seems essentially embedded within a Japanese cultural framework. However, from this extract we do not see whether he realizes the cultural implications of this word. The teacher follows up on Tai's comment in order to elicit some of the cultural assumptions underlying his explanation. Specifically, the teacher questions whether explanation would constitute excuse making, even when there is an explicit recognition of fault (It was my mistake). In Line 11 Tai suggests that this statement would index 'sincerity'. In Line 16 Seiji also concurs with the assessment that explaining the circumstances of the incident would be viewed negatively in Japanese interaction. Thus, through the talk a relative consensus is built up concerning the preferable structure of an apology in Japanese. In this kind of talk we see evidence that the students are going beyond a comparative description of linguistic practices. The students are exploring how the structure of the speech act relates to particular cultural ideas and the consequences that might result from failure to adhere to these norms (Liddicoat, 2006).

An important issue here is how the affordances for learning were shaped by the task framing. In order to establish a context for intercultural comparison, rather than framing the task as one requiring cultural generalizations, the teacher prompts the learners to reflect on what some differences might be vis-à-vis this particular situation. Whereas cultural generalizations can be made without analysis by falling back on well-known stereotypes, what is important about this task framing is that it engenders a focus first of all on the communicative context. In fact, there is evidence in the talk that maintaining the use of the dialogue as a reference point allowed the students to make use of meta-pragmatic awareness from the earlier discussion. This is first evident in Line 2 in the way Tai appropriated the meta-pragmatic label 'point of regret' for representing part of the speech act set. This shows that

Tai is using the terminology for mediating his meta-pragmatic awareness, thereby making knowledge gleaned from the previous task available for further reflection and use. Later in Line 5 when the teacher wished to shift the focus to a different element of the apology set, he quotes from the dialogue rather than assigning a meta-pragmatic label. Through quoting from the dialogue, the students are required to consider what is achieved by this particular utterance in interactional terms. Hikari is quick to do this in Line 6, recognizing the utterance as an explanation. Thus, this is another way in which the teacher helps the learners make use of their meta-pragmatic awareness for intercultural comparisons.

Another issue of importance which stems from the interaction above is how the teacher takes part in the cross-cultural comparison by offering his own interpretation regarding the significance of language used in the dialogue. In dealing with culture and cross-cultural comparisons, the teacher is inevitably placed in the position in which he or she has to provide some kind of explanation regarding what is normal or preferable behaviour in the target language and to offer an account of logic behind such judgements (Kohler, 2015). This can be seen in Line 17 where the teacher's contribution to talk shifts from asking questions to offering an interpretation regarding why apologies in English tend to be accompanied by some kind of explanation of the circumstances involved. When this occurs, ideally it is best if learners see this not as a definitive explanation but as a useful reference point to be taken on board and tested against future interactional experiences. Further, it is not necessary for teachers themselves to feel under pressure to offer the authoritative word on aspects of language and culture, but rather to see themselves as instruments in the developmental process (Kohler, 2015). Teacher interpretations are a valuable resource which suggest perspectives on pragmatic phenomena that can be taken into account as learners continue to learn about and use the language.

Interrogating Appropriateness of Language Use

Complimenting is another speech act which can be highly face threatening and can have serious implications for the making and breaking of interpersonal relationships. Our assumptions about what is permissible in terms of types of compliments, when they can be given and who they can be given to derive from our perceptions of many sociocultural variables, including social distance, gender, workplace communication, and many others (Golato, 2005). Although there is significant similarity in the semantic formula used for compliments in different languages, ideas about what can legitimately be complimented on are necessarily more variable (Wolfson, 1981). They are thus an interesting and important area of linguistic behaviour for learners to reflect on, not simply in order to learn how to give and respond to compliments in the target language, but to develop heightened awareness of the interpersonal function of compliments and insight into the range of normative ideas that can surround their usage, as well as to develop the ability to take up multiple perspectives as what may be perceived by some as inappropriate complimenting behaviour.

Language input: Complimenting

The language input adopted for this speech act was referred to as the 'Jane and Phil dialogue' (Figure 3.3). This is a controversial dialogue which contains an appearance-related compliment from a male supervisor to a female subordinate in the workplace. There is thus much scope for reflecting on how norms relating to gender, workplace interaction and hierarchy constitute a frame of reference for learners' interpretation of the appropriateness of the interactional choices within and how the speakers manage the situation.

Phil is Jane's supervisor in a small IT company. This conversation occurs in the office.

Phil: Hi Jane. Wow, have you lost weight?

Jane: Oh, um, I'm not sure..........probably not.

Phil: Oh no...you really look great!

Jane: Oh... By the way, I have finished checking these documents.

Figure 3.3 Jane and Phil dialogue
Source: McConachy (unpublished resource).

Interpreting intentions behind complimenting

Rather than approaching the discussion of this dialogue through a linguistic focus, an entry point for analysis is created by attention to the perceived feelings of the dialogue characters at various points within the interaction. This quickly allows for the issue of appropriateness to be brought out. The discussion below involves Seiji and Tai, with some analytical scaffolding work from the teacher as well.

Extract 3.7

1	**Teacher:**	Okay, so I'd just like you to discuss how you think the people here feel in this little interaction.
2	**Tai:**	Maybe he likes Jane so much and he is attracting.
3	**Seiji:**	Attracted to Jane? He's attracting Jane?
4	**Tai:**	Yeah, he's attracting Jane.
5	**Seiji:**	He's attracting her?

6 **Tai:**   Ah, yes. Because 'have you lost weight?' is so personal, ah,
                  it's not usual when supervisor greets their employee.
7 **Teacher:** Do you think it is appropriate?
8 **Tai:**   Um, it might be a kind of sexual harassment.
9 **Teacher:** Oh yeah? Do you think so too Seiji?
10 **Seiji:**   Yes, it's inappropriate.

The initial analytical focus on the perceived feelings and communicative intentions of the dialogue characters is first oriented to by Tai, who seems to interpret Phil's comments on Jane's appearance as indicating some kind of special interest in Jane. In lines 3–6 there is an exchange which aims to clarify Tai's use of the phrase *'he is attracting'* from line 2. In English *'attracted to'* would imply an emotional state, whereas *'attracting'*, although grammatically awkward, would imply that there is a bigger agenda. Seiji is thus attempting to ascertain exactly the interpersonal intent that is being ascribed to Phil by Tai. While this might appear like a vocabulary issue on the surface, it is also a meta-pragmatic issue which requires Seiji to draw on his own assumptions in order to try to make sense of Tai's comments. What this highlights is that collaborative analysis of a conversational extract or textbook dialogue engages learners in multi-layered interpretive processes, whereby they not only have to interpret the text but also the interpretations which others offer about the text. Moreover, these attempts at clarification also constitute scaffolding for the development of meta-pragmatic awareness as individuals are prompted to not only specify what their judgment is, but what underlies it. This takes further shape from line 6 where Tai explains that he sees Phil as strategically deviating from normative communication patterns between a supervisor and an employee in order to index some kind of special affection for Jane. This is justified by reference to the meta-pragmatic judgement that the comment is 'personal', thus not usual in this kind of workplace interaction. Through the talk thus it is revealed that Tai is looking at workplace hierarchy as a frame through which to evaluate this interaction, which the teacher makes use of in line 7 to elicit an explicit judgment on the appropriateness of Phil's comments. Tai acknowledges the potential for Phil's behaviour to constitute sexual harassment, which is aligned with by Seiji. It can be seen through the exchange that as students are challenged to articulate the rationale for their interpretations of the character's intentions, they are prompted by both peers and the teacher to give more specific articulation of the assumptions underlying their judgments, which reveals the various frames which are operating in their meta-pragmatic awareness.

Exploring constraints on speaker choices in interaction

In examining an interaction in the classroom, particularly from the perspective of the intentions of the speakers, one thing that can become overlooked is the role of the hearer in the process, not only how they interpret what has been said but also the various constraints on how what has been said is responded to (Padilla Cruz, 2013). This is an important area for inter-cultural learning as it very closely relates to how students view the roles of participants in an interaction and their ideas about what should and should not be said within these roles. In the interaction below, Hikari and Misato reflect on the appropriateness of Phil's comments from Jane's perspective and draw out a number of frames of reference underlying their judgements through the talk.

Extract 3.8

1 **Hikari:** He is her direct supervisor, so he shouldn't say something about her body matter. Jane didn't want to be asked about this matter, so she wanted to cut off this conversation and change to business matter.

2 **Misato:** I think if Phil was not her direct supervisor she could say something more, but he is her direct supervisor so she cannot.

3 **Hikari:** I also think Phil maybe wanted to make Jane more feel happy or maybe he just wanted to start conversation or to have communication. I'm not sure.

4 **Misato:** He just think this sentence is start to good conversation, but Jane don't think so.

5 **Hikari:** Yeah, she couldn't accept.

6 **Misato:** But she can't *hitei suru* (reject) ... she can't ... she can't ...... deny it, so I'm not sure.

7 **Hikari:** I also think it is good example of this type of generation and business situation.

8 **Misato:** So I think he didn't understand Jane's feelings. He said, 'No, you look really good'. Maybe he had misunderstanding.

In the talk above it can be seen that a number of frames emerge in the ways the students interpret the dialogue characters' interactional deci-sions. As can be seen in Line 1, Hikari's comment first of all functions to foreground hierarchy as a frame for evaluating the complimenting behav-iour. Rather than gender, here she cites Phil's superior status in the work-place as a reason for negatively evaluating his question about Jane's weight. She specifically takes up Jane's perspective and that she had wanted to divert attention away from her physical appearance. As an aspect of con-text, this hierarchy frame is oriented to Misato in Line 2, here more clearly being given as a constraint on Jane's responses. Again, in Lines 5 and 6 Hikari and Misato construct an account of Jane being unable to accept

Phil's greeting, but yet at the same time unable to strongly reject it, presumably linking back to Misato's comment in Line 2 where she mentions Jane's subordinate status as constraining her reaction. Thus, we see the two students utilizing their understandings of workplace hierarchy as a frame for evaluating the appropriateness of the language used, for interpreting Jane's feelings, and for explaining her choice of interactional strategy.

However, the students are not simply looking at the interaction from Jane's perspective. In Line 3 the focus of the analysis shifts as Hikari attempts to interpret Phil's intention in the interaction by describing the potential functionality of his opening question in this interaction. To do this she needs to draw on her meta-pragmatic awareness, including knowledge of what forms can constitute compliments in English alongside her perceptions of the sociopragmatic appropriateness of such a question. In the end, although she recognizes the potential for such a question to constitute a compliment or greeting, she is unable to make a definitive determination. The act of interpretation brings her to face ambiguity and, with the help of Misato, to explore various interpretive possibilities. What is most important is at the end of Line 4 where Misato highlights a potential gap in the understandings of the interaction by the dialogue characters. What this symbolizes effectively is that they are interpreting the speech act from the perspective of the way it was taken up by the interlocutor rather than as a simple matter of speaker intentions encoded in language forms. This allows attention to be paid to the negotiated nature of the subsequent turns in the dialogue. In Lines 5 and 6 they are exploring the dilemma that Jane faces in being unable to accept the compliment, yet unable to reject it. Then in Line 8, Misato focuses on Phil's second turn in the dialogue as evidence that he has been unable to pick up on Jane's discomfort as expressed through her reactions.

The students explore the feelings and intentions of the dialogue characters and consider how workplace hierarchical structures may have influenced Jane's strategic use of language in expressing or concealing her discomfort. In the process of analyzing this dialogue the students have had to look especially closely at the relationships between utterances (discourse) and consider the potential meanings of utterances from multiple perspectives. Thus, they have viewed the interaction from each speaker's perspective, and then considered the implications of unrecognized intentions or conflicting frames of interpretation in interaction. Importantly, they refer explicitly to workplace roles as a key feature of context influencing the significance and appropriateness of language use contained within the short dialogue. While the students have not yet reflected on the deeper assumptions underlying their judgements, the initial interpretations generated in this stretch of classroom talk generate a foundation for more focused reflection, as can be seen below.

Scaffolding the construction of justifications for judgements

The previous two extracts show how learners engage with the dialogue to explore the potential feelings and intentions of the dialogue characters as manifested at different points of the interaction. They also build initial evaluations as to whether the compliment in question can be viewed as appropriate or not. In the talk below, a number of scaffolding strategies can be observed for pushing the students to consider in more depth the impact of contextual factors on the interactional features observed in the dialogue. The students' meta-pragmatic awareness develops as interpretations are elaborated and justified in response to teacher questioning.

Extract 3.9

1	**Teacher:**	How about if they've had a very long working relationship?
2	**Seiji:**	But, but, in this conversation, they don't seem to have long time.
3	**Teacher:**	Why do you think so? What evidence can you see in the conversation?
4	**Seiji:**	Um, … if they have known each other for a long time Jane might say at least 'thank you'.
5	**Teacher:**	Ah, right, yeah. Good point. You think that she's really not comfortable.
6	**Seiji:**	Yeah.
7	**Tai:**	She might say, 'stop kidding me'.
8	**Teacher:**	If they had a close relationship?
9	**Tai:**	Yeah.
10	**Teacher:**	Oh, I see. And a little bit more friendly?
11	**Tai:**	Yeah
12	**Teacher:**	So you think her reaction is a little bit cold?
13	**Tai:**	Yeah, she rejected.
14	**Teacher:**	How about the last comment by Jane?
15	**Tai:**	She changed the subject.
16	**Teacher:**	Yeah. Yeah, she didn't respond at all. Just quickly changed the subject.

The discussion above is launched by the teacher, who encourages students to consider the scenario from different angles and articulate in more detail the specific assumptions they are relying on when making judgments of appropriateness/inappropriateness. Specifically, the teacher prompts the students to consider whether Phil's language would still be inappropriate in the case that Jane and Phil had been colleagues for a long time. It is Seiji who first engages with this question, suggesting that there is no evidence to imply a long working relationship. At this point in line 3 the teacher therefore offers two follow-up questions which direct attention back to the dialogue so that this point can be substantiated in more concrete terms. What Seiji does next is important, as he points out the absence of any sort of thanking behaviour, the implication being that Jane has not recognized or refuses to recognize Phil's language as a compliment. Tai builds on this notion in line 7 by also providing an example of language that might indicate more familiarity in this case. Thus, it can be seen that the two students collaboratively construct a 'negative evidence' strategy to sustain joint interpretation of the situation. Furthermore, we see implicit here in their responses an understanding of the fact that compliments in English usually do attract some kind of response, such as thanking behaviour when accepted. Another important dimension of this interaction is that in exploring the possibility that Jane and Phil had had a long working relationship, it was the focus on Jane's reactions – an orientation to speech acts in discourse – which provided a framework for the 'negative evidence' explanatory strategy. In other words, students are not only looking at the relationships between utterances and context, they are directing explicit attention to the co-text of particular utterances (Lo Castro, 2003) and how this ties in with what is going on in the conversation as a whole. In this extract, this 'discourse perspective' on utterances thus constitutes a framework for the construction of more nuanced interpretation.

With the help of teacher scaffolding and peer scaffolding, both Tai and Seiji have moved from consideration of an aspect of context (the speakers' level of familiarity) to consideration of how such familiarity might be indexed linguistically within this particular context, thereby explicitly connecting the sociopragmatic and the pragmalinguistic dimensions of language use within their interpretations (Thomas, 1983). The teacher scaffolds the analysis through presenting potentially relevant contextual variables for consideration, by prompting elaboration of students' viewpoints, and by reformulating them so as to help constitute a coherent narrative. The hypothetical condition presented to the students for consideration in line 1 provides an alternate frame for them to re-evaluate their analyses (Meier, 1997), which then creates the conditions for the 'negative evidence strategy' to emerge. In the construction of this strategy, the students do scaffolding work for each other. Although Seiji and Tai collaboratively constructed the case against Phil and Jane's familiarity, it was Seiji's modeling of the strategy that initiated the co-construction. What this example illustrates is that peer scaffolding in meta-pragmatic analysis is constituted not only by the content of students' interpretations, but by the particular forms and strategies through which the content is articulated. More specifically, this kind of analytical discussion provides a context for the appropriation of mediational tools which can be used to develop students' abilities as effective analyzers of languages and cultures (Liddicoat & Scarino, 2013).

Contextual modification for deepening reflective analysis

In conducting contextual analysis, learners draw connections between observed features of language use and the aspects of context which they believe are relevant to shaping interactional decisions. While this is useful for drawing out assumptions relating to the interaction as presented, it can leave other related assumptions hidden. Hypothetical modifications to context constitute a valuable tool for shifting perspectives and deepening analysis. As one example of this, the extract below shows the teacher scaffolding a perspective shift based on modification of the context. Specifically, students are asked to consider the potentially differing implications of the language used in the dialogue if Phil's language had been uttered by Jane and vice versa. This leads to exploration of two social dimensions – gender and hierarchy – and more detailed elaboration as to how these notions inform students' interpretations of the situation and judgements of appropriateness.

Extract 3.10

1	**Teacher:**	Okay, so let's imagine it's the same conversation, but we change the place of Phil and Jane. So this time, Jane says 'Hi Phil. Wow, have you lost weight?' and Phil says 'Oh, I'm not sure. Probably not'. Would anything change? Would the conversation still be inappropriate or do you think it might be okay?
2	**Seiji:**	So, I think it's much more inappropriate because ...... to say 'have you lost weight?' to supervisor is too friendly and ....
3	**Teacher:**	To say that to a supervisor is even more inappropriate? Do you think it's more inappropriate to say to a man or a woman?
4	**Seiji:**	It's unusual to mention the weight about men.
5	**Teacher:**	Oh yeah? Is it usual to say it about women?
6	**Seiji:**	Um, not usual, but if talking about weight I think it's for woman ...... women care more about their weight than men.
7	**Teacher:**	Does everyone agree with that?
8	**Misato:**	Many people think all women care about her own self.
9	**Teacher:**	And men don't care about it so much?
10	**Misato:**	I think many men care about his weight, but generally people don't think so.
11	**Teacher:**	Hikari, what do you think?
12	**Hikari:**	Um, I think if the Phil is Jane's direct supervisor, Jane shouldn't say such a thing to her boss. But at the same time, on the other hand, for my working environment I and my co-workers often say such a thing to the head of the store.
13	**Teacher:**	Is it okay?
14	**Hikari:**	Because he is very friendly person, so we often say such a thing.

In engaging with the adjustment to the scenario proposed by the teacher, Seiji quickly reveals his perception that the new scenario would be even more inappropriate, drawing on assumptions about workplace hierarchy as justification. This invocation of hierarchy as a meta-pragmatic frame can be contrasted with Extract 3.7, where asking about weight was interpreted as inappropriate for gender reasons. Thus, the hypothetical modification to the dialogue has created an environment in which different types of assumptions are activated and brought to bear within the classroom talk for the purpose of analysis. From this perspective, the teacher's strategy in line 3 is particularly significant, as his questions function to confirm Seiji's interpretation, and then to re-include gender as a frame in the analysis. Following this, a number of gender-related assumptions are articulated in the form of generalizations about either men or women, such as line 4 (Seiji) and line 8 (Misato). While not rejecting generalizations overtly, the teacher takes explicit questioning strategies which encourage the students to consider the possible application of their generalizations to the other gender. For instance, in lines 5 and 9, the teacher responds to student generalizations about women, by asking whether the student thus implies that whatever has been said does not apply to men. This questioning leads students to elaborate on and in fact hedge their generalizations somewhat. Therefore, by keeping gender at work in the analysis and prompting students to make explicit the culturally derived assumptions informing their views of gender, the teacher is in effect helping the students to deal with any potential tensions in explanatory frames. Through making explicit not only the frames themselves, but the cultural assumptions that constitute such frames, there is the potential for synthesis and thus the development of a more sophisticated meta-pragmatic awareness.

Although Seiji and Misato focus mostly on gender, Hikari, on the other hand, orients again to notions of workplace hierarchy, as it pertains to the Japanese context, as a frame for her interpretation. In this process, she brings a personal account to the analysis, mentioning that in her workplace (in Japan) the staff do make comments like this to their boss (line 12). When invited to comment in more detail, Hikari suggests that the potential offensiveness of comments about weight is offset by the particular familiarity that exists with her boss due to his friendly demeanor (line 14). In this classroom discussion, the hypothetical modification to the scenario functions as an effective catalyst for probing assumptions relating to the meta-pragmatic frames (gender and hierarchy) activated for interpreting and evaluating the language use contained within. In justifying their evaluative judgments, thus, the moral order is appealed to primarily through these two dimensions of social relations (Kádár & Haugh, 2013). Through justifying their interpretations in response to the emergence of an evaluative frame within the interaction, students become more explicitly aware

of some of the cultural assumptions which underlie their own interpretations of the dialogue.

Exploring the Impact of First Language Assumptions on Interaction with 'Foreigners'

Although the development of meta-pragmatic awareness often means
engaging learners analytically with L2 input, reflection on interactions
which take place in the learners' L1 can be a valuable resource for learning
due to the added need to view the L1 and the construction of meaning from
a distanced perspective which is rarely practised in daily life (see also
Chapter 4). Reflection on intercultural interactions in the learners' L1 also
provides a way for learners to explore interculturality within their own
language, specifically by considering how non-conventional language use or
application of diverse cultural frames of understanding to the L1 might
influence the construction and interpretation of meaning (Kramsch, 1993).
When the focus remains on the L2, there is the danger that learners will see
interculturality as something that is inherent to the L2 but see their own
language in rigid terms. Shifting the perspective towards intercultural communication in the L1 is a useful way of opening learners up to the dynamic
nature of all communication and the meanings and impressions that might
be at stake when cultural assumptions applied to a particular language
diverge. This section looks at the way in which learners engage with a dialogue that depicts an intercultural interaction in the Japanese language and
how this brings out for discussion various assumptions regarding compliments and perceptions of the influence of in-group/out-group status on
interaction.

Language input (complimenting in Japanese)

The dialogue in this section (Figure 3.4 below) presents an interaction
between an Australian man living in Japan (James) and a middle-aged
Japanese woman (Kazuko) at a train station in Tokyo. The dialogue shows
Kazuko approach James while waiting for a train and initiate a conversation
by asking where he is from. Although James is able to understand what is
said to him, his Japanese skills are quite limited, as indicated by being unable
to pronounce the name of his country accurately and making a serious grammatical mistake. In spite of his apparent low level of proficiency, he is complimented by Kazuko for his Japanese skills. Due to being situated in the
students' L1 and involving a Japanese character who initiates an interaction
with a non-Japanese person in Japanese, this dialogue constitutes a resource

A middle-aged Japanese woman (Kazuko) begins a conversation with a young Australian man (James) while waiting for a train on the platform at a station in Tokyo.

Kazuko: お国はどちらですか？
          Okuni wa dochira desu ka?
          Where are you from?

James: 僕は<u>ア</u>ーストラリアから<u>行きました</u>。
          Boku wa <u>A</u>asutoraria kara <u>ikimashita</u>.
          (I <u>went from A</u>astralia)

Kazuko: あら、日本語お上手ですね。
          Ara, nihongo ga ojyouzu desu ne
          (Wow, you are good at Japanese)

James: いいえ、日本語は<u>ありません</u>。
          Iie, nihongo wa <u>arimasen</u>.
          (Actually, <u>there is no</u> Japanese)

Figure 3.4 Kazuko and James dialogue
Source: McConachy (unpublished resource). Notes: Underlining indicates grammatical or phonological errors. The Romanized script and English translation are presented for the convenience of the reader here, but were not included in the original dialogue as all participants could read Japanese characters.

for reflecting not only on potential differences in complimenting conventions, but also on deeper cultural assumptions or stereotypes involving 'foreigners'.

Exploring and evaluating motivations behind linguistic choices

As illustrated in previous sections, scaffolded contextual analysis leads learners to draw interpretations regarding the ways in which a wide range of sociocultural variables such as age, gender, setting, social distance, etc. may influence the linguistic choices made by speakers. The interpretations that learners construct are obviously dependent on the variables that learners view as relevant to a particular interaction, which is in turn shaped by their existing meta-pragmatic awareness and broader assumptions about social relations. Contextual analysis of interactions in the students' L1 can function to elicit these assumptions in different ways to L2 interaction, particularly assumptions about preferable interactional strategies for communication with non-native speakers, which are in turn linked to stereotypes and ideological dimensions of meta-pragmatic awareness (Verschueren, 2004). This becomes salient in the extract below as students are asked to take an evaluative stance on the language used by the Japanese character in the dialogue.

Extract 3.11

1	**Teacher:**	Okay, here you can just discuss what's happening in the conversation and also think about whether the lady's comment is appropriate or not.
2	**Seiji:**	The first phrase is I think a little hard to understand for foreigner because '*Okuni ha dochira desu ka yori mo, doko desu ka or doko kara kimashita ka?*' is better. (It's better to ask '*doko desu ka?*' or '*doko kara kimashita ka?*' than '*okuni ha dochira desu ka?*').
3	**Teacher:**	Maybe she's not used to talking to foreigners. She's not adjusting her language at all. How about the man's response? So, he says some strange Japanese, but what does she say?
4	**Tai:**	Yeah, I heard that most students who learning Japanese learn when they were said 'Your Japanese is good', they learn they have to say 'not so much'. So, I'm just curious he thinks about this.
5	**Teacher:**	Yeah. Maybe he really thinks that his Japanese is bad because it is bad. I mean in this case, he can't say the name of his country properly. It's not terrible. Maybe he has just come to Japan, but it's not '*jyouzu*' (good).
6	**Hikari:**	But I think this is very funny because she just asked in Japanese language and of course the foreigners couldn't answer well, but I think the woman is very usual Japanese woman because she think the Japanese language is really difficult for every foreigners, so maybe she thought maybe her language level for foreigners is very low, and she thought he was good at speaking Japanese.
7	**Teacher:**	So, do you think that he felt good about her comment?
8	**Tai:**	Maybe not.
9	**Teacher:**	Maybe not? Why not?
10	**Tai:**	He knows about his Japanese speaking level.
11	**Teacher:**	Right? What do you think about that?
12	**Tai:**	I think he knows it is ulterior motive.

This discussion is framed by the teacher as an examination of what's 'happening in the conversation', which implies that the students should look beyond the language forms for some kind of action. The discussion is further framed as an evaluation of the Japanese woman's comment (compliment), although the perspective from which the evaluation might be conducted is not specified. Seiji is first to orient to the task in Line 2 by taking up the issue of appropriateness from a sociolinguistic perspective, although not of the compliment, but of the opening question. Here he is contrasting Kazuko's opening question with functionally similar but more grammatically straightforward forms, which he regards as more appropriate for use with a 'foreigner' in this case. The assumption that seems to influence this comment is that as a foreigner this man is unlikely to be a competent speaker of Japanese, and it is therefore preferable to initiate the interaction with relatively simple language. Although this is a somewhat stereotypical initial interpretation, the teacher orients to Seiji's evaluation by suggesting that the woman's use of grammatically complex forms – that she did not engage in foreigner talk (Ferguson, 1971) – might indicate a lack of experience in speaking with foreigners in Japan. The teacher then shifts the focus to the man's response to the opening question by prompting the students to look for 'strange Japanese'. This characterization was intended to help the students focus on the limited nature of the man's Japanese as evidenced in his first turn in order to provide an entry point into examination of the compliment. In contrast to the teacher's intent, Tai in Line 4 takes up the man's compliment response, which he seems to view as strange because it conforms to the Japanese pragmatic norm that compliments should generally be rejected. What is interesting is the way in which Tai invokes his own anecdotal knowledge to consider the potential impact of formal education in the Japanese language on this man's compliment-response strategy. This shows that Tai is considering the nature of the meta-pragmatic awareness which is informing the man's pragmatic strategy in this dialogue. While Tai interprets the man as strategically conforming to Japanese pragmatic norms, the teacher in Line 5 highlights the possibility that the man is rejecting the compliment because it conflicts with the reality of the situation. The implication here is that the rejection of the compliment may actually be informed by Anglo-English pragmatic norms that language users should strive to represent reality as it is (Wierzbicka, 2006).

In Line 6 Hikari re-initiates an explicit focus on the thoughts of the woman and the role that her perception of the man's status as a foreigner may have had on her linguistic choices. Hikari first of all regards it as unusual that the woman initiated the interaction in Japanese because she assumes that the woman would share Hikari's perception that it is natural for non-Japanese people to be unable to speak Japanese well. Therefore, according to Hikari's interpretation, it is possible that the woman's compliment was sincere based on the low expectations she would have naturally have had towards the man. It is thus her grammatically complex opening questions that appear to be out of place for Hikari. While noticing the stereotypical formulations, the teacher doesn't directly respond to Hikari's characterization. Instead he prompts reflection on how the man may have felt upon being complimented, which helps the students relativize their perspective (Byram, 1997). In Line 8 Tai takes on the perspective of the man, suggesting that the man is likely not happy about the woman's comments because, as he explains in Line 10, the man 'knows about his Japanese speaking level'. The implication here is that the propositional content of the woman's words appearing untrue may make the man uncomfortable. Thus, in this analysis, Tai reveals a number of things. First, he implicitly reveals his understanding of the Anglo-English norm that compliments should generally be given sincerely. The second aspect of interest here is that Tai has viewed the man as applying the norms of his L1 (English) in trying to interpret the woman's comments. Thus, Tai has showed understanding of the potential for discomfort when a mismatch of pragmatic norms occurs in intercultural communication. When prompted again by the teacher for more information in Line 11, Tai then reveals that the non-Japanese character may be attuned to the fact that the Japanese woman is trying to achieve something socially. Here we see Tai depict the dialogue character as a man feeling uncomfortable due to gaps in pragmatic norms, yet still trying to make sense of the interaction from the woman's perspective. What Tai brings out here is a quite complex understanding of not only pragmatic norms, but also sense-making processes and their emotional dimension in intercultural interaction.

Throughout the discussion here the students are viewing the interaction specifically from the perspective of speaker intentions and considering the potential for perception of a speaker as cultural outsider to work as a frame of reference affecting linguistic decision-making (Moody, 2014). The evaluative nature of the discussion prompts the students to link two aspects of their interpretive architecture – assumptions about the function of compliments and assumptions about foreigners speaking Japanese – which helps to reveal how stereotypical assumptions about cultural outsiders ('foreigners', in this case) can affect how the significance of linguistic choices is interpreted. At this point, several competing interpretations have been offered regarding the potential intentions behind the compliment and compliment response and the meta-pragmatic assumptions that the dialogue characters may be drawing on in the interaction. The talk in Extract 3.12 represents a continuation of the discussion above, but sees a significant shift in perception by Hikari that occurs as she personalizes the situation and develops alternative insights regarding the intercultural implications of the linguistic choices in the dialogue.

Extract 3.12

1	**Hikari:**	Now I realize that the man just want to show his irritate. He doesn't feel good because of the Japanese lady's words.
2	**Teacher:**	How do you know?

3	**Hikari:**	From the conversation. But at the first time I read this conversation I thought if the conversation happened to Japanese, from foreigner to Japanese, so for example, 'Can you speak English?' and I say 'Oh, not so much'. And the foreigner maybe say 'You are good at speaking English' and maybe I say 'No. No'.
4	**TM:**	Well, let's think about that. So, I could say 'Can you speak English' and you could say 'Ah, English is no', and then I could say 'Oh, it's good!'.
5	**ALL:**	(laughing)
6	**Teacher:**	How would you feel?
7	**Hikari:**	Ah, behind my face ... I feel good ...
8	**Teacher:**	Oh, really?
9	**Hikari:**	... about such a words.
10	**Teacher:**	Really? I usually don't feel good when I hear this comment. Because I mean, if I'm having a very difficult discussion in Japanese then I guess it doesn't matter, but if I just say *'ocha wo kudasai'* (some tea please), you know I feel it's strange for someone to say that is especially good Japanese. It's no big deal right? I kind of feel like it's *'baka ni shite iru'* (making fun of me).
11	**Seiji:**	Many people in Japan, um, might guess that foreigner don't even try to speak Japanese well, so it's just surprising. So, they might say it.
12	**Teacher:**	Yeah, many people have that image.
13	**Misato:**	So, even when foreigners say *'ohayou gozaimasu'* (good morning) or *'arigatou gozaimasu'* (thank you), many Japanese say, 'Oh it's good'.
14	**Tai:**	But, when I was working, many foreigners come my shops and most of them can speak Japanese. So, yeah, I noticed about this.
15	**Teacher:**	Oh? Do you try to speak to them in English first?
16	**Tai:**	No. I speak Japanese first. So, if she or he can't speak Japanese, I change to speaking English.

What is particularly significant about this extract is Hikari's shift in interpretation and the nature of the reflective process (revealed in Line 3), which led to this shift. Hikari's comment in Line 3 reveals that she had first interpreted the man's emotions by imagining herself in a similar position. Rather than picture herself as the Australian man, in her imagination she had inverted the situation to involve her as a Japanese person being complimented on her English by a native speaker of English. In Line 4 the teacher describes such a hypothetical scenario for the class and asks Hikari how she would feel upon being complimented (Line 6). Interestingly, although she has arrived at the interpretation that the man may be unhappy about the compliment, she articulates in Lines 7 and 9 that she personally would not be unhappy about being complimented on her English, even if it wasn't very good. It would appear that Hikari has first interpreted the compliment from a Japanese cultural perspective in which the truth value of the compliment is not necessarily important. Upon further reflection, she seems to have noticed that the man may have been interpreting the compliment from a different cultural frame and thus may have been irritated by the compliment. Although Hikari does explain in Line 3 that this reinterpretation is based on the language used, she does not explain what linguistic evidence specifically she is drawing on. Implicitly here it seems that through reflecting on the reasons for her own perceptions, she has gained an awareness of the consequences of differing frames for interpretation in relation to speech acts in intercultural communication (Kecskes, 2014).

In Line 10 the teacher initiates a shift in the focus on the discussion by expressing his personal feelings about being complimented by Japanese on his Japanese skills, despite only engaging in trivial language use. What this does in the interaction is to generate an explanation from Seiji (Line 11), which is then followed up by Misato (Line 13). Here, there seems to be agreement that Japanese people tend to regard non-Japanese as uninterested in the Japanese language; therefore the simplest signs of competence are likely to elicit praise (Nishiyama, 2000). Line 14 is interesting, however, as it shows Tai drawing on his experience to explain how interacting with many non-Japanese people as a shop worker led him to awareness of the fact that many non-Japanese people actually can speak Japanese. From this realization, thus, he has formulated the policy of always speaking Japanese as the default language, and then switching to English if necessary. Tai is therefore drawing on intercultural learning which occurred outside the classroom to shed insight on the discussion of intercultural issues in the classroom.

Throughout this section, the teacher has assisted students to consider complimenting behaviour and various intents behind this behaviour from multiple perspectives. Importantly, students have also reflected on the perlocutionary dimension of complimenting behaviour – the effect that a compliment has on an interlocutor – and specifically how this effect depends on culturally shaped assumptions about what can and should be complimented (Barnlund & Araki, 1985). The act of looking at the interaction from multiple perspectives has also highlighted the potential influence of ethnic and cultural stereotypes in determining what is complimented and how positive intentions (even when informed by stereotypes) do not necessarily facilitate rapport when cultural interpretations of the compliment diverge. The meta-pragmatic awareness that is developed throughout this section is not knowledge of L2 pragmatic norms, but awareness of potential divergences around the interpretation of compliments within intercultural communication.

Chapter Conclusion

This chapter has shown some of the ways in which language learners mobilize existing knowledge and develop meta-pragmatic awareness through contextual analysis centred on textbook or teacher-constructed dialogues. The orchestration of contextual analysis in the classroom by the teacher engages learners in the active interpretation of aspects of language use and encourages them to see language use as a form of social action. What comes across strongly is that contextual analysis aids the development of meta-pragmatic awareness when learners are encouraged to view the exchange of meanings from a discourse perspective (Kasper, 2006). Viewing language use from a discourse perspective involves continuous movement of the lens through which learners view the interaction. This means that, in order to interpret the significance of a given turn at talk, students need to pay attention to the utterance/s, to the surrounding utterances and to the nature of the sociocultural context as a whole. Thus, students may focus the lens to examine utterances within a turn, then shift the lens out a little more to see how these are taken up in subsequent lines of talk, and then shift the lens out even further when looking at the interaction as a whole and the relationships between the characters. In other words, learners focus both on the context of situation and the context of culture (Halliday, 1978; Malinowski, 1923). Although learners may first of all pay attention to a single utterance or talk of turn, as learners consider the feelings and intentions of speakers they shift to interpreting language as a socially negotiated and interactively co-constructed phenomenon. Interpretation is thus driven by inferencing which operates as students engage with language at multiple levels (Lo Castro, 2003). This in turn helps learners develop insight into the fact that the negotiation of meaning within discourse always entails a process of active construction on the basis of assumptions and expectations about interpersonal relationships.

Contextual analysis within classroom discussion allows learners to take up multiple perspectives on any given interaction and to explore potential divergences in the goals of speakers and the way in which they orient to each other's communicative moves within interaction. Through reflection, learners articulate a range of assumptions behind their interpretation of language use, which suggests to learners the nature of their own interpretive architecture. The development of meta-pragmatic awareness through contextual analysis thus involves not only developing awareness of the pragmatic norms of the L2 but, equally importantly, bringing into awareness the nature of one's own interpretative architecture (McConachy, 2013). Such a process is highly scaffolded by the teacher, who creates initial entry points for analysis, directs learners' attention to various aspects of sociocultural context, presents alternative scenarios and interpretations, prompts intercultural comparisons, and continually encourages learners to elaborate on and justify their interpretations. Learners are not necessarily encouraged to see the materials they engage with as an embodiment of a monolithic external norm, but are rather encouraged to construct interpretations and engage with the interpretations of others in a way that promotes complexity of attention to language use as a form of social action. Within the context of this goal, it is not essential that teachers have access to authentic materials, and lack of authentic materials is not a barrier to learning. Contextual analysis based on available materials is a useful way of helping move learners beyond a view of language as code and draw them into the kind of interpretive engagement with language that is essential for developing an intercultural perspective on language use in the long term.

4 Reflection on Experience as a Resource for Intercultural Learning

Introduction

Learners' relationship to the target language is complexified when they have opportunities to use it as a tool for constructing and interpreting interactional encounters outside the classroom. Whereas examination of language use in conversational transcripts or textbook dialogues allows learners to practice interpretation from a distanced perspective, the experience of observing and using the language outside the classroom brings to the learner a different kind of cognitive and affective stimulation, as well as different insights drawn from the experience (Roberts *et al.*, 2001). Similarly, learners' accumulation of experience of using their L1 in a range of contexts brings to them a stock of normative expectations and other assumptions for interpreting social behaviour and negotiating meanings in a range of contexts with a variety of interlocutors. As discussed in Chapter 2, the interpretation of interactional experience, whether in the L1 or L2, is necessarily filtered through a learner's existing interpretive architecture – the complexly interwoven amalgam of cultural assumptions, explicit knowledge, schema, scripts and stereotypes. Throughout the language learning experience, learners draw on and add to their interpretive architecture not only by acquiring new linguistic knowledge but also by adding new sociocultural knowledge and using reflection to modify and reorganize existing knowledge (Kecskes, 2014). Each experience of interaction also draws on and feeds back into the interpretive architecture, with the potential to bring about meaningful insights, depending on the nature of the reflective engagement with the experience and level of significance imbued to the experience. It is the recognition of this importance of analyzing and reflecting on experience that underlies much of the work on critical incidents in the intercultural field (e.g. Snow, 2015; Spencer-Oatey, 2013), as well as more recent work on the autobiography of intercultural encounters (Byram *et al.*, 2009) and learning within the context of study abroad (Holmes *et al.*, 2016).

Critical incidents, by definition, focus on problems in communication. They typically present a communicative encounter between two or more individuals from different cultural (usually, national) backgrounds and present a misunderstanding or other negative outcome which is assumed to arise out of a mismatch of cultural norms and assumptions. Critical incidents can be useful to a certain extent for engaging learners in reflection on potential causes of misunderstanding and generating insight into the fact that, even when speakers have good intentions, unacknowledged assumptions infused with strong affective power can lead to misunderstanding and other negative outcomes in communication. However, there is also a danger in using critical incidents that learners will fall back on essentialist notions of culture where cultural differences are assumed to exist simply based on national identifications (Holliday, 2010). This can lead to intercultural analyses where assumed differences are used an 'excuse' for negative trajectories (Abdallah-Pretceille, 2006; Dervin, 2011). Rather than an exclusive focus on cultural differences, the approach in this chapter is more aligned with the work on AIE, which emphasizes first and foremost the importance of scaffolded reflection in helping learners make sense of their own interactional experiences in both native and foreign cultural contexts.

There are two main features that characterize the approach in this chapter. The first is that processes of reflection are explicitly anchored in aspects of pragmatics, such as common conversational routines and speech acts. This provides a linguistic grounding for reflection on broader sociocultural norms and intercultural comparisons (Dervin & Liddicoat, 2013). The second is that I focus on the role of 'experience talk' within reflection on experience and how it works to scaffold learning. The term 'experience talk' is used to refer to the various descriptive, evaluative and explanatory accounts of interactional experiences that are collaboratively constructed among classroom participants on the basis of reflection. It will be shown in this chapter that experience talk not only reveals participants' perceptions of interactional norms, but it also makes visible important aspects of their interpretive architecture in ways that are conducive to the development of an intercultural perspective on language use. This includes learners developing insight into the fact that interaction between individuals is not simply a negotiation of meanings in a narrow sense but also images and projections of self and other, as well as interpersonal evaluations (Kramsch, 2009).

Reflecting on Interactional Experiences in Students' First Language

For the language learner, reflection on interactional experiences in one's L1 plays an important role in the development of an intercultural perspective on language use in that it allows learners to externalize their taken-for-granted assumptions about interaction and the social relationships that interactions function to sustain. Importantly, this involves learners mobilizing their own interactional experiences as a way of illustrating, justifying or challenging normative ideas about L1 use, as well as considering how assumptions and experiences drawn from the L1 may influence perceptions of L2 pragmatics (Pizziconi, 2009). Within the process of constructing experience talk in the classroom interaction, learners attempt to reconcile accounts of individual experiences with their own knowledge and explore various interpretations and evaluations of cultural practices.

Intercultural comparison and evaluation deriving from first language reflection

When students are constructing an account of L1 norms within the foreign language classroom, it is perhaps not surprising that they explicitly invoke the L2 as a point of comparison and contrast. In some cases this may simply serve the purpose of developing an account of linguistic differences, but in other cases the L2 might be brought in within more of an evaluative frame to take up a positive or negative stance on aspects of the L1 (McConachy & Liddicoat, 2016). In such cases, learners appeal to broader perceptions of the roles and relationships of individuals involved in order to develop more detailed interpretations. This can be observed below, where the interaction begins with students mobilizing their meta-pragmatic awareness of a particular interactional routine in customer-service discourse in Japan, but which then provides an entry point into reflection on cultural characteristics embodied in the interaction, which in turn functions to incite intercultural comparisons. The specific interactional routine under consideration involves the purchase of a coffee at a typical café in a major Japanese city (Extract 4.1). The experience talk which emerges on the basis of reflection in this extract pertains not to a particular experience, but to the generalized images students have constructed on the basis of experience. In other words, they are articulating what is normal for them.

Extract 4.1

1   **Teacher:**   So I've got a question to ask you. When you go into a café or a coffee shop or a shop like that in Tokyo, what will it be necessary or usual to say to the counter staff? And what will they say to you? Okay, so you'll have to think carefully. From when you enter the shop, how does communication start and proceed? Please discuss this in pairs.

2   **Tai:**   If I'm in the clothing store or something ... I buy something ... ah ... I say 'onegaishimasu', but in the food store I don't say anything. Just if staff is friendly I smile. How about you?

3	**Misato:**	Usually they say first, 'Please next' in coffee shop or café, and they say, 'For here or to go⸮'
4	**Tai:**	And what do you say⸮
5	**Misato:**	I only say menu
6	**Tai:**	Just one⸮
7	**Misato:**	Just one. What else do I say⸮
8	**Tai:**	Maybe nothing⸮
9	**Misato:**	I don't communicate with them. But usually they are polite than foreigner staff.
10	**Tai:**	Oh.
11	**Misato:**	So I get a little bit nervous.
12	**Tai:**	Yeah. It different from foreign shop. I'm working at the Gap and doing register usually. Most half of customers say nothing. I'm a little bit irritated.
13	**Misato:**	(laughing). So I'm customer like that.
14	**Tai:**	It's not good.
15	**Misato:**	So sometimes I feel pressure from them because they seem to be hurry so I'm sorry. But especially in Disneyland they are very kind. They wait me.

What is interesting in this interaction is that although it begins with students articulating their perception of a cultural script for a customer-service interaction in Tokyo, intercultural comparisons are constructed to illuminate the perceived manner of Japanese customer service. Upon being prompted through the task framing in Line 1, Lines 2–9 see the students reflecting on their experiences to engage their L1-based interpretive architecture and build a descriptive account of a typical interaction in a coffee shop in Tokyo. As requested by the teacher, the students are taking a sequential view of interaction – walking (talking) through the sequence of turns of talk that would constitute the typical interaction according to their perceptions. It is in Line 9 where Misato shifts from description to evaluation of practices by formulating a dichotomous comparison in which Japanese staff are placed in contrast to 'foreigner staff'. Here she emphasizes her perception of the relative 'politeness' of Japanese staff and then in Line 11 positions herself in relation to this politeness by saying that it makes her nervous. The notion of politeness remains unpacked here, and although Tai doesn't comment on Misato's attribution he does orient to her use of the category 'foreign', using it to construct an intercultural comparison of his own in Line 12. Here, he invokes the notion of 'foreign shop' in order to establish a frame of reference for taking a critical perspective on what he perceives as the impolite behaviour of Japanese customers at his workplace (a clothing store popular among young Japanese). The implication seems to be that 'foreign' customers interact more with the shop staff.

Although the scale of comparison being constructed by the students is problematic in that it is framed in terms of 'Japanese staff' versus 'foreign staff', at this point this is functioning as an initial frame for comparison which obviously has validity for them at this stage of development. These categories can be seen as constituting frames in the students' interpretive architecture and can be modified in response to further input. Similarly, although the concept of politeness itself is also yet to be problematized, the generation of personal accounts of interactional phenomena based on reflection on experience help to construct an initial framework within which learners can take up evaluative positions (including critical perspectives on practices) and to compare and contrast these practices with other languages and cultures (Liddicoat & Scarino, 2013). Whereas the talk here has been mostly descriptive and evaluative, in Extract 4.2 below students move to an explanatory mode in response to teacher prompting. Specifically, Tai and Misato are considering the observation made in Line 12 of the previous extract that Japanese customers tend not to speak much to store staff during a transaction.

Extract 4.2

1 **Tai:**   Why do you think Japanese don't greet with shop staff?
2 **Misato:**   So, I think, in my case the process of buying something is manual, so I think I don't have to say something. So, it's like *me wo mireba wakaru* (I think that they will understand what I want just from eye contact).
3 **Teacher:** So you might want to think about why is manual style good in Japan and what does it do for you? How does it help you or how does it help the staff?
4 **Tai:**   Most staff is working as part time job and they are not professional, like high school student, so companies should make a manual because they don't know formal language.
5 **Misato:**   I think so. It save time to teach new staff how to communicate with customers.

In Line 1 Tai initiates an explanation-seeking frame for the discussion pitched at the level of 'Japanese people'. What is interesting is that although Tai's question is framed as a generalization, Misato invokes the term 'in my case' to frame her response as a personal one rather than a generalization. Misato is thus positioning herself as one of those 'Japanese people' who typically don't say much to store staff. Her interpretive repertoire is constituted by the view that such interactions tend to be highly scripted anyway (according to the 'manual'), and it is therefore unnecessary for her to say anything beyond the minimal requirements for completing the transaction. She appeals to a notion of implicit communication ('*me wo*

mireba wakaru'), against which her interactional behaviour can be rational-
ized. What is particularly significant in Misato's formulation is that her
interpretation has been developed to consist not simply of an account of
practices, but of the cultural logic which she uses for interpreting practices.
In this regard, it is highly indicative that Misato uses the L1 to express this,
as it shows she is drawing directly on cultural knowledge embedded in the
Japanese language which functions as a part of her interpretive
architecture.

In following up on Misato's Line 2 comment, the teacher's contribution
in Line 3 can be regarded as having two functions. First, it attempts to re-
frame the cultural analysis from a functional perspective. In other words,
students are encouraged to consider pragmatic norms not as self-justifying,
but as being retained for serving a purpose (Agha, 1998). Secondly, the
teacher's question shifts the mode of analysis from an individual perspective to a more generalized perspective on interaction. What emerges from
Tai in Line 4 is a kind of sociolinguistic perspective, which suggests that
companies will aim to standardize the interactional routines of customer
service staff based on the assumption that this is necessary to ensure that
everyone can use formal language. Through his comment Tai reveals the
cultural assumption that being able to use 'correct' (formal) Japanese is
usually something reserved for people who have completed formal school-
ing and taken up full-time jobs. Misato aligns with Tai's assessment in
Line 5, adding an economic perspective to the analysis – that standardizing
interactions also saves time when training employees. Here the reflection is
not so much on the cultural knowledge underlying interpretation of interaction per se, but is rather geared towards exploration of aspects of the social
structure that contribute to the formalization of particular ways of speaking
(Bourdieu, 1990).

Over the two extracts presented above, students can be seen to draw on
their meta-pragmatic awareness for customer-service encounters to construct descriptive, evaluative and explanatory accounts of interactional
behaviour that they regard as typical. Experience talk emerges to give a level
of specificity to the description of practices, which in turn helps to shift the
interaction towards evaluation of practices. The talk becomes most obviously meta-pragmatic in the evaluative and explanatory accounts as students
invoke notions such as politeness, construct intercultural comparisons and
appeal to cultural common sense (Kádár & Haugh, 2013). The intercultural
dimension surfaces most obviously in the use of a monolithic 'foreigner'
against which standards of politeness in Japanese customer service can be
understood. It is clear that stereotypicalized perceptions of foreigners are
functioning as a resource for interpretation, but the students' awareness at
this point is yet to incorporate a critical dimension in which constructs such
as 'Japanese', 'foreign' or 'polite' might be more insightfully deconstructed
(McConachy & Liddicoat, 2016).

Experience talk for grounding exploration of speech act norms

Traditional views of meta-pragmatic awareness within SLA have emphasized the ability of learners to recognize L2 speech act realization patterns in terms of triadic mappings between form, function and context (e.g. Schmidt, 1993). For example, the ability of a learner to state that 'in Japanese you can say express thanks by saying *"sumimasen"* or *"arigatou gozaimasu"'* would constitute evidence of awareness of form-function mapping. For a learner to state that 'you should use *"sumimasen"* if the act is unexpected' would add a layer of contextual understanding. It would also hint at awareness of the connection between notions of interpersonal rights and obligations and speech act behaviour (Spencer-Oatey, 2008). As McConachy and Liddicoat (2016) have argued, in intercultural language learning such awareness constitutes a foundation for understanding, but it is necessary to go beyond such descriptive formulations to explore underlying cultural assumptions and the complexity of judgements of appropriate language use in context. One way of opening up to complexity is by developing learners' ability to search their interactional histories for instances that can help illustrate how L1 forms are used and how they can be variably interpreted. In the talk below, students are drawing on a previous discussion in which it had been mentioned that although the Japanese word *sumimasen* can be used for thanking, it can also be used for apologizing (Sugimoto, 1997). Therefore, in order to explore the students' meta-pragmatic awareness of *sumimasen*, students have been asked to identify instances in their own interactional histories in which the word had been used. Extract 4.3 shows how experience talk can function to ground exploration of the contextual conditions relating to utterances and the cultural frameworks that are implicated.

Extract 4.3

1	**Teacher:**	Alright, then. So please try to find some of your own experiences where perhaps you said *'sumimasen'* or perhaps someone said it to you.
2	**Tai:**	Ah, yes. I have. I get the bed from the elevator, that elevator was on the second floor and I want to go next floor. So the person who came in the other side, I let her go first, and she said *'sumimasen'*. And it means 'Thank you'.
3	**Seiji:**	Oh. I was with my friend of the university and she came from Hokkaido and her father came to see her so we are waiting for coming him in Takadanobaba Station together. And her father came the station and I met him and suddenly he gave me souvenir from Hokkaido. And then I said *'sumimasen'*, but it is 100% 'Thank you'.
4	**Teacher:**	In that case why couldn't you say *'arigatou gozaimasu'*?
5	**Seiji:**	Um, I haven't expected at all that he gave me so it was too sudden for me.

6 **Tai:**   Maybe it's Japanese custom when we are given something
              a gift we have to reject.
7 **Teacher:** Oh, right? In this case you cannot reject it because he
              bought it for you. Like you couldn't say, 'kekkou desu'. You
              have to take it.
8 **Seiji:**   Um, I said, 'Oh, can I really accept this?'
9 **Teacher:** Right.
10 **Seiji:**   And he said, 'It's okay'.
11 **Teacher:** Hmm, that's interesting.
12 **Tai:**   Maybe if he says 'arigatou gozaimasu' firstly, it is rude.
13 **Teacher:** Why?
14 **Seiji:**   Maybe it's custom or culture.
15 **Tai:**   It seems that he waited for it.
16 **Teacher:** Oh, I see. So he should show the feeling that it is not
              necessary? Is it trying to lower your position or...
17 **Seiji:**   nande nan darou ne, demo ... (Yeah, I wonder why ... hmm ...)
18 **Teacher:** Would you say 'arigatou' if he were equal?
19 **Seiji:**   Rejecting at least once or showing rejecting is kind of polite
              so 'sumimasen' is kind of the rejection. So it seems to be polite.
20 **Teacher:** Interesting. How about if you went to Hokkaido and you
              gave something to him? Do you think that he would say,
              'sumimasen'? Or would he say, 'arigatou'?
21 **Seiji:**   He might say 'arigatou'. Nande nan darou ne! (I wonder why!)
22 **Tai:**   (Laughing)

In line with the task framing, the interaction begins with Tai and then
Seiji contributing a short example each from their experience which serves
to illustrate the function of *sumimasen* to accomplish thanking, but with
slightly different nuances in each example. Tai's example illustrates use of
sumimasen to thank someone for their consideration while simultaneously
acknowledging that imposition has been borne. Meanwhile, Seiji's example
illustrates the use of *sumimasen* to express thanks for a gift from someone
older and with moderate social distance (Sugimoto, 1998). At this point, the
teacher directs attention to Seiji's example in order to scaffold comparison
with another way of thanking in Japanese and draw out the students' understanding of the contextual constraints on these forms in more detail.
Whereas Seiji responds in terms of his own personal interpretation of the
situation, Tai begins to formulate a cultural norm. While Seiji explains that
he couldn't use *arigatou gozaimasu* in this case because the gift was unexpected (Line 5), Tai interprets the situation in terms of a *'Japanese custom
[that] when we are given a gift we have to reject'* (Line 6). In essence, he is connecting specific speech act norms to broader norms of social behaviour. In
Line 7 the teacher prompts Seiji to reflect on this notion of rejection specifically in relation to this experience, which leads him to elaborate on the

nature of the linguistic strategies he used to accept the gift humbly (Lines 8 and 10). Building on this, Tai adds that using *arigatou gozaimasu* instead could come across as rude (Line 12).

It is notable that the teacher encourages the students to unpack the cultural assumptions underlying these norms, through prompting the students to formulate explanatory accounts (Line 13), by reformulating these accounts (Line 16) and by prompting consideration of other contexts (Lines 18 and 20). Throughout this extract as a whole, students collaborate to construct an account of *arigatou gozaimasu* as inappropriate for Seiji's situation due to failing to index the necessary hesitation expected when receiving a gift in Japanese culture. On the other hand, *sumimasen*, in combination with explicit confirmation strategies articulated by Seiji in Line 8, allow for the gift to be received in a culturally appropriate way. The teacher and students can be seen to be working together to unpack some of the cultural assumptions that surround the acts of thanking in Japanese and the constraints on how thanking can be manifested linguistically. In this way, experience talk which requires elaboration of the interactional specifics of the situation, including the context and the language used by participants in the interaction, plays an important role in that it functions to effectively 'ground' the analysis. Contextual specifics are made increasingly salient and students are able then to construct an interpretation of cultural norms that might influence how language use in the situation could be interpreted (McConachy, 2013).

In terms of meta-pragmatic awareness development, a particularly important feature of the talk emerges in Lines 17 and 21, where the Japanese phrase *'nande nan darou ne'* represents a juncture in which Seiji notices the limitations of his meta-pragmatic awareness to account for his intuitive knowledge. Both students clearly sense that these two utterances are different, but explication of these differences proves to be harder than expected. As a learning process, coming to the limitations of one's ability to account for an observed feature of language use provides a platform for the creation of a more complex meta-pragmatic awareness which can be used to explore the deeper cultural influences on language use. This can be observed below. Here we see students working from their gaps in awareness to reflect further and, through the interaction, to develop a more sophisticated explanatory account invoking Japanese cultural concepts.

Extract 4.4

1 **Teacher:** So, just before we were thinking about the differences between *'sumimasen'* for 'Thank you' and *'arigatou gozaimashita'*. During the break have you thought about this any more? What are you thinking Seiji?
2 **Seiji:** Um, I think its difference comes from hierarchy.
3 **Teacher:** What kind of hierarchy? Age?

4	**Seiji:**	Yeah, or situation. Like I imagined that if the inferior gave some gifts to superior, superior might say *'arigatou gozaimasu'*. And in contrast, a superior gave something to an inferior, an inferior might say *'sumimasen'*. I just think so. So I think it is because of hierarchy system.
5	**Teacher:**	Okay. So do you think that they are just saying 'I'm sorry' or the feeling is really 'I'm sorry'?
6	**Seiji:**	... feeling ...... um little bit feel sorry because superior is thinking of the inferior. Superior *ga kidukai wo shimeshita* (The superior showed concern), so it's ... inferior might think ...
7	**Teacher:**	It's not necessary?
8	**Seiji:**	... um no ... if I were inferior I feel I let him to do so. So it's little bit impolite.
9	**Teacher:**	So you think it's connected to the idea of *kidukai*? So basically you are saying that somebody in a lower position should not make someone in a higher position do *kidukai*. But if they do, then you should say *'sumimasen'*?
10	**Seiji:**	It just my opinion but I think so.
11	**Teacher:**	Could you agree with that Tai?
12	**Tai:**	Yeah, I often do the mistakes when I got the gift. I don't know this comes from my personality or experience, but when someone give me the gift I say *'arigatou gozaimasu'* most times.
13	**Teacher:**	Do you think other Japanese people would think it's bad?
14	**Tai:**	Hmm, maybe. Yes I think so.

It can be seen that further reflection has helped the students come up with a more sophisticated account of the use of *sumimasen* and *arigatou gozaimasu*, this time rooting their explanations in explicit meta-pragmatic concepts, including Japanese emic concepts (Haugh & Hinze, 2003). Throughout the talk, the teacher constantly prompts students to specify in detail the nature of their ideas as they emerge. The first concept to emerge is 'hierarchy', which Seiji invokes in Line 2 as an aspect of context influencing thanking behaviour in Japanese. Upon being questioned regarding the meaning of hierarchy by the teacher (Line 3), Seiji constructs quite an elaborate meta-pragmatic explanation (Line 4) to illustrate the relationship between the pragmalinguistic and sociopragmatic dimensions of *sumimasen* and *arigatou gozaimasu*. Using hierarchy as his grounding concept, he suggests that a superior would be likely to use *arigatou gozaimasu* when receiving something from an inferior, whereas an inferior would be likely to use *sumimasen* in the reverse situation. Important in the lines that follow is the further emergence of cultural concepts to elaborate on the constraining role of hierarchy in thanking behaviour. In Line 5 the teacher's question is aimed at digging out whether these utterances are simply used ritualistically or whether speakers actually experience feelings that correspond to the illocutionary act. Seiji reveals in Line 6 and Line 8 that the use of *sumimasen* by an inferior in this case would actually accompany a feeling of being 'sorry' due to the fact that receiving a gift from a superior implies that the inferior has made the superior show '*kidukai*' (concern). It can therefore be seen that the focus on the emotional dimension of language use has helped Seiji reflect on his own knowledge and develop more sophisticated meta-pragmatic awareness, explicitly linking the linguistic with the cultural. Of additional importance here is that this telling by Seiji is highly scaffolded by the teacher. The teacher's reformulation in Line 9 can be seen to make use of the L1 metalanguage introduced by Seiji in Line 6 in order to reformulate the ideas from Seiji's contributions in Lines 4 and 6 to tie them together in a coherent whole. That the teacher has effectively synthesized Seiji's interpretation is confirmed in Line 10.

It is noteworthy that the reflection as scaffolded in the talk allows Tai to explicitly position himself vis-à-vis L1 interactional practices. He in fact reveals in Line 12 how he often does not use *sumimasen*, preferring to use *arigatou gozaimasu* regardless of social hierarchy. Nevertheless, he reveals in Line 14 that he maintains his interactional preference even while recognizing that generally people may not approve of it – in fact framing his own behaviour as a 'mistake'. His meta-pragmatic awareness therefore consists of knowledge of interactional conventions and the coercive implications that they can have, leading him to position himself as atypical with regard to aspects of Japanese pragmatics. In other words, he characterizes his own practices as culturally illegitimate according to a perspective on Japanese culture in which internal diversity is not highly tolerated.

As above, further targeted reflection on language forms used for thanking enabled the students to bring out aspects of their interpretive architecture. Specifically, learners have been able to explicate their understandings of the norms associated with thanking and how these are influenced not only by aspects of context such as social distance, but also by underlying values which permeate broader social relations. The students incorporate the Japanese emic concept of *kidukai* to develop an explanatory framework (Haugh, 2003) as a part of a more nuanced cultural interpretation of linguistic behaviour. Meta-pragmatic awareness therefore clearly goes beyond a mapping of forms, functions and contexts. Meta-pragmatic awareness here links forms, functions, notions of interpersonal rights and obligations, and contextualizes these elements within culture-specific logic (McConachy & Spencer-Oatey, forthcoming).

Evaluating and explaining cultural practices

Reflection on how people interact in particular situations inevitably involves not just description and explanation of practices, but also interpersonal evaluations on the basis of practices (Houghton, 2012). As an interpersonal evaluation that is particularly salient in everyday discourse, attributions of politeness or rudeness also emerge in accounts of interactional experiences that students reveal in the classroom. In Extract 4.5 students are reflecting on customer-service interactions in Japan, particularly the meta-pragmatic judgement of one student, derived from his own experience, that many customers tend to be 'rude'. The basis of such a judgement is explored by the classroom participants and is supported by an account of experience from the teacher's perspective (a cultural outsider). This addition of an outsider perspective in particular functions to generate explanatory accounts from students.

Extract 4.5

1	**Teacher:**	Tai, I remember before you said that you get irritated by customers who don't say much when you serve them. So I want to ask you all, generally do you feel that the customers are rude in Japan? If you are just watching other customers, do you feel that they are rude?
2	**Tai:**	60 or 70% are rude.
3	**Teacher:**	Yeah? Why do you feel they're rude exactly?
4	**Tai:**	I feel they don't think that I'm a human
5	**Teacher:**	Not worthy of respect?
6	**Tai:**	Um, they don't think I have feeling.
7	**Teacher:**	Yeah, when I first came to Japan that was my impression too. They, I felt that the customers treat them like they don't have feelings. They ask them a question, like you know, 'atatamemasuka?' (Shall I warm this up?), and they don't say yes or no. If they don't say anything it means yes, I guess. Or maybe they moved their face a little bit that I couldn't see. But they didn't say 'onegaishimasu' (yes, please) or 'kekkou desu' (no, thanks). They didn't say anything like that. That was my first impression.
8	**Seiji:**	Oh … Um, I think the Japanese tend to be more shy compared with Western people and the Japanese tend to, um, tend to want some …
9	**Tai:**	distance?
10	**Seiji:**	… distance between staff and customer because they don't know each other, so they might think that they don't have to be, like, friendly.
11	**Teacher:**	Right. Yeah.
12	**Seiji:**	So, I don't think it's rude, but, um, I want it to be kind of changed.
13	**Teacher:**	Yeah, I know what you're saying. I think that is probably not shyness. Shyness is usually when you want to talk, but you can't. Like, you think 'I want to talk more' to some

		people, but 'I can't do it'. Probably, what you're saying, it's interesting, you could say it's social distance. (Writes it on the board). So you feel comfortable if there is some distance between you and the staff perhaps.
14	**Tai:**	Yeah, I think social distance is actually correct in Japan because at Gap, ah, my elder ask us to communicate with customers like 'This is good clothing', but someone, I say, for example 'This is nice', it depends on person, but most of them feel uncomfortable.
15	**Teacher:**	Right.
16	**Tai:**	Embarrassed.
17	**Teacher:**	Yeah. Yeah, they're not comfortable having a kind of personal conversation in a customer setting.

The most significant aspect of the above is the ways in which experience talk, from the teacher and students, functions as a tool for cultural exploration. In a previous discussion Tai had relayed to the class his negative impression of Japanese customers based on his experiences as a sales clerk at a clothing store. Line 1 of this extract sees the teacher use this evaluation as a frame for discussion, here prompting further reflection on the attribution of 'rudeness' to Japanese customers. Although Tai asserts in Line 2 that he sees 60–70% of customers as rude, at this point he does not explain how this concept of rudeness is manifested in interactional terms. The teacher's turn in Line 3 is an attempt at prompting reflection for eliciting such an explanation, although what Tai offers in Lines 4 and 6 is more a characterization of his own emotional reactions to interaction. Therefore, the nature of Tai's conceptualization of the culturally laden notion of rudeness remains somewhat obscure. From this perspective the teacher's contribution in Line 7 can be considered significant as he aligns with Tai's general characterization and draws on his own experiences observing Japanese interaction, which helps to specify how rudeness can be manifested interactionally from the teacher's perspective.

Although it is now the teacher's construal of rudeness which has come under attention, the effect this has on the unfolding interaction is significant. Specifically, the provision of this outsider perspective appears to stimulate Seiji in Line 8 to generate an explanation for the phenomena mentioned in the teacher's experience talk. Here he formulates a dichotomy between Japanese and 'Western' people in order to attribute to Japanese people the characteristic of 'shyness', thus explaining their reluctance to interact with service providers. While the generation of the culturally variable notion of 'shyness' provides an alternative frame for the exploration of interaction, from this comment it cannot be ascertained whether Seiji sees this characteristic as culturally variable or not. His shyness explanation seems to be tied up with the concept of 'distance', which Tai helps him formulate (Lines 9–10). Seiji's Line 10 comment elaborates this relationship in a little more detail, where the idea comes out that Japanese people recognize friendliness – presumably characterized by more active verbal exchanges – as contingent on the degree of familiarity with a particular speaker. Interestingly, in Line 12 Seiji evaluates this phenomenon as not being rude, but at the same time as something he would prefer was not the case. It appears that, although both students are working at generating cultural explanations for interactional behaviour, they are in alignment to a certain extent regarding the 'rudeness' characterization, thus constituting a somewhat critical perspective on aspects of their own culture.

In Line 13 the teacher offers an interpretation of the phenomenon, which takes the form of a reaction to Seiji's shyness explanation, that is, that the lack of interaction on behalf of Japanese customers is not a matter of 'shyness' so much as a matter of greater social distance being the norm in such situations. The explicit introduction of the concept of social distance appears to provide a resource for Tai's contribution in Line 14, where he aligns with this assessment by the teacher. It is important that here Tai brings his own experience into the analysis to assert in specific interactional terms the legitimacy of his cultural explanation. In other words, by sharing his experience of attempting to engage with Japanese customers on a personal level in a workplace context, his experience talk here thus functions to illustrate the notion of social distance and at the same time to substantiate its validity as a construct for explaining Japanese customer behaviour. The value of the experience talk here is not simply that it helps to reveal more specifically the conceptualization of culturally variable notions; it is also important that it helps to evidence one cultural explanation over another for the participants in the talk.

The significance of the classroom talk above for intercultural learning is that it shows cultural explanations being generated in order to explain, and in some sense justify, attributions such as 'rudeness' or 'shyness' which stem from evaluations of observed interactional practices (McConachy & Hata, 2013). Particularly interesting is the way in which students again brought in 'Western people' as an outside reference point in order to illustrate a perceived feature of Japanese people. Although this particular comparative frame itself was not challenged in the extract of discussion above, the attribution of shyness was interrogated in order to move beyond the level of commonplace cultural generalizations. Rather than accept the essentialist notion that 'Japanese are shy', the teacher pushes students to consider alternative explanations. Through the talk, the particular interpersonal concepts such as 'shyness' which inform students' interpretations of linguistic behaviour (and are necessarily tied to stereotypes of one's own and other groups) are able to be articulated with more specificity and examined on the basis of reflection (Kádár & Haugh, 2013).

Coming to generate explanations for cultural behaviour, then zooming in on the concepts which are invoked in explanations provides a useful interpretive lens within classroom talk for developing meta-pragmatic aware-ness. However, in generating explanations for behaviour, there is always the danger of underestimating the role of context on that behaviour, especially when this involves intercultural comparisons. As in the previous extract, the claim is made that social distance between customer-service providers and customers in Japan limits the possibilities for more personal talk. However, interactional patterns, even within a similar type of discourse, can be prone to variability, particularly variability according to region (Coulmas, 2013). This is an issue which is taken up below, as a challenge emerges to the asser-tion made earlier by Tai and Seiji that Japanese customers are uncomfortable interacting on a personal level. The students and teacher draw on their expe-riences to present examples that problematize this assertion.

Extract 4.6

1	**Hikari:**	I think we can't say so for all the situation, for all the cases in Japan, all part of Japan because when I went to Shikoku and to Kochi even they get on the bus they just say *'ohayo gozaimasu'* or *'sayonara'*.
2	**Teacher:**	To the bus driver?
3	**Hikari:**	Yeah, to the bus driver, and so it happened in Kanazawa and Osaka. When I went to Osaka every time I bought something, something happened to our conversation. They add something special to customer and so they enjoy the communication.
4	**Teacher:**	Yeah, I've experienced the same thing actually. Like when I go surfing in Chiba, it's quite a country area, so you know, if I go into a shop, they greet me and I greet them and I've seen other Japanese people greeting them as well. You know, not really casually, just like *'A, konnichiwa'* or something like that. So, I thought it is different to Tokyo.
5	**Tai:**	I think it depends on population.
6	**Seiji:**	It's just my opinion, but people in Tokyo is more cold than people in Osaka.
7	**Teacher:**	Oh, yeah, you've said that before.
8	**ALL:**	(Laughing)
9	**Tai:**	Yeah, my friends who came from Osaka said the same thing.

Hikari launches the discussion with a challenge to the assertion that Japanese people are reluctant to engage in personal interaction in service encounters. She does this by highlighting the importance of regional vari-ability, which is exemplified by instances of her own experiences interacting outside Tokyo (Lines 1 and 3). Hikari's contribution functions to frame the exploration of diversity in terms of regional variability, which is also taken up by the teacher in Line 4 with instances from his own experience. Tai's contribution in Line 5 is interesting as it frames the issue of diversity as related to population rather than region per se. This thus represents the generation of an alternate lens for understanding cultural diversity. Seiji, on the other hand, chooses to formulate a dichotomy between Tokyo and Osaka (Line 6), implying that the reluctance to communicate in service encounters is just one manifestation of people in Tokyo being 'cold' in comparison to people in Osaka. Although Seiji has been a resident of Tokyo for several years, he is originally from Osaka, so the dichotomous nature of the formulation here can be considered as derived from his specific frame of reference as a resident in both cities. In Line 9 Tai reports that he had heard a similar characterization made by his own friends from Osaka. In a sense, this contributes to validating the Tokyo – Osaka dichotomy within the talk, although the notion of 'coldness' has not really been talked through at the level of interactional specifics in this extract. What is particularly important is that the students are engaging in exploration of diversity in relation to practices in their own culture, which functions to challenge previously made characterizations concerning 'shyness' expressed as reluctance to interact in service encounters (Extract 4.5). The exploration of diversity in this extract can therefore highlight for the students the difficulty with making generalizations and the fact that unanalyzed aspects of one's own experience may in fact contradict one's own previously made assessments of culture upon reflection. In essence they are still making generalizations; however, through the talk they have moved away from the idea of a homogenous national culture through exploration of regional variability (Dervin, 2011).

Section summary

As demonstrated throughout this section, reflection on L1 interactional experiences constitutes a valuable tool for uncovering the elements and relations between the elements that constitute students' interpretive architecture. Specifically, learners use reflection to articulate the schema and scripts they apply to specific interactional practices and settings and how they attribute particular interpersonal evaluations such as politeness to specific aspects of speech acts and interaction. Learners develop awareness of the general contextual contingency of linguistic actions and of the subtle norms and assumptions that pervade everyday sense making. Collaborative reflection in cases such as this where students share an L1 creates a context for discovery of both similarities and differences in the ways in which students interpret and evaluate interaction, and awareness of the fact that each student interprets culture from his/her own individual standpoint, constituted by the history of his/her own personal experiences (Scarino, 2009). Culture-specific meta-pragmatic constructs (such as 'kidukai') emerge in the talk within explanatory frames that serve to deepen the collaborative analysis. This section also shows that even when the focus of reflection is on L1-based experiences, learners' perceptions of 'others' – frequently articulated as 'foreigners' or 'Westerners' in this chapter – are active in learners' minds and are used to construct accounts of cultural similarity or difference, often in essentialist ways. While some might argue that such reflective activities simply encourage learners to stereotype, it is clear that scaffolding strategies can be used to prompt students to fully articulate the nature of their interpretations and challenge simplistic explanations. It is better for the influence of stereotypes to be exposed rather than ignored (Houghton, 2012).

Reflecting on Experiences of Intercultural Communication in the Foreign Language

For language learners, reflection on experiences of intercultural communication in an L2 provides a range of opportunities for exploring the ways they draw on cultural assumptions to interpret interactional features as well as the interactional context (Byram *et al.*, 2009). Unless individuals are highly proficient in an L2, the cognitive load involved in L2 intercultural encounters can mean that there is little room left over for monitoring the specific pragmatic details of an interaction and how one made sense of them at a cognitive and affective level. It is for that reason that the classroom can provide opportunities for more focused reflection on the nature of learners' interactional experiences and help them reinterpret these experience with insight gained from peers and teachers. However, while it might be relatively easy for learners to offer descriptive, evaluative and explanatory accounts of interactional experiences from their L1, it can be a challenge to reflect on L2 interactions. This section shows some of the ways in which reflection on the pragmatic dimensions of intercultural interactions can provide opportunities for intercultural learning.

Interpreting and evaluating perceived cultural difference

When reflecting on experiences of intercultural communication in a foreign language, there can be a tendency for learners to focus on aspects of interaction that they perceive as somehow different from interaction in the L1. Although perception of difference does not necessarily indicate actual difference, it is important that learners are able to articulate their perception of difference in order to make it available for collaborative examination. In other words, it is the subjective perception of difference and its articulation within experience talk that provides fertile ground for digging out some of the assumptions that underlie how learners interpret communicative encounters in culturally unfamiliar contexts. In Extract 4.7 students are reflecting on one of Misato's experiences when interacting in San Francisco, which is framed as one example of cultural difference. The nature of the difference is explored from a comparative perspective and cultural explanations generated.

Extract 4.7

1	**Teacher:**	Okay, so let me ask you: how have you felt when you've been travelling overseas and the shop staff have spoken to you in a different way than in Japan?
2	**Misato:**	So, when I went to San Francisco the staff asked me, 'Where did you come from, Tokyo or Osaka?' I said, 'I from Osaka', and last he asked me to shake hands.
3	**Tai:**	Weird
4	**Misato:**	Yeah, at last I feel a little strange. So because he asked me many things.
5	**Tai:**	Yeah, I think maybe he was too friendly.
6	**Misato:**	And it because I foreigner and tourist so maybe he was too friendly, I think.
7	**Tai:**	Ah, but I think the relationship between customer and staff is equal in….
8	**Misato:**	Abroad?
9	**Tai:**	Abroad? Yeah, I don't know about that, but maybe Western.
10	**Teacher:**	Yeah, that's an interesting point. I actually feel like sometimes the shop staff are up here and the customer is down here. Sometimes in Australia you are friendly to them but they are not so friendly to you. It's kind of reversed.
11	**Misato:**	I think it's because in Japan, there is the concept of 'okyakusama wa kamisama' (The customer is God). So many customers are arrogant, I think.
12	**Tai:**	Ah, but this idea 'Customer is God' was not natural in Japan because I learned that in tourism class. One hotel manager thought up have this idea and ordered his staff, 'Don't be rude to customer'. Until then, the staff say something impolite to customer like, 'This is not my job'. But now, even some job is not staff's job, they do it.

The discussion is initially framed by the teacher as one in which students should look for examples of cultural differences encountered in their own experiences and reflect on how they reacted emotionally to those perceived differences. Misato is the first one to orient to the framing of the discussion by relaying an experience interacting with a sales clerk in San Francisco (Line 2). While Misato here describes rather than evaluates the interaction, Tai characterizes it in Line 3 as 'weird'. Misato's next turn (Line 4) is interesting as it sees her align with Tai's evaluation (strange) and describe in more detail what it was exactly that she interpreted as 'different'. This thus shows how perceptions of pragmatic or interactional differences can function as a trigger for interpersonal evaluation (Roberts, 1998). Misato points to the fact that the service provider she interacted with asked her many questions. She therefore works to illustrate the construct of strangeness which is at play in the evaluation of cultural difference. In Line 5 Tai responds to the addition of detail given by Misato, this time shifting his evaluation from 'strange' to 'too friendly'. What is interesting again is that in Line 6 Misato adopts the concept of 'too friendly', orienting to Tai's characterization. However, in Line 6 it is important that rather than attempting to explain her experience in terms of national characteristics (e.g. North Americans are too friendly), she focuses on the nature of the sociocultural context of interaction, specifically the social roles of the speakers. Reflection allows her to explore the potential role that her positioning as a cultural outsider and tourist had on the interaction. In effect, the experience talk provided a context in which she can re-evaluate whether what she experienced is really representative of cultural norms, or whether it is a contextually situated accommodation by her interlocutor to her status as foreign tourist (Schegloff, 1996).

In Line 7 there is another interesting shift as Tai begins constructing a cultural explanation for the perceived 'friendliness' of the American interlocutor. What he draws on here is the notion of 'equal', which can perhaps be regarded as an interpretation of social distance, or more specifically lack of social distance in this case. One thing that is significant is that in the act of attempting to make this attribution, he struggles at the end of Line 7 to find the appropriate referent for the attribution. In Line 8 Misato offers 'abroad', which would set up a dichotomous contrast between Japan and the rest of the world, something Tai rejects in Line 9, eventually choosing to adopt the referent of 'Western'. The teacher's contribution in Line 10 brings Australia into the discussion as a reference point, which functions to establish the nation as a framework for comparison in the remainder of the talk. Although the nation is still very broad category for intercultural comparison, it nevertheless represents a narrowing down of the frame of reference being used for intercultural comparison.

Further, the teacher's suggestion that customer-service providers in Australia can sometimes demonstrate less friendliness than customers seems to prompt Misato to articulate an explanation for how power distance – specifically the high status attributed to the customer – influences customer-service discourse in Japan. What she comes up with in Line 11 is a commonly cited catchphrase in Japan (The Customer is God) which she believes functions to shape people's behaviour in customer-service encounters. Articulating this specific cultural formulation illustrates the role of commonly circulated cultural ideas which inform speakers' meta-pragmatic awareness in processes of meaning making (Niedzielski & Preston, 2009). In Line 12 Tai makes an important contribution to the interaction by utilizing knowledge gained from formal learning to problematize the notion that Japanese service providers have always treated the customer like a 'God'. He explains that the catchphrase mentioned by Misato was in fact something made up for the purpose of improving the attitude of Japanese workers in a previous era.

What Tai's example achieves in this discussion is that it highlights the fact that culture is created, and that the cultural knowledge which we tend to fall back on may in fact be arbitrary. He therefore builds on Misato's turn to illustrate the ideological dimension of meta-pragmatic awareness (Coupland & Jaworski, 2004).

The interaction here shows how experience talk serves the function not simply of illustrating perceived differences, but of highlighting the fact that perception of difference can lead to negative interpersonal evaluation. What is most important here, however, is that attributions such as 'weird' or 'friendly' are not the conclusion of the talk, but lead to further reflection which aims to generate multiple explanations for the behaviour under attention. This extract shows that it can in fact be attributions made by other learners listening to the experience that lead to co-construction of a particular stance on interactional features and what they mean in interpersonal terms (Liddicoat, 2007). The other learners help to construct particular frames of analysis within the experience talk and give shape to trajectories that lead to meaningful learning. While learners will not necessarily immediately revise attributions, the attempt to explain behaviour from multiple perspectives indirectly challenges them, as is the case in the talk above where the notion of friendliness was briefly discussed in relation to multiple customer-service contexts in Japan and abroad. Further, cultural explanations can be problematized and, in the process, expose the ideological nature of particular meta-pragmatic formulations (Agha, 1998). Learners' interpretive architecture will necessarily contain many assumptions about the nature of their own and other cultural groups that have been ideologically constructed and tend to remain unproblematized. It is in noticing the ideological dimension, and hence the arbitrariness, of cultural concepts and explanations that provides an important catalyst for learners to re-examine their perceptions of behaviour and decentre from taken-for-granted assumptions (Kramsch, 1993).

Re-evaluating negative evaluations of intercultural experience

Learners' accounts of their experiences interacting in a foreign language overseas are bound to include not only examples of excitement and friendship, but also examples of misunderstanding and frustration which lead to negative interpersonal evaluations (Spencer-Oatey, 2008). Although it is not the goal of classroom teachers to forcibly change learners' perceptions of negative (or positive) interactional experiences (Houghton, 2012), it is possible that experience talk can lead to new insights, either self-generated or offered by others, which lead to a reappraisal of the experience. In the extract below, experience talk can be seen to function as a resource for the re-evaluation of a negative intercultural experience, which in turn leads to heightened awareness in one particular learner of herself as a culturally situated interpreter of interaction.

Extract 4.8

1	**Seiji:**	While Golden Week I went to Australia, Gold Coast. And I went to clothes shopping with my family and we were looking for some swimming wear because we were planning to go to Great Barrier Reef, so we needed swimming pants, so I asked the shop staff and she was so friendly! 'Okay, I'm gonna looking for you', or something, she said. And I had conversation with her, like she said, 'I wanna go to Japan', so I recommend her the places like Kyoto or Osaka, and she like said, 'Thank you' and 'Have a nice trip'.
2	**Hikari:**	It friendly
3	**Seiji:**	It doesn't occur so much in Japan so first I was surprised, but I felt like 'Oh, it's culture difference'. So how about you?
4	**Hikari:**	So, when I went to the Netherlands, it's just my first impression but almost all public staffs very rude.
5	**Seiji:**	Oh really?
6	**Hikari:**	Yeah, really awful, especially the staffs at the station counter. So, most of staffs are very elderly women, but they are very rude and *'sugoi'* …
7	**Seiji:**	*'Sugoi'?*
8	**Hikari:**	Severe or just too…
9	**Seiji:**	Cold?
10	**Hikari:**	Cold. I think especially for foreigners or Asian girls. But when I entered to Germany and Belgium, so everything changed completely, so everyone very friendly and even I didn't need any information from others, I could walk by myself, but every strangers spoke to me and …
11	**Seiji:**	Tried to help you?
12	**Hikari:**	'Are you okay' or just take me to the sightseeing places and very gentle.
13	**Seiji:**	Did you feel happy?
14	**Hikari:**	Yeah. So, and I realized I loved Belgium, such a country.
15	**Seiji:**	But you will go to Netherland, so…
16	**Hikari:**	But maybe I just *henken* (biased) because I was just nervous at my examination and entrance test, so maybe it's not real. Maybe I was just too sensitive about others.
17	**Seiji:**	I have no imagine about Netherlands. It's not famous in Japan is it?
18	**Hikari:**	Not famous. On the other hand, in the Netherlands, there are many immigrants from other countries, Africa or such people. They are very very mixture culture. So, such an environment make such a situation, but maybe I made a mistake.
19	**Seiji:**	You should have decided other country?

20 **Hikari:**   Yeah, yeah, maybe the Holland is good country, but it was just my first impression, so it will be changed in the future.

21 **Seiji:**   But the staff of train at first when I came to Tokyo I felt they are cold. I ask them, 'Where is somewhere?' and it's just my opinion, but those who are in Osaka are more kind and they told me what I don't want to hear. 'You also can ......', etc.

22 **Hikari:**   Now suddenly I realize that I was too expected to the Dutch people to be more friendly and kind for foreign people. I don't care daily in Tokyo to station staff to be more friendly and I don't care so much their attitude. But for others more expected.

In Line 1 Seiji offers an account of an experience from when he was travelling with this family in Australia earlier in the year. He describes an interaction with a sales assistant in which the assistant was 'friendly' as exemplified by her attempts to find just what he wanted and her attempts to personalize the conversation. One thing that is important in Seiji's talk in Line 3 is that it includes an account of how he interpreted the experience at the time. He first recalls his emotional reaction to difference (surprise), which he then interprets on a cognitive level as a cultural difference. Seiji's talk is therefore revealing the processes of interpretation, in this case highlighting the fact that his response to difference in interaction was to interpret it as a cultural difference rather than a random encounter with an unusually friendly sales clerk.

Due to foregrounding the notion of friendliness, Seiji's experience talk can be seen to constitute scaffolding in that it prompts Hikari to reflect on an intercultural experience of her own in which she perceived the staff as being the antithesis of friendly. In her account which begins in Line 4, Hikari is initially unreserved in her negative evaluation of the staff she encountered in The Netherlands (Lines 4, 6, 8, 10), although she does not specify what is was about the way they interacted which gave her the impression of rudeness. From Line 10 she reflects on subsequent experiences in Germany and Belgium which serve to illustrate the elements she perceived as lacking in The Netherlands and thus contributed to her negative image. Her experience talk in Line 10 draws on the attribute of friendliness, which she illustrates through descriptions of the way in which local people interacted with her. What the talk is achieving here is to reveal the meta-pragmatic awareness Hikari has concerning the way people are supposed to interact in their roles as service providers. Although the culturally relative nature of the concept of friendliness is yet to be taken up, it can be seen that friendliness has been operating as a frame throughout the experience talk by both students to this point, which has allowed for further reflection on experiences and illustration of the notion through description of interactional characteristics. Furthermore, through his contributions to this point Seiji can be seen to scaffold the telling of Hikari's experience, through helping her formulate attributes (Lines 7, 9), interpreting her experience and offering words to co-construct descriptions of behaviour (Line 11), and prompting telling of emotional reactions to interaction (Line 13). All of these contributions can be regarded as a kind of peer scaffolding in that they help Hikari bring out her experience for further reflection and reinterpretation, which is what happens next.

Line 16 sees a shift in the tone of the analysis as Hikari seems to bracket her negative evaluation of The Netherlands. Here she recognizes the possibility that her perceptions and construal of interactions may have been blurred by the specific personal circumstances she was in at the time. Here Hikari has not discussed her perception as being culturally situated per se, but she certainly seems to decentre from the perspective that what she interpreted at the time was a matter of culture. Upon being indirectly prompted for more information about The Netherlands by Seiji (Line 17), Hikari goes on in Line 18 to offer her interpretation that the multi-ethnic nature of the country may have created 'such a situation'. The 'situation' to which Hikari refers is most likely that being of foreign appearance affords you no differential treatment in interaction, which Hikari may have been hoping for due to her English. She does, however, hedge this interpretation at the end of Line 18, indicating awareness that her own perception may be relative. Furthermore, in Line 20 she explicitly expresses her openness to reviewing her evaluation of The Netherlands as a country. It shows that in the act of engaging in experience talk characterized by description and evaluation, she has come to reflect on and in fact begin to suspend the legitimacy of her interpretation of her own intercultural experiences.

In Line 18 there is another important shift in the talk which is achieved by Seiji reflecting on how he felt when he first moved to Tokyo from Osaka. He recalls ascribing the attribute of 'cold' to station staff in Tokyo, whom he regarded as considerably less helpful than those in Osaka. In his talk here, he maintains the legitimacy of this attribution, albeit hedging it slightly. What is particularly significant is how this experience talk, which is articulating perceptions on variability in her own culture, leads Hikari to further reflection and a reinterpretation of her own intercultural experience. As a result of reflection she achieves three noticings (Line 22). The first is that station staff in Tokyo are not especially friendly. The second is that she has never thought this to be a problem. The third and most important noticing, which emerges in relation to the aforementioned two, is that she had had different expectations for the people in The Netherlands and the people in Japan. In other words, Seiji's commentary has helped bring perceptions of Japanese norms into awareness for Hikari, which she has then used as a resource for reflection, leading to awareness of the fact that she had much higher expectations for people outside Japan than she does typically for people in Japan (Hinton, 2015). Thus, it can be said that here Seiji's more specific articulation of his meta-pragmatic awareness has facilitated reflection and noticing for Hikari.

As can be seen above, when applying L1 cultural scripts to encounters in an L2 context, there is the potential for negative evaluations or stereotyping when interactions fail to play out according to one's expectations. Reflection on such negative experiences can help learners describe, and subsequently become more aware not only of the nature of their own expectations, but the nature of their own evaluations (Houghton, 2012). Specifically, through reflecting on and describing experiences, learners can develop insight into and understanding of the ways that their evaluations are informed by their own experiences as a communicator in their own cultural contexts. Such insight suggests to learners the cultural situatedness of their own interpretations and evaluations and those of others, which is one catalyst for decentring (Byram *et al.*, 2001). In this extract, the moving between cultures is particularly salient within the reinterpretation of intercultural experience. Through such an analysis, facilitated by the classroom interaction, Hikari seems to have become aware of the potential impact of latent cultural expectations on the act of interpretation in intercultural contexts.

Exploring the implications of pragmatic differences in intercultural communication

Experience talk in the classroom can involve not only interactions that the learners themselves have participated in, but also ones that they have observed overseas. When offering accounts of such experiences thus, learners combine roles of observer and analyst for the purposes of reflection (Scarino, 2009). This can provide affordances for a more distanced analysis of the consequences of pragmatic differences in interaction. In the extract below, reflection on an intercultural interaction observed by Tai in France between Japanese tourists and local sales clerks functions to highlight the potential for negative interpersonal evaluation in intercultural interaction.

Extract 4.9

1 **Tai:**   This February I travelled to Paris. It was a HIS option tour so all customers were Japanese and I observed their action at cash register and they didn't say anything.
2 **Misato:** They didn't say 'Thank you' or anything like that?
3 **Tai:**   And *bonjour* or anything.
4 **Misato:** So, I think when I go abroad my attitude to customer service changes because they say something so I think 'Thank you'.
5 **Tai:**   But most of Japanese don't change their style and maybe I thought the shop staff was frustrated because when I greeted her in French she smiled.

Building on earlier discussions in which the tendency for Japanese customers to avoid engaging in conversation with sales staff in Japan had been taken up (Extract 4.1), Tai here reports (Lines 1, 3, 5) an instance when he had observed Japanese customers behaving in a potentially rude way in France due to not greeting sales staff. The experience talk here is thus rooted in observation rather than direct involvement. The issue that is raised here seems to be that a behaviour (greetings) which may not be necessary in one cultural context may in fact be necessary in another, and lack of awareness of this fact or lack of attempt to accommodation to local cultural norms may lead to negative impression formation (Hinton, 2015). In Line 3 Misato appears to align with the notion that a certain amount of accommodation to local cultural norms is necessary, indicating her own habit of doing so in response to the cultural experience she encounters. What is significant in this extract is that Tai is aware of the gap in normative behaviour in the respective contexts and is able to use this awareness to consider the consequences of mismatch. In this sense, Tai positions himself as an intercultural mediator on the basis of his meta-pragmatic awareness. As Liddicoat (2014) has argued, the act of intercultural mediation is first and foremost an interpretative activity in which the individual considers the impact of different cultural behaviours or frames of reference on intercultural communication. Tai shows that he not only mediates, but is also able to translate insights derived from mediation into his own interactional decisions. That is, as a result of observing lack of greetings and considering this to be problematic, he makes a decision to greet service staff in French, which leads to a positive outcome. In other words, Tai's experience talk in this extract constitutes an account of his own intercultural learning in context. In the talk, Tai positions himself as observer and analyzer of intercultural interaction and recalls in the talk not only what he observed but how he interpreted it. He further positions himself as performer and intercultural mediator in that he has used analysis based on observation in order to strategically formulate his own interactional decisions. One important feature of this, therefore, is that the experience talk provides a context for the development of awareness of oneself as an intercultural speaker/learner (Liddicoat & Scarino, 2013).

In intercultural communication, the potential for negative interpersonal evaluations can be hard to predict without knowing which norms or cultural frames of reference will be applied. For language learners, one way in which implications of applying native interactional norms in foreign norms can be made salient is by considering instances of intercultural communication in the learners' L1. The extract below represents a discussion which builds on the theme which emerged in Extract 4.9 regarding the implications of differences in pragmatic norms in intercultural interaction. Whereas the discussion in Extract 4.9 had been concerned with Japanese people interacting in another language and culture, in Extract 4.10 the teacher shifts the focus to the potential implications of applying greeting conventions from Australian English in a Japanese context.

Extract 4.10

1 **Teacher:** Okay, so just before we were talking about speaking another language in a Japanese way could give a bad impression. I mean, they could seem rude to the local people. Remember I told you that in Australia the customer and shop staff often use, 'How are you?' Okay, how about if I went into the convenience store in Japan and greeted them with '*O genki desu ka?*' (How are you?)

2 **ALL:** (laughing)

3 **Teacher:** How would that be?

4 **Seiji:** Um, it's not rude, but it's strange.

5 **Teacher:** Yeah? Why is it strange?

6 **Seiji:** Because...

7 **Hikari:** Not so common.

8 **Teacher:** Oh, yeah, right, maybe that's one reason. I guess the question itself is not strange, but just asking that question in that particular situation in Japan is strange. What situation could you ask that question and it would be okay?

9 **Tai:** Ah, if I know much the shop staff.

10 **Misato:** In my hometown, when my grandma go to local shop they ask each other '*O genki desu ka?*' and they talk too much. It's too long because they know each other too much.

11 **Teacher:** What are they talking about?

12 **Misato:** I don't know. Um, it's maybe about me. So grandson or granddaughter or neighbours.

13 **Teacher:** Right, so they talk about kind of personal stuff.

This discussion begins with the teacher outlining a hypothetical scenario in which the teacher transferred norms for greeting store staff in Australian English when speaking Japanese. The immediate response is laughter (Line 2), followed by an evaluation as 'strange' by Seiji in Line 4. The teacher prompts Seiji to reflect on what exactly is strange, which he is unable to articulate. Instead, Hikari offers an explanation of it being 'not so common'. What the teacher does next is to emphasize that perhaps it is not the routine itself which is strange, but the context in which it is being applied as a result of pragmatic transfer from the speaker's first language. The teacher therefore alternatively encourages the students to consider the type of context in which it would be appropriate. Tai suggests that it may be acceptable if there is familiarity with the shop staff (Line 9). Misato then (Line 10) draws on her own experience of observing her grandmother interacting with local store staff in which '*O genki desu ka?*' is used. Misato's contribution here is significant in that the provision of this account functions to illustrate the notion of familiarity and to foreground the importance of context in determining interactional possibilities, thus highlighting intracultural diversity.

The talk in this extract shows that interactional routines, while being culturally variable, are not necessarily incompatible. In other words, while 'How are you?' and 'O genki desu ka?' are not interchangeable in some customer service encounters, in others they may be. What is significant is that a routine which was first evaluated as 'strange' was in fact, upon further reflection, revealed to be a valid interactional possibility within certain Japanese interactional contexts. What was achieved as a result of reflection within the discussion was not only insight into culture-internal variability, but also awareness that similarities between cultures can be discovered when we look at interactional practices as contextual phenomena rather than as being homogenous within the nation (Dervin, 2011).

Chapter Conclusion

Reflection on learners' interactional experiences is a valuable learning practice in the foreign language classroom. Constructing an account of interactional experience within classroom talk is not simply a matter of telling others about something that has happened (Cazden, 2001). It is an interpretive activity through which learners draw on aspects of their interpretive architecture to construct descriptive, evaluative and explanatory accounts of interactional practices they have encountered within and across languages and cultures. Such talk involves reference to culturally based expectations about interpersonal and interactional roles and relationships, sequencing of actions within an event, and notions of appropriate speech act realization in context. It can be said that experience talk helps transform the experiences of individual learners into a text which can be interpreted by other learners who then themselves engage in forms of questioning, as well as take up a range of evaluative stances and construct explanations in relation to aspects of the experience. This comes to constitute a communal learning resource (McConachy, 2013).

The various descriptive, evaluative and explanatory frames which are articulated within experience talk each provide opportunities for intercultural learning. Experience talk which derives from collaborative reflection on interactions in an L1 shared by the learners helps learners describe their sense of L1 interactional norms and how contextual influences affect the meanings and impressions derived from use of particular language forms. Rather than abstract discussion of norms, the description of individual experiences within experience talk allows for reflection on the basis of norms to be more 'grounded'. This does not mean that learners from the same national background will necessarily agree about what is typical in regard to ways of interacting. In fact, the contextualizing effect of experience talk provides opportunities for developing awareness of diversity within and across languages, as each student brings his/her own experiences to bear in the analysis

(Kramsch, 2009). In this sense, experience talk provides a framework within which learners can evaluate whether the image they have of what is 'typical' is really supported by their own experience (Deutscher, 1973).

The description of experience, with particular attention to what was said by whom and when, also facilitates learning in the ways it elicits evaluations by other learners. These evaluations become manifest in experience talk in various ways, but often in the form of interpersonal evaluations wherein particular ways of interacting (as revealed by the narrator of the experience) are evaluated as 'weird', 'cold', 'friendly', 'rude', etc. Although such evaluations can be ethnocentric, what is important in terms of teaching and learning is that these evaluations are further examined (Liddicoat, 2006). This occurs most obviously through experience talk when an individual makes an interpersonal evaluation such as 'The speaker was rude', and is then required to describe the interactional characteristics upon which such a judgement is based for the other classroom participants. In other words, experience talk can function to 'operationalize' the concepts being used to frame the evaluation, for the other class participants and oneself. This means that the justification of evaluation of practices requires that the nature of the practices is further elaborated on so that individuals can illustrate the characteristics they have ascribed (Tusting et al., 2002). This dialectical relationship between description and evaluation which unfolds in the talk thus works to prompt further interpretation, draw out aspects of learners' interpretive architecture and translate it into meta-pragmatic awareness.

Importantly, descriptive and evaluative accounts also pave the way for explanatory accounts within which learners attempt to give reasons for interactional phenomena in L1 and L2 contexts. These explanatory accounts reveal how learners perceive the influence of context on language use, as well as how they see cultural differences in interaction. It is this level of explanation that particularly taps into learners' stereotypes of their own and other national cultures, often manifesting in essentialist notions of Japanese people being shy or 'foreign' or 'Western' people being friendly and outgoing. As highlighted in this chapter, when constructing intercultural comparisons, the specific referents invoked can be problematic. While dichotomous formulations which compare 'Japanese' against 'foreigners' invoke somewhat dubious categories (Houghton, 2012), they can still be useful as a starting point for articulating the perceived cultural characteristics of these groups according to the students' perspectives. Experience talk allows for a range of explanatory accounts to be constructed, but also allows for them to be made the object of examination, as the collaborative nature of discussion and strategic teacher scaffolding pushes learners to justify their explanations or revise them to be more precise. Experience talk which moves from description to cultural explanations provides a fertile context for intercultural learning, as multiple perspectives can be taken not only on the nature of the linguistic moves which constitute practices, but also of the normative relationships between language and context, and the specific cultural concepts and assumptions which frame how the significance of language use is interpreted. This in turn allows for attention to the language ideologies which tend to persist in a given nation (Jaworski *et al.*, 2004; Warner, 2011).

It is centrally important to recognize that whatever experiences learners bring with them to the act of learning, the contingencies of the classroom interaction shape the potential for experience to be made meaningful for learning. In other words, it is the interpretive capacities and engagement of classroom participants that transforms experience into meaningful experience talk. Questions and comments from the teacher and other learners help the author of a particular experience reflect on, and in some case, reinterpret a previous interactional experience in a new light (Brooks & Donato, 1994). It can thus be said that for the author of the experience, the potential for learning from experience talk is highly contingent upon the ways in which others orient to him or her. Those who interpret the experience and engage in experience talk also develop insight into their own interpretive architecture and hone their interpretive capacities (Liddicoat & Scarino, 2013). There is therefore a crucial role for the teacher to scaffold learners' reflection on experience and the development of talk that is conducive to learning. Particularly important to teacher scaffolding are questioning techniques which prompt students for elaboration in the area of description, and justification in the area of evaluation and explanation. Teachers take constructive moves that help learners more effectively interpret, and thus become more effective interpreters.

5 Combining Performance and Reflection for Learning

Introduction

Whether in communication in one's L1 or a foreign language, language constitutes a fundamental semiotic resource for identity construction (Harre & van Langenhove, 1999; Kramsch, 2009). The foreign language classroom is a place where learners engage with new linguistic forms and practices, reinterpret old ones, and gradually construct a sense for how languages work and how they can work with languages for identity purposes. Different languages not only provide different structural resources and interactional resources, but also come with different cultural constraints on how everyday conversational routines and speech acts are conventionally expected to be performed (Kecskes, 2014). Therefore, right from the beginning of the learning process, learners are faced with the issue of impression management and how the things they say and the way they say them in the foreign language might lead to them being evaluated as a particular kind of person. Moreover, identity is not only individual but social as well. Adding a new language to one's communicative repertoire does not mean leaving old affiliations behind, and many learners will wish to position themselves as members of particular social and cultural groups, old and new. The question of how 'to be' within the foreign language is thus an exceedingly complex issue that presents challenges on both a cognitive and an affective level (Liddicoat, 2005). Theorizing on the theoretical and pedagogical significance of learners' productive language use in classroom performance tasks has been dominated by the cognitive perspective of mainstream SLA theory, particularly Long's (1983) interaction hypothesis. This hypothesis frames the role of performance in terms of the opportunities created for noticing incongruous aspects of one's use of linguistic forms, which can trigger readjustments to facilitate interaction and acquisition. This perspective is useful in understanding how structural aspects of the linguistic system are acquired. Within such a paradigm, however, it is difficult to explain how learners interpret the social significance of the language forms they encounter and how they go about appropriating particular ways of speaking or writing to show something about themselves (Firth & Wagner, 1997).

When we move beyond sentence-level discourse and into the realm of pragmatics, we ultimately require a perspective that can accommodate learner subjectivity and the cognitive and affective dynamics that occur as individuals learn to interpret language use as social action and explore the possibilities for adding to their communicative repertoires (Ishihara, 2010; Kramsch, 2009). Within an intercultural orientation to language teaching and learning, classroom performance tasks are meaningful not simply in that they allow for output and interaction, but because they also provide a forum for reflection on the significance of one's language choices and for practising intercultural mediation. In other words, classroom performance tasks are not simply chances to do things with words, but also to experience 'the impact of foreign cultural norms on one's sense of identity' (Crozet, 1996: 52) and to reflect more specifically on how to strategically position oneself through one's linguistic choices. This perspective has also been argued recently by van Compernolle (2014), who highlights the role of performance tasks in developing learners' sense of agency in the L2. This chapter adopts the perspective that reflection on performance tasks, particularly role-plays, helps learners become aware of many assumptions they have about the L2 and its use in context. This in turn is facilitative of meta-pragmatic awareness development which is useful for more strategically considering the nature of the meanings and impressions that learners want to construct. This chapter looks closely at the ways in which learners variously combine the learning roles of 'performer' and 'analyzer' (Liddicoat & Scarino, 2013) in relation to role-play tasks and the affordances for intercultural learning that are generated in the process. The chapter presents data of learners' role-play performances, together with reflections on role-plays in order to illuminate some of the ways in which reflection works for learning.

Reflecting on the Significance of Noticed Aspects of Performance

In order to develop the ability to be a reflective user of the L2 and develop a sense of agency, learners need the ability to notice and describe the features of their own language use inside and outside the classroom. This is not necessarily in order to then bridge the gap between one's own language use and that of native speakers, but to objectify one's language use and consider how it relates to one's own interactional goals and sense of self (Liddicoat, 2005). This section shows how reflection on one's own L2 use, combined with observation of the performance of peers, can be used to explore the initial assumptions learners have about how interactions might work in particular contexts of communication in the target language.

Observing, noticing and reflecting on aspects of performance

Extracts 5.1 and 5.2 below show Hikari and Seiji performing a role-play in which they assume the respective roles of counter staff and customer for the purchase of a drink at a coffee shop in the United States (as they decided). Although the role-play itself was unscripted, such customer-service interactions had been the focus of reflective discussion earlier in the lesson. A similar role-play had also been performed by Misato and Tai earlier. The pedagogical intent of this task was to give the students a chance to experiment with greeting forms used by service staff and language forms used for ordering, and to use reflective discussion to explore the assumptions which lay behind students' interactional decision-making. Thus, students were instructed to perform the interaction as they saw appropriate. The reflective discussion in Extract 5.3 brings together perspectives of the performers of the interaction (Hikari and Seiji), and also Misato and Tai who were asked to observe the interaction. The combination of perspectives helps to reveal the logic behind learners' choices in the role-play and other options which might be available.

Extract 5.1 Role-play
Hikari (Counter Staff) and Seiji (Customer)

1 **Hikari:** Hello
2 **Seiji:** Hello
3 **Hikari:** Aa, ah, sorry … Hello, what would you like?
4 **Seiji:** Can I have a hot coffee?
5 **Hikari:** Sure. It's 220 yen.
6 **Seiji:** Okay.
7 **Hikari:** Have a nice day.
8 **Seiji:** Too fast, but okay thank you (laughing)

Extract 5.2 Role-play
Seiji (Counter Staff) and Hikari (Customer)

1   **Seiji:** Hi, how are you?
2   **Hikari:** Hello
3   **Seiji:** Hi, hello (laughing) …… How are you?
4   **Hikari:** Ah, yeah, good. (laughing)
5   **Seiji:** That's good … So, what would you like?
6   **Hikari:** A coffee please
7   **Seiji:** Okay. It costs 220 yen.
8   **Hikari:** (Gesture: Placing money on the counter)
9   **Seiji:** Thank you.
10 **Hikari:** Thank you
11 **Seiji:** Have a nice day

Extract 5.3 Reflective discussion

1	**Teacher:**	So, how was it?
2	**Hikari:**	Ah, we didn't use 'Here you are'.
3	**TM:**	Oh, okay. Just gave them the coffee. Maybe it's not such a big problem. Yeah, saying, 'Here you are' with a positive intonation is a good thing, but probably a lot of places don't. They just give it to you. Especially if they are busy.
4	**Misato:**	I think Seiji said 'How are you?' many times.
5	**Seiji:**	(Laughing)
6	**Hikari:**	Many times.
7	**Teacher:**	What happened?
8	**ALL:**	(laughing)
9	**Seiji:**	Ah, I said, 'How are you', but she didn't say 'I'm fine' or something like that, so I said again.
10	**Teacher:**	Oh, right. Right ... In a real situation do you think the shop staff would ask twice?
11	**Seiji:**	I don't think so.
12	**Teacher:**	Why not?
13	**Seiji:**	Why not?
14	**Teacher:**	Don't they want to know the answer?
15	**Seiji:**	Mm. They don't mind if customer is fine or just kind of rule.
16	**Misato:**	Mmm
17	**Teacher:**	Yeah, just like a greeting?
18	**Seiji:**	Yeah.
19	**Teacher:**	Yeah, I think so too. Most of the time, in my experience anyway, it's just a greeting. So if they said, 'Oh, how are you?', and you said 'Oh, hi', there wouldn't be a problem. I do this a lot because sometimes even I don't know what to say.
20	**Seiji:**	It's normal?
21	**Teacher:**	A lot of people do it, but other times it's just like a set response: 'Oh, good thanks' or 'Not bad' ... 'Pretty good, and how are you?' Most of the time, I think, they don't really care, in a city anyway. If it's in a country area, then you actually might have a conversation. You could be in the store talking for 10 minutes before you buy anything.
22	**ALL:**	(laughing)

The reflection on performance is first given a specific focus through Hikari's comment in Line 2, where she reveals her noticing that her group had not used 'Here you are' when handing over the product to the customer. Although Hikari does not explicitly frame this aspect of her role-play as a 'mistake', she has approached the task of looking for performance differences from a perspective in which she discovers what is 'missing' in her own performance. Such an approach may indicate that she views this type of interaction as tightly 'scripted', which it tends to be in Japanese. The highly scripted nature of many customer-service interactions in Japan had been discussed in a previous task (see Extract 5.2). In Hikari's case here, observation of performance and noticing can been seen to inform her construction of a descriptive account of difference rather than an explanatory one. The teacher contributes his own interpretation in Line 3, which functions to show Hikari that the element of her own performance she had taken up was not necessarily problematic.

The second aspect of performance taken up in this discussion is brought out by Misato in Line 4 where she refers to Seiji's use of 'How are you?'. In their role-play, Hikari had failed to respond to his question, leading him to ask again. When prompted to reflect on this aspect of his role-play, Seiji offers an explanatory account which amounts to a justification of his interactional choices (Line 9). His comment here reveals his meta-pragmatic awareness of *How are you?* as the first part of an adjacency pair, which Hikari failed to orient to in terms of articulating the expected response (Liddicoat, 2007). Therefore, as a repair strategy Seiji offered the question again. The articulation of Seiji's meta-pragmatic awareness in Line 9 is significant as it allows the teacher to make use of it to prompt further reflection in the subsequent lines. In Line 10 the teacher sets up an alternate layer of comparison by prompting the students to consider whether a service provider would be likely to insist on an answer to 'How are you?' in a real-world situation. Seiji is very quick in the next line (11) to respond in the negative, the reason for which he articulates in Line 15. His comments reveal that he recognizes the question as largely formulaic, which makes salient a contrast between his meta-pragmatic awareness and his performance in the role-play. What this shows is that this layer of reflection and comparison in relation to perceptions of real-world interaction has provided a context in which Seiji could more fully reveal his meta-pragmatic awareness and also articulate a reason for the apparent gap between his awareness and performance (Bardovi-Harlig & Griffin, 2005). There is a question of how to interpret the significance of the gap between Seiji's performance in the role-play and his meta-pragmatic awareness revealed in the reflective discussion. The degree with which he was quickly able to articulate the pragmatic norm in the reflective discussion leads me to believe that his choice to re-cast the question *How are you?* was an attempt to allow his partner to fulfil her role in the interaction – the default response in the adjacency pair. In other words, it was strategic behaviour, thus evidence of meta-pragmatic awareness functioning as a resource for analysis within performance.

An additional aspect of the teacher's scaffolding which deserves discussion is the ways he framed his interpretation of interactional norms. In Lines 3, 19 and 21 the teacher offers his perspective on several aspects of customer-service interaction. What is important is that, while interpreting pragmatic norms, the teacher is careful, through use of hedging devices, to emphasize the variability of practices. Specifically, the teacher frames the practices as variable in Line 3 (... *is a good thing, but probably a lot of places don't*), contextualizing his perspective on the practices in Line 19 (*Most of the time, in my experience anyway* ...), and the city/country dichotomy used to emphasize contextual variability in Line 21. When working with pragmatics-based ideas, there is tension between the need to frame aspects of interactional practices as normative – and by implication learnable as 'knowledge' – while at the same time stressing the diversity inherent in interactional practices. For intercultural learning, 'knowledge' of interactional norms and 'awareness' of the inherent diversity of any interactional practice are both important (Liddicoat, 2005). Without one or the other, the development of the ability to deal flexibly with novel contexts and diversity in even seemingly stable contexts is unlikely to be possible. What the teacher does through his commentary on pragmatic norms in this extract is to facilitate a view of interactional norms as preferred ways of doing things rather than as scripts to be adhered to, even within interaction which is more on the scripted side such as customer-service encounters.

In this task, learning based on reflection is as an essentially collaborative enterprise in two ways. First, reflection was engaged in as a result of observing the performance of another group and comparing it to one's own group. Compared to simply reflecting on one's own performance, such inter-group comparisons provide a broader context for noticing aspects of one's own performance due to the fact that the performance of others can be used as a reference point for reflection. This can be seen at work in the noticing provided by Hikari in Line 2. Conversely, inter-group comparisons based on observation also allow for the noticings of the observers to be noticed and then reflected on by the performers. This can be seen in Misato's contribution in Line 4. As in this case, when an aspect of one's own performance is taken up by another student, it can lead to talk in which students articulate their meta-pragmatic awareness by explaining for the other students and teacher why they did what they did. Reflection within such a process therefore allows for meta-pragmatic awareness to operate for combining 'performance' and 'analysis'. In such a way, classroom learning can help learners develop the ability to shift perspectives from observer to performer and back again, becoming more aware of the features of their language use and the assumptions from which it derives.

Exploring perceptions of pragmatic differences and the impact on performance

In some cases, aspects of student performance can be made the object of reflection by the teacher. In other cases, reflection on aspects of peer performance can emerge from the observations of peers. This section highlights the role of collaborative reflection in prompting examination of an aspect of performance that had been difficult for a particular student during a role-play. Specifically, the role-play required Hikari to initiate an invitation to go out for a drink with Tai (a friend within the context of this role-play), mainly because Hikari wanted to seek his advice about some troubles at work. Reflective discussion in Extract 5.5 reveals that broaching the reason for the invitation was difficult for her, something which she attributes to a pragmatic difference between Japanese and English. Whether or not this assessment reflects actual differences in pragmatic norms, the reflective discussion allows for students' current meta-pragmatic awareness to be revealed and then utilized for considering alternative interactional options for future performance. During the role-play, Misato and Seiji observed the nature of the interaction.

Extract 5.4 Role-play

1	**Hikari:**	Hello Tai
2	**Tai:**	Hi Hikari
3	**Hikari:**	How are you?
4	**Tai:**	Good. And you?
5	**Hikari:**	Ah, yeah, a little bit. I'm just good, but I have some problem with my co-workers, so I was wondering if I have some words with you if you listen to my trouble in my workplace, so … so and I am thinking to go to somewhere to drink with you, so how about Saturday night? Are you okay to go drinking with me?
6	**Tai:**	Oh, it's okay.
7	**Hikari:**	It's okay?
8	**Tai:**	But I have to finish my report until 8:00, so is that okay?
9	**Hikari:**	You are making your report? Are you okay? Thank you. I must take over two hours to speak all long stories.
10	**Tai:**	(Laughing). Yeah, I like listening to somebody's complaints.

Extract 5.5 Reflective discussion

1	**Teacher:**	So, did you notice anything in that role play?
2	**Misato:**	It seems to take a long time to make the invitation by explaining a lot.
3	**Teacher:**	Actually, I didn't know if you were inviting him or just wanted to talk about your problems now.
4	**Hikari:**	Ah, maybe I have to start from my offer.
5	**Teacher:**	In that case, what could you say?
6	**Hikari:**	What could I say ……
7	**Teacher:**	You said, 'I'm having some troubles at work, so …'
8	**Hikari:**	So, 'I'd like you to listen my problem …'
9	**Teacher:**	Yeah, it sounds kind of heavy if you say, 'I'd like you to listen to my problem'.

10	**Hikari:**	Really?
11	**Teacher:**	Yeah, I think you don't need to say 'problems'. 'I'm a bit stressed at work, so if you have some time next Saturday it would be nice if we could meet and talk. And I also want to hear about your situation.'
12	**Hikari:**	Oh, I see. Actually, I wanted to say main point faster like English way, but it is difficult.
13	**Teacher:**	Yeah, it's very very interesting. Before you start the role-play you have a plan in your mind of what to do, but when you do the role-play, often what you do and say in the role-play is different to what you thought you would do.
14	**Hikari:**	Yeah.
15	**Teacher:**	So, you understand it, but when you do it you do it differently.
16	**Tai:**	Maybe it is easy to do role-play as Japanese way.
17	**Teacher:**	Right? That's an interesting comment. What do you mean Tai?
18	**Tai:**	I think that it is hard for Japanese to say invitation directly at first.
19	**Teacher:**	Oh, okay. Yeah, there may be something cultural here. I mean, if you feel this is unfamiliar, then it might be difficult to follow this. Just do it however feels right for you.

The discussion is launched by the teacher who elicits comments regarding what the students had just observed in order to draw out any noticings. Misato comments in Line 2 that she had noticed that it took a long time for Hikari in the role-play to get to the main point. The teacher in Line 3 also aligns with this assessment. From this point, the evaluation of this aspect of interaction prompts reflection oriented towards the exploration of possibilities for revision of performance. In Line 4 Hikari suggests that perhaps she should have started with the offer (invitation), and the teacher prompts her to consider how this could be achieved exactly (Line 5). In Line 6 Hikari is searching for linguistic possibilities but having trouble. What the teacher does here is to repeat what she actually said in the role-play (Line 7), which seems to allow her to reformulate this in Line 8. The teacher's action here is significant in that by repeating for Hikari an aspect of her own performance it makes it accessible to her for attention (Schmidt, 1993) and for exploring alternatives. There is an important juncture at Line 12 as Hikari reveals the nature of her intended performance and that she perceives it as being constrained by a cultural difference. Hikari had in fact been trying to get to the invitation faster, something which she characterizes as the 'English way'. She seems to be having difficulty with the idea that an invitation can be offered earlier in an exchange without needing to go into a lot of background details first to frame the invitation. This would seem to represent an element of knowledge within her interpretive architecture that inductive rather than deductive discourse is preferable for this kind of interaction (Scollon & Wong-Scollon, 2001). Tai similarly comments that 'maybe it is easy to do role-play as Japanese way' (Line 16) and that beginning with the invitation may be culturally unfamiliar for Japanese people (Line 18).

Although it cannot always be assumed that students' perceptions of cultural differences automatically accord with actual differences, these two students do align with each other to co-construct an account of difference. Tai's comment in Line 16 shows awareness of the potential relationship between culture and discourse structuring, as well as the need for individuals to find ways to mediate between these differences when constructing performance in an L2. Reflection has allowed for exploration of a gap between intended performance and actual performance and awareness of how preferences for discourse structure embedded in the L1 can influence not only one's performance, but also one's cognitive and affective reactions to that performance. The students are drawing on culturally situated frames of reference from their interpretive architecture and becoming aware of them through the talk, generating insight into the fact that performance in an L2 is a matter of mediating between linguistic and cultural resources from multiple languages and is, as such, intercultural (Liddicoat & Scarino, 2013). The teacher takes up this issue in Line 19, highlighting that a lack of familiarity with cultural difference in discourse may make it difficult to conform to, if that is one's aim. The teacher points out here, however, that conforming to the norms is a choice rather than a requirement. In essence, the teacher alternatively implies to the students that what is needed is the construction of an interactional solution which is comfortable, thus leaving the agency with them.

Evaluating Aspects of Performance

Beyond becoming able to describe aspects of the classroom performance of the self and others, it is vitally important that learners are afforded opportunities for exploring the value judgements which they make in relation to particular pragmatic features. This means exploring the basis of meta-pragmatic judgements which invoke evaluative terms such as 'polite', 'rude', 'formal' or 'casual', particularly focusing on how learners utilize these terms and what they mean by them (McConachy & Hata, 2013). In a given interaction inside or outside the classroom, a learner may wish to position himself or herself as 'polite'; however, without deeper consideration of the meaning of such a culturally variable notion, it is difficult to construct an informed basis for intercultural mediation. The extracts in this section show the role of reflection in generating initial evaluations of performance, which are then reflected on to reveal the meta-pragmatic constructs through which learners frame their own performance. This in turn provides a resource for helping the students consider the impact of cultural framings on the positioning of self in interaction and what some of the possibilities for intercultural mediation are.

Meta-pragmatic evaluation and reflection on one's own performance

This section shows reflection for self-evaluation of performance leading to the emergence of a cultural construct to frame the evaluation. The role-play data (Extracts 5.6 and 5.7) show the students conducting role-plays involving a request from a student to an English-speaking non-Japanese professor. This particular role-play context was chosen by the students after the teacher asked them to come up with a communicative situation involving a certain amount of social distance. Extract 5.8 shows the reflective discussion, framed explicitly by the teacher as evaluative in nature.

Extract 5.6 Role-play
Hikari (Professor) and Misato (Student)

1	**Misato:**	(Knocking on imaginary door)
2	**Hikari:**	(Seated behind table) Yes? Come in.
3	**Misato:**	Hello.
4	**Hikari:**	Hello.
5	**Misato:**	Professor, are you busy now?
6	**Hikari:**	Yeah, really busy.
7	**Misato:**	Oh? Um, so I was wondering if you could do me a big favour. Today I need to write application for another university and I would like you to check my papers. So, could you do that?
8	**Hikari:**	When do you plan to submit your application to the university?
9	**Misato:**	Ah, it's next month.
10	**Hikari:**	You have more one month.
11	**Misato:**	Yes, but I'd like to write more good paper so.
12	**Hikari:**	Yeah.
13	**Misato:**	If you have time, I want you to check my paper.
14	**Hikari:**	Should I check it immediately?
15	**Misato:**	Ah, no. If you do that by next week, it's okay.
16	**Hikari:**	Oh? Okay, sure. (Laughing)

Extract 5.7 Role-play
Seiji (Professor) and Tai (Student)

1	**Tai:**	(Knocking)
2	**Seiji:**	Yes ... yes ... come in.
3	**Tai:**	Ah, professor ...

4	**Seiji:**	Hi
5	**Tai:**	… I have a … I want a favour.
6	**Seiji:**	Okay. Sit here.
7	**Tai:**	I wrote your last assignment, but I worry if I could write good quality or not.
8	**Seiji:**	Is this time your only free time or could you … could you … see another time?
9	**Tai:**	Yes, I can. Ah, how much time can you spend?
10	**Seiji:**	Oh, about ten minutes.
11	**Tai:**	So I wonder my report doesn't have much information from books. I wonder I should put more information.
12	**Seiji:**	I think so, but it doesn't relate to the evaluation, so you don't really have to worry about it.
13	**Tai:**	Oh? Thank you. When I wrote this report I became to be interested in this subject, so I want to meet you another time. Okay, so when you have free time?
14	**Seiji:**	My office hours are Monday afternoon and Fridays from 9:00 am to 10:30 am.
15	**Tai:**	Can I come?
16	**Seiji:**	Yes, you can come.
17	**Tai:**	Oh, thank you. Okay, thank you very much.

Extract 5.8 Reflective discussion

1	**Teacher:**	So basically I want you to just evaluate your own role-play. So just tell me, do you think it went well?
2	**Tai:**	I think I made a mistake.
3	**Teacher:**	What did you do?
4	**Tai:**	Oh, not so formal.
5	**Teacher:**	What was not so formal?
6	**Tai:**	About style of asking is a little bit sudden.
7	**Teacher:**	Did you feel that Seiji?
8	**Seiji:**	Um, it was just role-play, so I didn't focus on his mistake, but I just concentrated on acting.
9	**Teacher:**	Oh, so you were kind of thinking about your role as professor and didn't notice what he said.
10	**Seiji:**	(Laughing) *hisshi datta* (I was struggling).
11	**Teacher:**	Oh really?
12	**Seiji:**	(Laughing)

In orienting to this task, Tai launches his self-evaluation with the comment that he had 'made a mistake', which is revealed in Line 4 to be one related to formality. From this comment it can be seen that he is clearly evaluating his performance from a pragmatics perspective rather than a grammatical one. It seems that the perception of power distance in this relationship enacted in this role-play task has prompted Tai to monitor his language use in view of its appropriateness for the context he is interacting in. That being said, the explicit framing of this aspect of his performance as a 'mistake' would seem to indicate a view of linguistic politeness in English as being rather prescribed and obligatory. It is important to note the critical perspective emerging from reflection on performance here, in that it differs decidedly from purely descriptive 'I did X' or explanatory 'I did X because ...' accounts of performance. Rather than offering justification for his performance, Tai's comment in Line 6 shows what it was about his performance that he regarded as problematic. In other words, by highlighting the specific interactional feature (lack of preparatory moves), he reveals the nature of the concept of formality within his interpretive architecture that shapes the evaluation of his performance.

Thus, we see reflection here functioning as a resource for critical self-evaluation, the concept used for framing the self-evaluation (formality) emerging through illustration in the subsequent talk. Notions such as formality are highly culturally embedded as well as culturally relative (Haugh & Hinze, 2003), and it is an important aspect of developing the capacity for intercultural mediation that learners are able to explain and illustrate what they mean. For them, the notion of formality seems to be linked to the assumption that it is necessary to be articulate and respectful when interacting with a professor. Now that Tai is experiencing a gap between intended and actual performance, he is looking for ways to construct appropriate formality for himself and the professor character in the role-play. In the talk below, there is a broadening of participation as the students engage in a kind of problem-solving discourse regarding how to achieve more formality in future performance.

Extract 5.9 Reflective discussion

1	**Teacher:**	So, in a real situation what would you do differently?
2	**Tai:**	I ask his permission at first.
3	**Teacher:**	What kind of permission?
4	**Tai:**	Time.
5	**Teacher:**	Oh, so you'd knock on the door and what would you say?
6	**Tai:**	Hmm, 'I want to talk about my report' or something.
7	**Teacher:**	'I want to talk' is very direct, isn't it?
8	**Tai:**	Ah, 'I have a problem'.
9	**Teacher:**	Hmm, that's very direct as well.
10	**Teacher:**	(To the class as a whole) What would be the best thing to say?
11	**Misato:**	Do you have time to talk with me?
12	**Teacher:**	He might be thinking, 'Maybe I have time, but it depends on what you want'. So, you could say something like, 'I was wondering if we could talk about my essay' or 'I was wondering if I could ask you some questions'.

13 **Seiji:**   Oh, it sounds good.

14 **Teacher:** Okay, so anyway, if we go back to the start. So you knock on the door and the professor says, 'Come in'. What do you say?

15 **Seiji:**   This is Seiji from the Department of French Literature.

16 **Teacher:** You could say that, but it sounds like a phone call.

17 **ALL:**   (Laughing)

18 **Teacher:** If for example the door to the professor's office is closed and so they can't see who you are, you could say 'This is Seiji Kim'. But if you open the door ......

19 **Seiji:**   Hi?

20 **Teacher:** 'Hi, Mr or Mrs ...' Just going immediately into the topic is a little bit rude. (Writing on the board) 'Hi Professor so and so' ... I hope you're not busy. If you have some time, I was wondering if you could ......'.

In Line 1 the teacher prompts reflection on how things could be done differently in a real context. In essence, this is an opportunity for Tai to consider how he could revise his performance to achieve the formality that he desires. In Line 2 he refers first of all to the need to ask permission to talk to the professor before moving into the request, but the language he offers for achieving this in Lines 5 and 8 would not convey the formality he is looking for. Tai has made the judgement that somewhat formal language is necessary in view of power distance, but he is unsure as to the specific language that can realize this. What this talk is showing is the teacher and Tai working together to explore the linguistic possibilities for actualizing Tai's desired notion of formality. It is important to note that as Tai's initial critique of his performance (Extract 5.7) was framed by the culturally variable notion of formality, the reflection on performance and comparison with ideal performance prompted by the teacher here engages Tai in intercultural mediation work as he strives to find a linguistic solution to the issue of how to construct formality in English.

From Line 10 there is a broadening of participation in the problem-solving discourse as the teacher invites comments from the other students. The focus here is still on how to best formulate a formal pre-request to a professor. Whereas Misato views the appropriate step as checking if the professor has time (Line 11), the teacher suggests that it might be better to make clear the purpose of the visit first (Line 12). In Line 14 the teacher leads the students back to the initial stages of discourse, prompting them to articulate how the scenario would unfold in terms of sequences of speech acts. Seiji focuses on first of all introducing himself to the professor (Line 15), which the teacher takes up in the subsequent lines, finally engaging in meta-pragmatic explanation regarding how to pull together the utterances of the speech act set into a coherent whole (Line 20). In this section of the extract therefore, the teacher is scaffolding collaborative reflection on the speech act of requesting, assisting the students to articulate their meta-pragmatic awareness, which then becomes a resource for further reflection as students generate multiple accounts of linguistic possibilities for the act.

In terms of reflection on performance, the significance of the discussion above stems from the fact that meta-pragmatic awareness is developed within the context of exploration of the possibilities for revised performance. From this perspective, the performance in the role-play of one student (Tai in Extract 5.7) and the subsequent evaluation of self-performance (Extracts 5.8 and 5.9) has constituted a kind of 'text', which is used in the current extract for exploring interactional possibilities, first by the individual in question, then by the group. In order to explore interactional and intercultural possibilities for the context under attention, students are required to utilize their meta-pragmatic awareness, which is further reflected on and re-evaluated. In this regard, it is important to note that although there is a high amount of teacher talk, the nature of the talk is such that it promotes reflection and the generation of further participation (Cazden, 2001). The reflective processes in which the students engage are significant because the articulation of possibilities in regard to a particular interactional problem gives shape to the students' existing meta-pragmatic awareness and, through the interaction, allows for gaps in knowledge to be recognized and consolidated. Such a process allows for awareness to be developed as the initial point of noticing becomes more specific as a result of further reflection and elaboration through the talk. Meta-pragmatic awareness of the target language, as it is developed in this sense, then constitutes a resource for intercultural comparison and exploration. This will be taken up below.

Reflecting on the possibilities for intercultural mediation

Reflection on the nature of meanings and impressions that one wants to construct in the foreign language necessarily mobilizes learners' meta-pragmatic awareness of the L2, but it does not necessarily address cultural assumptions derived from the L1 which may impact on how learners perceive contexts of use and how to go about engaging in particular communicative encounters. Bringing in reflection on L1 interactions can help highlight these assumptions and also give clues to learners about how to mediate between cultures in the construction of their own interactions (McConachy & Liddicoat, 2016). As one instance of this, the extract below shows reflection for intercultural comparison and exploration which builds on the meta-pragmatic awareness developed earlier in the discussion (Extract 5.9). Specifically, as the previous extract had involved the development of meta-pragmatic awareness regarding how to initiate a conversation and lead into a pre-request with one's professor, the students now consider how interaction in Japanese might play out in a similar context. However, the focus of discussion in this extract is not the request sequence per se, but the pragmatics of entering the physical space of someone who is considered as being in a higher status position than oneself in order to initiate communication.

Extract 5.10 *Reflective discussion*

1	**Teacher:**	Okay, so in this kind of situation in Japan, how do you think you should behave? If you had to go to the professor's office to ask them to do something for you, how would you do it? Is there a rule about knocking in the case of high status?
2	**Seiji:**	Maybe knock three times.
3	**Tai:**	I do twice.
4	**Teacher:**	Okay, so you knock on the door. Then?
5	**Misato:**	*'Shitsurei shimasu'* (Excuse me)
6	**Teacher:**	You have to say *'shitsurei shimasu'*. All right. What would you do in English?
7	**Tai:**	In English?
8	**Teacher:**	Yeah, so before you talk to a Japanese professor you might feel like you need to say *'shitsurei shimasu'*. How about if you needed to talk to a non-Japanese professor in English? For example, you might feel that you should say something, but you don't know what to say.
9	**Tai:**	Yes.
10	**Teacher:**	What would you do? You want to show politeness to your professor because you are entering their space. What can you do?
11	**Seiji:**	If a professor didn't say, 'Come in'. If they just said, 'Yes', I would say, 'Can I come in?'
12	**Teacher:**	Yeah. If the professor didn't directly say, 'Come in', I guess you could ask yourself. So, anything else? Would you apologize?
13	**Hikari:**	Apologize? Like, 'Sorry for disturbing you'?
14	**Teacher:**	Something like that.
15	**Tai:**	I think usually we must. Yeah, but my professor prefer to being friendly. So I can't find way to apologize.
16	**Teacher:**	You're talking about your Japanese professor?
17	**Tai:**	Yes. He likes us to be friendly.

In initiating this task the teacher makes explicit the context (maintaining coherence with the previous discussion) and frames the purpose of discussion in terms of identifying likely interactional 'differences' between Japanese and English. The English side of the equation had been the focus of the previous task, thus here it is primarily reflection on the Japanese side which allows for comparisons to be made. The discussion is launched by the teacher-prompted reflection first on any norms for knocking on the door of a high-status person (Line 1), then on procedures for entering the room (Line 4). In Line 5 Misato alludes to the fact that the Japanese phrase *shitsurei shimasu* would be needed when entering the room. Up until this point in the extract, the discussion consists of reflection and explication of L1 practices. What is most of interest is how Line 6 sees a shift to explicit comparisons between practices across languages. Specifically, the teacher prompts the students to consider the possibilities of expressing politeness when entering the professor's office in English, similar to what is achieved by *shitsurei shimasu* in Japanese. The teacher talk in Line 7 thus functions to illustrate that differences in cultural practices require mediation. Furthermore, here and in Line 10, the teacher is prompting the students to reflect on the nature of the differences in practices in order to help them generate interactional possibilities which would reflect a mediation of cultures. In the subsequent lines the students do not try to come up with an exact translation for *shitsurei shimasu*, instead taking a functional perspective – exploring phrases that would constitute a functional equivalent. In Line 11 Seiji suggests that if the professor had not explicitly invited him to come in, he would ask whether it was okay. Such a question thus would allow for indexing of recognition of the spatial boundaries, similar to what is achieved by *shitsurei shimasu*. He has used reflection on a C1 context to then explore the linguistic possibilities in the L2 for conveying an aspect of politeness similar to that achieved by an utterance in the L1. There is thus an explicitly intercultural orientation to the reflection here, which is being used to construct possibilities for performance in the L2.

In Line 12 the teacher initiates a question as to whether the students would apologize to a Japanese professor for dropping in. While in Line 13 Hikari offers an English phrase that could achieve this speech act, Tai refers to his experience when dealing with a Japanese professor of his who actually prefers students to be 'friendly'. What Tai's contribution in Line 15 shows is that although reflection allows him to recognize a pragmatic norm, reflection on his experience reveals diversity within the L1. In other words, his example constitutes an example of intercultural mediation of sorts within the L1 in the sense that Tai has had to negotiate a style of interaction with his professor based on the professor's preference for casual interactions with students. What is important in this interaction is that the discussion builds on the previous task in the sense that it constitutes exploration of the Japanese norms in a similar context, thus achieving intercultural comparison across tasks. Furthermore, noticings regarding the Japanese norms are again compared to English and students are encouraged to find intercultural solutions through reflection (Liddicoat & Scarino, 2013).

Reflecting on Emotional Reactions to Interaction

Considering how to position oneself through one's interactional choices in the target language is not simply a cognitive task but an affective one as well (Siegal, 1996). In fact, it is often emotional reactions (both positive and negative) encountered in the process of experimenting with new ways of interacting in foreign cultural contexts that suggest to learners the possibilities (and limitations) for self-presentation and relating to others (Ishihara, 2010). Learners inevitably encounter a range of emotional reactions during classroom performance tasks as well, which provide an important locus for examining the specific assumptions or conflicts from which emotions derive. Some of the ways such examination can be orchestrated by the classroom teacher and the outcome of reflection is the focus of the extracts that follow.

Reflecting on emotional reactions and difficulties in performance

Even in classroom performance tasks such as role-plays which are sheltered from the consequences of the outside world, learners can experience a range of emotions when trying out interactional practices in a foreign language, particularly when the practices themselves are performed differently from what a learner is used to (Kramsch, 1993). Reflection which helps learners explore the relationship between their affective responses to performance tasks and their perception of the task can help them better consider how they wish to come across in the target language. Moreover, such reflection can lead learners to generate their own questions of interest about how to interact. In the role-play task below (Extracts 5.11 and 5.12), the students are experimenting with aspects of interaction between a bartender and a customer which they had viewed on a DVD which is part of an English learning resource entitled *Beyond Talk* (Barraja-Rohan & Pritchard, 1997) at an earlier point in the lesson. The DVD had showed two different interactions, distinguished most obviously by the length of the conversation between the bartender and the customer. The interaction in the first scene had been rather short and transactional, centred on the business of buying/serving a beer. In the second scene the conversation is similarly initially 'centred' (Barraja-Rohan, 1999) by the beer order; however, there is significant topic development following this, including general enquiries into the customer's recent activities. When watching these scenes the students had been surprised by the interaction in the second scene, particularly by the fact that casual conversation on personal topics was embedded within the otherwise typical service transaction. Students had also commented that such an interaction would be very unusual in Japan. Therefore, the pedagogical intent behind this role-play was to allow the students to experience both types of interaction and to reflect on their emotional responses and any other impressions from the performance. For this task the students were asked to follow the interactional structure observed in the DVD scenes so as to allow targeted reflection in the post role-play discussion. In this case, Misato and Tai were asked to act out the short interaction and Seiji and Hikari were asked to attempt the longer one. For this longer role-play, Seiji and Hikari were instructed that they were free to develop the conversation in any way they liked and to cover various topics while still getting the main tasks of giving and receiving a drink order completed. This interaction was set up as one where the customer is a regular and has thus interacted with this particular bartender numerous times before.

Extract 5.11 Role-play

1	**Misato:**	Hi
2	**Tai:**	Hi, how are you?
3	**Misato:**	I'm fine, but not so bad. How about you?
4	**Tai:**	So, what do you want?
5	**Misato:**	Ah, so I want to have ... beer.
6	**Tai:**	Beer?
7	**Misato:**	Yeah.
8	**Tai:**	How much?
9	**Misato:**	Just a little bit
10	**Tai:**	Okay, here you are
11	**Misato:**	Thank you. So, today I had a trouble in the office. So, ...
12	**Tai:**	You don't drink beer?
13	**Misato:**	Okay, thanks

Extract 5.12

1	**Seiji:**	Hi
2	**Hikari:**	Hi, how are you?
3	**Seiji:**	I'm fine. And you?
4	**Hikari:**	Yeah, good. How's your life in your school?
5	**Seiji:**	It's good, but I have so many thing to do and I'm so tired, so ... French class is so difficult to follow.
6	**Hikari:**	Oh, really?
7	**Seiji:**	And, my professor is too strict.
8	**Hikari:**	Oh, but you look very good.
9	**Seiji:**	Oh, really?
10	**Hikari:**	What can I get for you?
11	**Seiji:**	I would like to have gin and tonic.
12	**Hikari:**	Okay, I'll make it for you.
13	**Seiji:**	So, are you busy now?
14	**Hikari:**	Ah, yeah, a little bit, but it's okay. Here you are.
15	**Seiji:**	Oh, thank you. So, have a nice day.
16	**Hikari:**	Yes, thank you. Bye.

Extract 5.13 Reflective discussion

1	**Teacher:**	So, how did that feel?
2	**Hikari:**	Strange.
3	**Tai:**	It's difficult to end the conversation.

4	**Teacher:**	Yeah, it is, it is. Well, especially if you are being a bartender. (laughing) But, I liked your strategy: 'Don't you drink¿'
5	**ALL:**	(laughing)
6	**Teacher:**	So, his strategy was to offer the drink again because it's probably an indirect way to end the conversation.
7	**Tai:**	Yeah, I wanted to say the bubble.
8	**Teacher:**	Hey¿
9	**Tai:**	The bubble is disappearing.
10	**Teacher:**	Oh, oh, 'Drink it quickly before the bubbles disappear'. Yeah, that would have been perfect I think. Any other comments¿
11	**Hikari:**	Um, if the customer come to the bar first time, what happened to them¿
12	**Teacher:**	Oh, what would they talk about¿
13	**Hikari:**	Yeah.
14	**Teacher:**	Probably they could just say something like, 'Are you busy¿'
15	**Hikari:**	Oh yeah¿
16	**Teacher:**	Just change it to a normal question. So, yeah, yeah, it's not strange.
17	**Hikari:**	Oh¿ (surprised intonation)
18	**Teacher:**	One thing in Australia that is quite different to Japan is that often the customer greets the store staff first. There is no 'irrashaimase'.
19	**Hikari:**	*Hee* (Japanese feedback token to show surprise).
20	**Teacher:**	So, yeah, you can be the first to ask a question like this or 'Are you busy¿' In that kind of situation it's not strange.
21	**Hikari:**	*Hee.*

In Line 2 Hikari had commented that this type of interaction had felt 'strange' to her in the role-play. It is assumed that she is referring to the phenomenon of a customer and service provider chatting about what may seem to be personal issues, although this is not specified in the discussion. In contrast, Tai's comment in Line 3 is framed not in emotional terms, but in terms of a particular aspect of interaction which had been problematic for him. What he points to here is difficulty in ending the conversation. Certainly this is an element of discourse which has been shown to vary within and across languages (Bardovi-Harlig *et al.*, 1991). However, in the context of this role-play, it is not a conventional conversational closing that Tai is trying to perform. He is actually trying to 'shut down' the conversation by orienting away from the turn towards a personal topic initiated by Misato in Line 11 of their role-play (Extract 5.13). Thus, this social action which Tai attempts to perform can be considered pragmatically complex and consequently involve a heavy cognitive load due to the performance pressure associated with a role-play (Livingston, 1982). In order to build on Tai's noticing, the teacher offers an interpretation of his strategy for ending the conversation to the class, which helps Tai to elaborate on his intention in Lines 7 and 9. The teacher's contributions to the talk here can therefore be regarded as scaffolding the formulation of Tai's account, which allows him to use his meta-pragmatic awareness to explain the gaps between his intended performance and his actual performance. In other words, Tai is able to elaborate what he was trying to achieve socially through the language which he used. Thus, we see in this case reflection on performance leading to noticing of aspects of difficulty, further reflection on which allows for intentions in interaction to be clarified through the classroom discussion. This ability to reflect on and notice aspects of one's performance and to be able to explain them in terms of one's communicative intentions is fundamentally important for negotiating meaning in intercultural interactions where individuals can interpret things in very different ways and explanation is often necessary for the purpose of clarification (Liddicoat, 2005).

Another instance of reflection as a catalyst for learning emerges in Line 11, where Hikari enquires as to what interaction would be likely to occur when visiting a similar establishment for the first time. In other words, reflection has assisted Hikari with considering other contexts and formulating questions of concern to her. In Lines 14 and 16 the teacher offers his own interpretation of the pragmalinguistic possibilities, and then draws specifically on his experiences in an Australian context to illustrate the fact that it is quite possible for a customer to be the initiator of a conversation (Lines 18, 20). Hikari appears to be surprised by this cultural difference, which can be interpreted from her use of the feedback token 'hee' for showing surprise in Japanese. In this section of the extract, Hikari has used reflection on the role-play performance to generate a relevant question regarding the impact that contextual variability might have on the interactional specifics in customer-service interaction. This highlights that one of the potentially important roles for reflection on performance is that it can promote consideration of alternative contexts, which functions to reveal gaps in meta-pragmatic awareness. Subsequently confronting gaps in one's meta-pragmatic awareness through explicitly formulating questions that allow for knowledge to be sought can be considered crucial for the development of the learners' interpretive capacity. In other words, learning how to ask questions regarding how particular pragmatic acts can be achieved, how they are likely to be interpreted in an L2 context and how they might be different to L1 communication is indispensable for the intercultural language learner.

Exploring the cultural basis of one's emotional reactions to performance

Although opportunities for reflection are often created in the classroom, it does not mean that reflection or learning stop there. Learners continue to contemplate what they have encountered in the classroom, how they responded to it on cognitive and affective levels and how their communicative repertoire is developing. This section shows a student (Tai) reflecting in his learning journal on an affective response he had to a particular aspect of interaction during a role-play in the previous class. This reflection generates exploration of the cultural basis of his reaction. Extract 5.14 presents the content of the role-play to which Tai refers in his learning journal entry (Extract 5.15). The commentary in the learning journal consists of sequential contributions to a discussion between Tai and the teacher which unfolded over a period of two weeks. Tai's contributions were written outside class, and the teacher's comments were written during the class when the journal had been handed in.

Extract 5.14 Role-play

1	**Tai:**	Hi Seiji
2	**Seiji:**	Hi.
3	**Tai:**	Was that book interesting? Fun?
4	**Seiji:**	Ah, yes it was interesting. But I have to tell you something.
5	**Tai:**	What about?
6	**Seiji:**	Ah, yeah. I brought your favourite book and I was reading it on the train. And I'm sorry … it was stolen by someone.
7	**Tai:**	Oh, really?
8	**Seiji:**	Yes. I'm sorry that it happened. It was completely my mistake. A drunken man was sitting next to me and while I was sleeping he might steal it because he was drunken. Anyway, I should have put it on my bag.
9	**Tai:**	Oh. Okay, so it's not your fault. I can buy a new one.
10	**Seiji:**	Oh, no, no, no. Please let me buy you a new one.
	Tai:	Okay, if you will.

Extract 5.15 Reflective discussion

1	**Tai:**	Today, I felt excuse wasn't necessary when Seiji was explaining what happened. I understood that wasn't excuse, but I couldn't help my feeling. I think the problem is the order of conversation. We explained what happened before apologizing in English and it sounds like excusing to me.
2	**Teacher:**	Do you think this is connected to the concept of 'moushiwakenai' in Japanese?
3	**Tai:**	Maybe. So, I looked up what 'moushiwakenai' means in the dictionary. It means, 'benkai no yochi ga naku, aite ni sumanai' (To have no room to make excuses and to be sorry to the other person) and 'moushiwake' means 'iiwake'. Originally 'moushiwakenai' means, 'It's completely my fault and I take responsibility'. So, I think it is usual Japanese apology. Maybe my feeling come from this. However, it is disappearing little by little in recent years.

4 **Teacher:** Why do you think '*moushiwakenai*' is decreasing?
5 **Tai:**   Because people don't take responsibility in Japan even they
              said it. I mean that '*moushiwakenai*' is losing its own meaning.
6 **Teacher:** What do you think the social causes are for this?
7 **Tai:**   I think a human relationship is one of the cause. These days,
              we can't have a good relationship with people who are not
              friends or family.

Translation of terms from above:

(1) *Moushiwake/Iiwake* = Excuse
(2) *Moushiwakenai* = I have no excuse

As the interaction above unfolded within Tai's learning journal several days after the class, it shows that he has continued to reflect on the role-play performed in the class with Seiji. Tai's reflection seems to have been prompted by a feeling that something was problematic in the discourse he encountered in the role-play, which he has identified as being related to the sequencing of information within the apology sequence. Specifically, he suggests that beginning the apology sequence with an account of the situation (Olshtain & Cohen, 1983) rather than an offer of apology straight up made it sound like an excuse to him. That Japanese apologies are more likely to begin with an offer of apology is an issue which has been discussed in the literature (e.g. Barnlund & Yoshioka, 1990; Sugimoto, 1997, 1998). It can be seen that Tai has used reflection on performance, prompted by his own emotional reactions, to identify a specific aspect of cultural difference as problematic for him.

The teacher's contribution in Line 2 is significant as it prompts Tai to reflect on how his perceptions of this aspect of discourse may be culturally shaped. Specifically, he prompts Tai to consider whether his perception may have been shaped by the Japanese notion of '*moushiwakenai*', which literally means 'I have no excuse'. In Line 3 Tai shows that he has not simply reflected on this notion, but has looked up its formal meaning in a dictionary, which has allowed him to reflect further on the meaning. This can be seen to have led Tai to recognize that this notion may have affected his emotional reactions to performance in class. There is a significant turn in the extract at the end of Line 3, where Tai offers the perspective that the significance of the notion of *moushiwakenai* may be decreasing in Japan. This is thus a shift from reflection on the meaning of the concept for exploration of one's own emotions to reflection on the role of the concept in the C1 in general – in other words, intracultural reflection. The teacher prompts Tai to elaborate on the reason for his opinion, offering his perception (Line 5) that these days people's uttering of the words *moushiwakenai* is not accompanied by acceptance of responsibility, which is required. In Line 6 the teacher further prompts Tai to reflect on the social causes for such a change. He offers his analysis in Line 7 that a weakening of the bond between strangers in Japanese society is leading to a lack of concern and responsibility. Reflection in this section of the extract has facilitated an analysis of social factors underlying perceived changes in cultural values which impact on interaction.

Reflection here can be seen to first of all provide a resource for the exploration of emotional reactions to specific aspects of in-class performance. The noticing gleaned from this reflection is then further reflected on in order to identify cultural frames (notion) shaping the perception of interaction. The cultural significance of the notion of *moushiwakenai* is explored, both as being an important notion in Japanese culture and as affecting one's own reactions to the L1 discourse encountered in class. This thus highlights the cultural situatedness of perceptions of discourse and the self as a language user. As Scarino (2009) points out, reflection on experiences in communication tasks can reveal to students gaps in knowledge which involve their own frames of reference. This is an important catalyst for reconsolidating their understanding of the specific linguistic constructions which constitute the interpretive architecture through which interpretation is conducted. The processes in this extract provide a context for talking through, exploring and understanding the ways in which culturally embedded concepts frame one's own emotional reactions to discourse. Particularly when adverse emotional reactions are experienced in interaction, individuals are in need of the capacity to articulate their feelings and explain them with reference to their own culture for the interlocutor to understand (Liddicoat, 2005). However, in order to be able to do that, the individual needs conscious awareness of the specifics of the cultural difference which is problematic. The reflective work which is accomplished by Tai together with the teacher in his journal can be considered as moving towards the development of such awareness through making explicit connections between the use of language and cultural ideas.

Reflecting on personality and identity in interaction

As discussed above, when learners are engaging with interactional patterns that they are not used to, this can generate particular cognitive and affective reactions but not always lead to explicit invocation of concepts such as personality or identity from learners. When this does occur, learners are seeing the foreign language not simply as tools for sending messages but as potential identity resources (Ishihara & Tarone, 2009). The question which they face is how the communicative affordances provided by the target language can be worked with or transformed for one's purposes. Below, the issue of personality and identity management emerges in one of Tai's journal entries in response to a role-play experience in class. The role-play he refers to was one performed with Hikari involving an invitation between friends, with Tai being on the receiving end of the invitation. For the role-play, the students were left with the decision as to the nature of the invitation and whether or not to accept it. The only specification from the teacher was that a reason be given in the case of turning down the invitation. In an earlier discussion students had remarked that indirect rejection is generally preferred in Japanese, whereas in English it is generally preferred to explain the unavoidable circumstances that lead to the rejection (Gass & Houck, 1999). This role-play was therefore an opportunity for learners to explore the possibilities within such an interaction.

Extract 5.16   Role-play

1 **Hikari:**   Hi, how are you?
2 **Tai:**   I'm good. How are you?
3 **Hikari:**   Yeah, good. And um, so I'd like to ask you that, we are now planning party next Sunday in student hall, so would you like to join us?
4 **Tai:**   Next Sunday? What time will it start?
5 **Hikari:**   The party will open 5pm.
6 **Tai:**   Oh, sorry, I can't go there.
7 **Hikari:**   Oh, really?
8 **Tai:**   Because, yeah, on Saturday I have to hand in report until 6:00, and I have three reports so maybe I will be writing it on Saturday, so I don't have time.
9 **Hikari:**   Oh, I'm sorry for hearing that. It's okay, I understood your situation.

Extract 5.17   Reflective commentary

Tai: I think that the last role-play was completely different from my personality. Usually I do not explain so much when rejecting. However, the conversation was better than before and it was comfortable for me. So, when I speak other language, I should create a new personality, like officially and privately. Of course it doesn't mean I should be a split-personality person. I feel when I'm speaking English, my personality become a little different unconsciously.

In his reflective journal Tai takes up the issue of the rejection of the invitation, where he reveals that this aspect of interaction is different from how he usually interacts. Tai draws an interesting analogy between the repertoires that individuals have for interacting in formal (official) and casual (private) contexts and the repertoires that individuals need for communicating in different languages (Davies, 2004). What Tai is essentially pointing to here is the issue of how to present oneself in interaction within the languages that one uses. His comment that he does not need to become a 'split-personality person' would seem to indicate that he is approaching the issue of identity management from the perspective of how to retain a coherent sense of self while presenting the self in different ways according to the language. This resonates with the idea that for the intercultural learner there is always the pressing question of 'how am I me when I speak this language?' (Liddicoat & Scarino, 2013: 23). The reflection on performance here has thus helped Tai to reflect on his emotional reactions to cultural difference, which has foregrounded for him the issue of identity construction for communicating across languages and cultures. The awareness of difference and the awareness of himself as an experiencer of difference has led him to the recognition of the need to reflect on and make use of the linguistic resources available to him in order to create intercultural positions as he interacts (Liddicoat, 2005). Although Tai comments that he perceives an automatic change in himself depending on the language, the awareness generated from reflection here can go towards a more conscious monitoring of his own positioning, both within and across languages.

Exploring one's positioning in performance

As learners become more accustomed to the process of reflection and more consciously monitoring their own cognitive and affective responses to interactional activities conducted within the classroom, they can start to consider the nature of their own intercultural mediation. The extracts below reveal a role-play and Misato's reflection on the role of culture in influencing her interactional choices and the presentation of self in both Japanese and English. For this role-play the students had been asked to perform the role-play based on a scenario involving obvious power distance between the speakers. In this case they opted to act out the situation in the roles of 'sempai' (roughly translatable as 'senior') and 'kohai' (roughly translatable as 'junior'), specifically with the sempai (Misato) inviting the kohai (Seiji) to do something.

Extract 5.18 Role-play

1 **Misato:** Hi Seiji
2 **Seiji:** Hi
3 **Misato:** So, I'm planning a drinking party next Friday night. My friends is coming and your friends is coming, so why don't you come our party?
4 **Seiji:** Ah, next Friday?
5 **Misato:** Night
6 **Seiji:** *Sempai*, I have so many things to do now, like you know. I, I can't answer to it now, so if I could go there I will call you later.
7 **Misato:** Oh, okay. See you.

Extract 5.19

1 **Misato:** I have recently noticed that I could understand not only cultural difference, but also myself (my personality) from role-plays. During role-plays, I feel sometimes 'I'm really Japanese'. On the other hand, sometimes I feel 'I'm a little bit far from Japanese, but near to English (Westerners)'. Anyway, in this role-play, I felt Seiji's reaction was really really Japanese. It is because his way to deny my offering was indirect and euphemistic. This character is the character of Japanese I think.

2 **Teacher:** This is really interesting. Could you tell me which role-plays (speech acts) you especially felt like this? Also, what kinds of cultural differences have you become able to notice easier?

3 **Misato:** I think I'm poor at weekend conversation because I don't ask about someone's weekend. When I meet friends that I haven't seen for a long time, I ask him/her 'How have you been recently?', but this does not mean asking about weekend, but his/her work, study, or places where they went for a job or holiday. If I talk about weekends I rarely ask, 'How was your weekend?' I think there is difference between things that people who speak English regard as private or public, and things that Japanese do. I always worry about which topic is private for him/her because I think this depends on not only cultural differences, but also each person's personality. If possible I want to avoid communication troubles but I realize these cannot be avoided! That is the communication!

The first comment offered by Misato in her learning journal is significant as it implies two related aspects of intercultural learning which are afforded by reflection on performance in the role-plays. The first is that she has come to a sense of progression in her own intercultural learning. Her Line 1 comment reveals self-awareness of her own emerging ability to identify cultural differences at the level of interaction. What is of further significance is that Misato's comment indicates that her developing meta-pragmatic awareness has come to allow her not only to perceive cultural difference, but to monitor her own and others' performance and to interpret the nature of cultural positioning in performance. In other words, she has become able to sense intercultural mediation at work, as indicated by her interpretation of 'Japaneseness' in Seiji's performance in English, which in turn helps her to reflect on her own intercultural positioning.

The teacher responds to Misato's commentary by prompting her to reflect on other cultural differences she has come to notice as a result of performance. Misato responds that the act of regularly asking about someone's weekend, which is an issue which had been discussed and experimented with in an earlier class, had been a little unfamiliar to her. What is significant is that Misato's analysis goes beyond a simplistic comparison of conversational routines, to reflect on the potential impact of divergent ways of construing cultural concepts such as 'personal' and 'private' across cultures. In other words, Misato identifies linguistic differences as stemming from culturally variable social constructs used to conceptualize and manage social relations (McConachy & Spencer Oatey, forthcoming). Furthermore, while recognizing the existence of cultural differences, Misato also shows recognition of diversity within cultures based on the personality of each individual. Misato reports that in her own interactions there is difficulty in determining how to perceive and respond to each individual's positioning within their own culture. She nevertheless explicitly recognizes the inherently dynamic nature of communication and that the negotiation of boundaries of appropriateness is one necessary aspect of interacting across cultures. Awareness of the cultural variability of the concepts which individuals use to manage their social relations and recognition of the existence of culture-internal variability is an important indicator that Misato is decentring from her own cultural assumptions (Kramsch, 1993).

Chapter Conclusion

Throughout this chapter it has been argued that reflection on performance in the classroom can promote intercultural language learning in several ways. The significance of the learning opportunities afforded by reflection on performance derives from the fact that the performance of each learner constitutes a 'text' which can be interpreted by the self and others. While this is also true in the case of experience talk (Chapter 4), the most significant difference involved with the interpretation of performance in classroom tasks is that the performance is equally available as text to all participants. Learners thus have the opportunity to interpret aspects of their own and others' performance, compare strategies for carrying out particular social acts, and reflect on how meanings and impressions can be constructed. This is a different engagement with language from simply developing knowledge of L2 norms. It is a process of active construction within which learners' own perceptions are brought into focus and used as a resource for considering options for interaction and what they can be used to signify in social terms (Kramsch, 2009; Liddicoat & Scarino, 2013).

Reflection on the nature of one's own performance within productive activities such as role-plays helps learners come to clarified understanding of what their own communicative intentions were at various points within an interaction and why they made the linguistic choices they did. Again, this is not simply a matter of comparing one's own performance with an idealized native-speaker norm, but a process of exploring rationales for linguistic choices. This is an important aspect of learning because it makes learners aware of the assumptions they have about how to carry out social acts in the L2 and also helps cultivate a view of language as a resource to be utilized rather than a rule-system to be obeyed. Importantly, in the act of reflection, learners focus closely on the nature of context and the kinds of interpersonal impressions they wish to construct through the L2. Through reflecting on concrete issues such as how to index formality in order to convey politeness to a professor, how to talk to a more senior student or how to carry out an invitation, learners activate assumptions rooted in L1-based cultural experiences and then explore how to achieve their interactional and interpersonal goals through creative linguistic choices. In other words, learners mediate between norms, assumptions and meta-pragmatic concepts (such as 'formality') drawn from the L1 (and their existing perspectives on language use) and try to reconcile them with the L2 linguistic resources at their disposal (McConachy & Liddicoat, 2016). Learners thus creatively engage with language as a system of meaning potential that can be creatively utilized for their own ends (Kearney, 2016). This shift in perspective towards language as a resource resonates with Kramsch's (2009) notion of symbolic competence, and the intercultural mediation that accompanies this shift can be seen as driving the development of agency in the L2.

Reflection on performance also creates affordances for learning through the way it facilitates learners' exploration of their own emotional reactions to aspects of interaction. The emotional dimension of reflection is important, as seemingly trivial differences (or perception of difference) in ways of carrying out conversational routines or speech acts can challenge learners' perspectives on how language should be used to instantiate particular interpersonal relationships (Saville-Troike, 2003). Reflection provides a way for learners to identify the specific nature of their own emotional reactions – what they felt 'uncomfortable', 'fun', 'difficult', etc. – and attempt to consciously tie their reactions to various pragmatic triggers. In other words, learners explore what they feel and why they feel that way in increasingly specific terms through reflection. Such a process is an important route to tapping into deep cultural assumptions that learners have about language use, interpersonal relationships and their own emerging identities as intercultural language users. The experience of emotionality and reflection on emotionality thus brings learners in a different way to the fundamental question of who they want to be when they speak the L2.

For the language teacher, creating a variety of opportunities for learners to reflect on one performance and observe others is a crucial pedagogical act for helping learners link their capacities as 'performers' and 'analyzers' of language and culture (Liddicoat & Scarino, 2013). This means helping learners develop a view of themselves as someone who does not just uncritically reproduce the language of a textbook or other pedagogical resource, but as someone who is able to analyze situations in contextual terms, mediate between assumptions drawn from different languages, and incorporate insights into their own linguistic production. Teachers help learners develop a perspective on language as a resource for language users and thus help learners see themselves as agentive beings who actively prepare for interactions and then use reflection on their interactions to think about future interactions. In role-plays and post role-play discussions as learning tasks, learners are not only learning specific features of interaction for the purpose of 'acquisition', but also learning how to talk about interaction and, more importantly, how to ask 'the right questions' about language in use that will help them formulate aspects of their own performance in more agentive ways. In essence, they are developing frameworks for talking about aspects of their own performance. Essentially, through such engagement in the classroom, students become socialized into ways of working with languages and cultures which will be important for intercultural mediation and serve as the foundation for becoming mindful analyzers and performers in intercultural communication.

6 Developing Intercultural Perspectives on Language Use

Introduction

As discussed in the Introduction to this book, theorizing around the nature of intercultural competence has tended to position the various knowledge, skills and attitudes comprising this competence as external to language. This has posed problems for language teachers who wish to develop intercultural competence in the language classroom, as it seems that intercultural goals are only indirectly related to the goals of developing the ability to use the L2. The incorporation of pragmatics into language teaching has helped draw learners' attention to some of the ways in which specific speech acts and features of discourse work in communication, but the focus has remained primarily on L2 linguistic realization patterns and culture has not been as well addressed (Alcón Soler & Martínez-Flor, 2008; Meier, 2003). As discussed in Chapter 1, this is due to the fact that the notion of 'pragmatic norm' is often seen in terms of the regularities in how native speakers communicate and what they view as appropriate language use. More recently, van Compernolle's (2010, 2011, 2014) work from the perspective of sociocultural theory has helped to complexify the ways in which we think about meta-pragmatic awareness. He has effectively highlighted the fact that the notion of context cannot be taken for granted, and that it is important to develop learners' broader awareness of the contingency of language use and the ability to reflect on how linguistic forms can be creatively used to generate a range of interpersonal meanings and impressions. However, in this work, the notion of meta-pragmatic awareness is still closely tied to the norms of native speakers and the role of learners' existing knowledge remains undertheorized. This book has thus aimed to resituate the notion of meta-pragmatic awareness within the framework of intercultural language learning.

The Role of Meta-pragmatic Awareness in Development

The distinctive point of departure in this book has been the recognition of the need to situate the development of meta-pragmatic awareness within an intercultural orientation to language teaching and learning. An intercultural orientation embodies the notion that the process of language learning is not simply the acquisition of a code, but a process of developing the ability to meaningfully and insightfully interpret and use features of the target language (Liddicoat & Scarino, 2013). Such a process involves learners in drawing on cultural frames of reference rooted in their knowledge of multiple languages, including their emerging knowledge of the L2. An intercultural orientation also embodies the notion that foreign languages will necessarily be used to communicate with a wide range of individuals from different backgrounds. In short, the language learning endeavour is seen as a process of developing the knowledge, skills and abilities necessary for intercultural communication through an L2. The argument that I have advanced throughout this book is that an important part of becoming able to use an L2 for intercultural communication is developing insight into the fact that language use achieves social actions and is thus interpreted on the basis of a wide range of assumptions about the social world. This is not limited to developing knowledge of the pragmatic norms of native speakers (although it would certainly include this, depending on the specific teaching context), but is more fundamentally oriented towards learners developing insight into how they themselves, as well as fellow learners, interpret the significance of particular ways of speaking in relation to aspects of sociocultural context and perceptions of broader social activities, relationships and identities. For learners, this requires tapping into their own taken-for-granted assumptions about the social world and how they influence perceptions of L1 and L2 language use. In other words, learners deepen their awareness of the fact that the interpretation of language use is never just about language (Fairclough, 2015). I have argued that such a process can be seen in terms of developing meta-pragmatic awareness, and that meta-pragmatic awareness is crucial to the learner's capacity for developing an intercultural perspective on language use over time. The focus in this book has not been on documenting the development of an intercultural perspective over time, but rather on the learners' interpretive engagement with aspects of language use in the classroom and the development of meta-pragmatic awareness within and across specific classroom interactions.

As discussed and illustrated throughout the preceding chapters, the development of meta-pragmatic awareness engages the learners' own existing assumptions about how language works as a tool for social action. In this sense, the learners' assumptions constitute the basis for the initial interpretive work done in a particular instance of analysis in the language classroom. However, in order to turn assumptions into awareness, the nature of the engagement with language is crucially important. Specifically, it is when the teacher constructs a focus on language as discourse that learners pay closer attention to the co-construction of meaning, the ways in which language is used to accomplish social acts, and the interpretive work which is implicated in such a process (Haugh, 2010; Kasper, 2006). Whether examining a dialogue or reflecting on an interaction they have experienced inside or outside the classroom, when learners look at utterances, not in isolation but in terms of their placement in relation to preceding and following talk, it helps them generate interpretations regarding the affective states of speakers and their communicative intentions, thereby mobilizing meta-pragmatic knowledge for the interpretation of language use as a social act (Lo Castro, 2003).

It is this attention to the structuring of pragmatic acts, together with reflection on the possible intentions of speakers in interaction, that draws learners' attention to the co-constructed nature of meaning and to the kinds of knowledge and assumptions that are implicated in the interpretation of communication. Furthermore, attention to language use from the perspective of what speakers may be trying to achieve socially in a given sequence of talk helps to highlight the role of language in helping individuals fulfil social roles while building and maintaining interpersonal relationships. At the same time, it helps learners consider the effect of individual utterances or turns of talk on an interlocutor and how meaning is dynamically negotiated on the basis of ongoing inferential work (Goodwin & Duranti, 1992). Emerging awareness of the linguistic features of speech acts and the ways that these and other pragmatic phenomena take place within the discursive construction of meaning is crucial for beginning to reflect on why speakers in interaction make the choices that they make, how speakers construct meaning over multiple turns, and what cultural knowledge informs and constrains the ways speakers interpret and evaluate contributions to talk (Kasper & Rose, 2001). This allows for a broader engagement of the students' interpretive abilities, which in turn provides a framework for reflective and analytical learning as the students reflect on their own cultural knowledge in order to make sense of the language they encounter (Kearney, 2016; Liddicoat & Scarino, 2013).

Classroom talk provides a context in which learner interpretations can be articulated, and articulation is instrumental in making the learners' ideas available for further reflection at the collective and individual level, gradually revealing the aspects of interpretive architecture through which interpretations are operating (McConachy, 2013). When the co-constructive moves of the teacher and learners help individuals articulate their perspectives on issues of pragmatic appropriateness and other evaluative issues, learners are able to draw on and make manifest the various ways in which conceptions of age, gender, workplace hierarchy, social distance and a host of other sociocultural variables and culturally variable concepts influence their judgements (Meier, 2010; van Compernolle, 2014). This becomes a learning resource for the individual learner and also for others. In many cases, a perspective on an aspect of interaction articulated by a particular student leads a separate student to reflect on an aspect of his/her own knowledge that had been taken for granted, thus bringing it to awareness. In this sense, individual interpretations themselves are tools for collaborative learning – an interpretation is an artefact of talk that promotes reflection and noticing of aspects of knowledge (McConachy, 2013). A crucial point here is that classroom talk also generates conflicting accounts of cultural phenomena which help to reveal the simplistic nature of many perceptions of cultural groups and communication styles (Dervin, 2011). It is in this sense that diversity of perspectives which emerge in classroom talk provide a catalyst for re-examining, complexifying and decentring from conventionalized ways of understanding, both in relation to the target language and the L1, as the justification of interpretation helps bring out underlying assumptions for scrutiny (Kramsch, 1993).

The success of reflection, however, is not guaranteed. Whether learners remain at the level of superficial interpretation of encountered input is crucially dependent on whether the dynamics of the classroom interaction prompt them to reflect further and open up to complexity. Scaffolding from the teacher and other learners which encourages an individual to describe a feature of language use in more detail, to consider language use in relation to context, to justify evaluative stances, to compare norms across languages and cultures and to consider alternative perspectives is essential in order to develop complexity of interpretation and enhance affordances for learning (Liddicoat & Scarino, 2013). The extracts of classroom interactions that I have presented throughout this book illustrate the varied ways in which teachers and learners work together to co-construct and co-scaffold particular perspectives on learning input and classroom experiences, not simply in the sense of prompting each other for more information but also by sharing tools for interpretation. Such dynamics are particularly salient in what I have referred to as experience talk.

Experience talk, as it is constructed through interaction among learners within the classroom, generates descriptive, evaluative and explanatory accounts of experience that create opportunities for learning. Such talk is particularly rich when the individual who is recounting an experience is prompted by questions and comments from the teacher and peers to elaborate on aspects of the experience, thus transforming the experience into a text which can then be interpreted and examined by all. When elements of an experience are articulated with sufficient specificity, learners can take a discourse perspective on interactional features of the experience, thereby considering the significance of who said what and in what order and why. Chapter 4 illustrates how this is meaningful for deriving learning on L1-based and L2-based experiences. Experience talk functions as a resource for learning within reflection on L1 communication primarily in that it exposes the cultural scripts for common interactions and the range of cultural assumptions about social roles and relationships that will tend to otherwise remain out of awareness. At the same time, experience talk generated by students who share the same L1 reveals not only diverse experiences of students but sometimes divergent and conflicting accounts which prompt re-examination of normative perceptions of L1 practices. In the extracts discussed in this book, the fact that features of Japanese language and culture were revealed to be variably interpreted by the classroom participants on the basis of their individual experiences helped to highlight the diversity of practices within the nation according to region, gender and other sociocultural variables. It furthermore suggested to learners that their own meta-pragmatic awareness – in terms of what they regard as typical and why – is shaped by their own personal experiences (Kramsch, 2009). From the perspective that this represents movement away from essentialist conceptions of language and culture, it can be considered significant.

When learners discuss their various experiences of interacting in foreign cultural contexts, experience talk also constitutes an important resource for exploring the basis of judgements made of foreign interactional practices and foreign speakers. Experience talk based on L2 interactions is particularly prone to evaluation, in that learners will tend to illustrate interactional encounters that have surprised them or which have led them to the subjective experience of cultural difference. From this perspective, the potential for intercultural learning derives most obviously from the ways in which learners are able to reflect on what they have experienced and how the interpretation of interaction has functioned as a tool for the evaluation of interlocutors. Without effective teacher scaffolding, there is of course the danger that learners will not re-examine their evaluations but simply justify them in a non-reflective way. It is for this reason that evaluative adjectives – notions such as 'cold', 'weird', 'rude', 'friendly' – are a key item of focus (Houghton, 2012; McConachy & Hata, 2013). When such evaluations surface in experience talk, effective scaffolding is necessary to prompt learners to 'illustrate' the attribute by describing the features of interaction that generated the relevant judgement. This generates collaborative reflection among learners as to how a particular student derived an evaluation of an individual from a different linguistic and cultural background (whether native speaker or not) based on what that person has said, how they have said it, and in what social role or interpersonal position they have said it. Evaluative adjectives only have meaning to the extent that they can be illustrated with specific behaviour. Therefore, explicitly relating behaviour to evaluative adjectives provides a resource for considering what it really means to be 'friendly', 'polite', etc., and how individual speakers possess unacknowledged assumptions about communication and interpersonal relations from which these evaluations arise. The semantic content of such notions is culturally specific, as are the ways in which such notions are conventionally applied to particular social behaviours (Kádár & Haugh, 2013). Experience talk constitutes a text which provides opportunities for the re/interpretation of experience and the development of meta-pragmatic awareness through generating insight into the cultural basis of meta-pragmatic judgements. This can be an important catalyst for re-evaluation of experience and decentring from previous, sometimes ethnocentric, interpretations (Byram, 2008).

In reflection by learners on their classroom interactional experiences, talk centred on role-play tasks can also become a 'text' with affordances for intercultural learning. In contrast to experience talk, what is distinctive about classroom performance is that the details of performance can be equally available as text to the other classroom participants, which allows learners to take up the interrelated roles of performer and analyzer (Scarino, 2009). Within the role of performer, learners experiment with aspects of discourse such as speech acts and conversational routines; in the role of analyzer they closely watched the role-plays of other groups and reflected, often in conjunction with peers and the teacher, on the cultural significance of what had been observed. The combination of these roles within role-plays and post role-play discussions provides a framework for exploring the learners' rationales for their linguistic choices, comparing norms of interaction across cultures, and considering the cognitive and affective implications of particular ways of interacting for the learner (Liddicoat & Scarino, 2013). When learners articulate rationales for their language choices it reveals their assumptions regarding how certain social functions can be achieved in the target language, including how this relates to notions of sociocultural context and the need to present oneself in a particular way socially. Importantly, the talk helps these assumptions become acknowledged and then used for considering how to structure the next performance.

The learners in this study were seen to notice the impact of Japanese cultural scripts for interaction on their own language use in English, particularly in role-plays. Learners drew on understandings of formality and politeness situated within a Japanese cultural context and considered how they could use English to convey similar interpersonal impressions. Classroom performance activities such as role-plays, combined with post-performance reflection, create affordances for practising intercultural mediation (Crozet, 1996). The classroom provides an important 'sheltered' environment in which learners can try out different ways of interacting and, through reflection, explore how the meanings and intentions they hope to bring to an encounter can be realized through the target language resources available to them. In this way, noticing, intercultural reflection and comparison are integral to developing the ability to communicate in the target language.

It is important to note that an engagement with otherness through a foreign language can incite a range of emotions, even within the relatively protected environment of the classroom (Saville-Troike, 2003). Learners experience a range of emotions which are brought about both in performance tasks in the target language such as role-plays and in analytical tasks which require reflection on the basis of their own ways of interpreting and evaluating language use. The learners in this study were actively encouraged to explore the role of emotion in interaction in various ways. In the contextual analysis activities in Chapter 3, students reflected on the role of language in indexing particular affective states and also how language can be used strategically in anticipation of and in response to the affective states of a range of interlocutors. Chapters 4 and 5 showed how students reflect more closely on their own affective responses to particular interactional experiences in English and Japanese, both inside and outside the classroom. Reflection helps learners articulate the nature of the emotions they experienced when experimenting with particular speech acts and conversational routines, as well as identify what triggered the emotions and why. This supports a process of conceptualization and an attempt to clarify how affective reactions relate to one's own assumptions and values. In this sense, affective reactions can signal to students where they currently stand in relation to particular ways of interacting in the target language and their own language/s, which in turn provides a resource for considering the possibilities for intercultural mediation in one's own performance repertoire. In connection to this, coming to understand the process of intercultural interaction and learning as both cognitive and affective suggests to learners the importance of viewing meaning making as a process in which speakers interact with their bodies, hearts and minds from their own culturally and individually structured standpoints (Kramsch, 2009).

To summarize, meta-pragmatic awareness can be developed within a range of classroom activities which engage learners in active interpretation of language use as social action and prompt them to reflect in diverse and complex ways on the basis of their own cognitive and affective reactions. Learners come to awareness of the various ways in which assumptions about social relationships, including stereotypes of self and other, influence the interpersonal impressions that are formed within communication. Moreover, learners come to awareness of the limitations of applying norms for appropriate communication from one context to another, especially norms derived from one language to the interpretation of language use in another. Such insights provide a tool for learners to reflect more closely on the nature of their own language use and the meanings and impressions they wish to construct.

Theorizing Intercultural Learning Practices

As the classroom interactions and learning in this book have been analyzed within the framework of intercultural learning practices proposed by Liddicoat and Scarino (2013), the analysis has implications for the conceptualization of these practices and the model as a whole. The first implication is for the conceptualization of *noticing* and its role in the learning process. In its present form, the model frames noticing in terms of Schmidt's (1993) notion of consciously registered input. When learners engage with new input and attempt to interpret it as socially meaningful, they begin to notice regularities in the input which they then attempt to understand. The attempt to understand salient features of the target language fuels the interpretation process, leading learners to reflect on what they are encountering and draw intercultural comparisons. Thus, what shapes the learning process in the first instance is the learner's ability to notice features of the input and make it available for conscious reflection. In this sense, it could be said that noticing is *input-driven*. However, what has come out strongly in this study is that, within learning centred on interpretation and reflection on language use, the objects of noticing (what is noticed) that lead to meaningful learning reside not only in external input but also in learners' own interpretive architecture. Through *reflection*, learners bring into awareness – consciously register – aspects of their own knowledge and underlying assumptions that inform their judgements of language use. Learners notice expectations they have about appropriate communication in the L1 and the L2, including how conversational routines and speech-act sequences play out, and how assumptions about interpersonal relationships, as well as cultural stereotypes, influence their perceptions of language in use. Noticing is embedded in reflection and manifests in awareness of aspects of one's own cognition. In this sense, noticing is *reflection-driven*.

In order to more fully articulate a theory of intercultural language learning, it is therefore necessary to recognize a distinction between input-driven noticing and reflection-driven noticing in the learning process. Input-driven noticing incites learners to try to interpret aspects of pragmatics (and other linguistic foci) as socially meaningful – that is, not just as a decontextualized code. It is this interpretation of language use as socially meaningful that leads to reflection on the significance of what has been noticed, which can be further analyzed from the perspective of how linguistic choices reflect speakers' roles and relationships, as well as other features of sociocultural context. However, the extent to which reflection becomes meaningful depends on whether learners' existing knowledge and assumptions can be effectively tapped into, noticed and communicated to others. If reflection simply triggers unanalyzed perspectives and interpretive repertoires, then the potential for learning is limited. Conversely, if reflection leads learners to notice aspects of their own knowledge and some of the unarticulated assumptions on which this knowledge is based, then the learner is able to more easily decentre from these perspectives, or at least consider them in a new light. Once noticed, the articulation of aspects of interpretive architecture can be transformed into an important form of meta-pragmatic awareness and feed into the learning process.

An important point to note is that reflection-driven noticing is not simply cognitive but also affective. As was particularly salient in Chapters 4 and 5, one of the common ways in which learners react to unfamiliar inter-actional conventions is by translating emotional reactions into value judge-ments of L2 practices or speakers as 'weird', 'friendly', etc. The cognitive act of labelling acts as a cover for an emotional reaction that tends to remain unanalyzed (Houghton, 2012). What is revealed in some of the classroom discussions is that one of the important ways in which reflection works is by helping learners focus on the nature of their own emotional reactions, to identify the reaction, and to attempt to identify where the reaction is coming from. The initial object of noticing is an emotional charge – such as an expe-rience of 'discomfort' or 'strangeness' – and the act of reflection helps the learner more consciously recognize – i.e. notice – the emotion, label it, and thereby bring it under more conscious attentional control so that different external triggers can be explored (Moon, 2004). When learners use reflection to specify the nature of their own emotional reactions in relation to particu-lar features of L1 or L2 language use, they are essentially linking the cogni-tive and the affective within meta-pragmatic awareness. This suggests the importance of looking at meta-pragmatic awareness within language learn-ing not simply as a matter of knowledge, but as a form of awareness within which the cognitive and affective domains of linguistic interpretation become linked.

That is not to say that learners always notice an aspect of their own knowledge or emotional reactions prior to the attempt to communicate it to others. It is frequently in the act of articulating one's own perspectives and reasons for these perspectives, particularly within small group interactions, that insight into the nature of one's own knowledge is gained. Languaging makes individuals' perspectives on language and culture available to others, and others' reactions scaffold further reflection on the perspective being articulated. In Swain and Lapkin's (1995) terms, languaging is a crucial instrument in reflection-driven noticing, as it helps the learner reflect to a point that deeper assumptions can be noticed. It is this dialectic between reflection and languaging as it emerges within classroom interaction that creates a space for decentring. This highlights one of the roles of *interacting* as an intercultural learning practice. At the same time, languaging based on reflection comes to constitute input for other learners, who are prompted to consider alternative perspectives on language and culture arising within classroom talk. This links with the practice of *comparison*. When learners reflect on the significance of input they have encountered, whether that be visual input such as a textbook or an experience shared by another learner or teacher, they not only interpret aspects of language and culture for them-selves, but they also interpret for others, and they are interpreted for by others (Liddicoat, 2014). In classroom learning, the individual perspectives of each student, shaped by their own history as a user of particular languages

in particular cultural contexts, come into contact with those of other learners and the teacher, thereby bringing together diverse perspectives on what
constitutes (un)usual, (in)appropriate and (im)polite ways of relating to
others through language. Learners thus need to transcend their own viewpoint by comparing and relating their own knowledge and assumptions with
those that are revealed by other classroom participants. In terms of complexifying our understanding of the intercultural learning practices, we need
to recognize that in the instantiation of these practices for learning, cognition is both individual and socially distributed (Duranti, 1997).

   This notion of reflection-driven noticing, shaped by the specific interactional contingencies of the classroom, brings a new layer of complexity to
our understanding of intercultural learning practices within the foreign language classroom. This is not to reject the importance of noticing form –
function – context relationships in the target language, but to suggest that
the reframing of meta-pragmatic awareness from an intercultural perspective, and recognition of the central importance of reflection, requires an
enlarged perspective on what is noticed, how it is noticed and why it is of
significance. Input-driven noticing and reflection-driven noticing are both
crucial elements in the cycle of intercultural learning practices and facilitate
learners' ongoing interpretive engagement.

   Although discussion of the intercultural learning practices of interacting,
noticing, reflecting and comparing in the literature to this point has been
focused on how these interpretive processes work for the purposes of learning, it is also beneficial to view these practices from the perspective of intercultural competence. The intercultural learning practices constitute a cycle
through which the individual is able more meaningfully and insightfully to
interpret the cultural input to which he or she is exposed, thereby using
experience to develop an increasingly sophisticated understanding of cultural
phenomena and an alertness to the potential for cultural difference in intercultural encounters. In interacting with individuals from a different cultural
background through the medium of a foreign language, one needs the ability
to notice how those present to the communicative encounter orient to features of interaction, in order to be able to reflect on what it signifies, to be
able to compare what one has noticed with one's existing assumptions and
expectations about social interaction, and to manage the construction of
meaning in a mindful way (Langer, 1989; McConachy & Spencer-Oatey,
forthcoming). From this perspective, the ability to engage in the practices
and to draw knowledge and meta-pragmatic awareness from this engagement can be considered an important part of intercultural competence
(McConachy & Liddicoat, 2016). From a long-term perspective, such a process shapes the development of an intercultural perspective on language use.
While language learners have the benefit of having the development of their
abilities scaffolded by the teacher, the ultimate aim is to become an individual who can draw on existing knowledge to engage in intercultural

learning practices in context, and thereby increasingly develop knowledge, insight and sensitivity for future intercultural interactions.

Developing Meta-pragmatic Awareness in Practice

What happens in language classrooms is largely constrained by the materials that teachers have available and how much freedom teachers have to decide the activities through which learners will engage with the materials. As was the case in the teaching drawn upon in this book, many teachers continually face the question of how to creatively utilize the materials at their disposal to construct a learning environment congruent with their pedagogical principles. What happens in classrooms also depends very much on how teachers see the object of learning. If teachers see culture as something that needs to be 'taught' as a body of knowledge, then it can seem like an insurmountable challenge for many. If teachers shift their perspective to see culture as something to be 'engaged with' rather than 'taught', then the burden is significantly lessened. When dealing with aspects of pragmatics, it is natural for teachers to want to expose learners to a variety of samples and to provide ample opportunities to put the language to use. Intercultural language teaching does not lessen the importance of exposure to input or practice. Rather, the suggestion is that learners benefit from the opportunity to reflect more closely on the nature of the input in terms of social meanings and to develop a view of their own L2 production as participation in meaning-making practices (Kramsch, 2009). The classroom is a site where learners become socialized into practices of thinking and speaking analytically about aspects of language and culture while engaging critically with a variety of pedagogical artefacts. The teacher's main role in implementing intercultural language teaching is helping learners interpret the linguistic and cultural representations they are exposed to, whether those are drawn from coursebooks, authentic materials, TV dramas, magazines, or any other source (c.f. Baker, 2015). This involves creating initial entry points for reflection and scaffolding discussions in a way that helps learners articulate their own perspectives while reflecting on those of others.

Creating entry points for reflection

The development of meta-pragmatic awareness as conceptualized and discussed throughout this book requires a large amount of scaffolding from the teacher in terms of crafting activities and facilitating interactions through which the learners can reflect, notice and compare aspects of pragmatics across cultures. This includes the creation of opportunities for analyzing aspects of language use in relation to context, considering the role of intention and co-construction in interaction, and exploring how cultural assumptions affect the ways in which individuals cognitively and affectively make sense of interaction. A fundamental part of this is encouraging learners to take a discourse perspective on language use and using this as a lens for exploring the cultural basis of meaning making. Unless learners are already highly capable of explicitly analyzing language in context, the teacher needs to play a key role in establishing explicit conditions that will promote reflection and analysis of language and culture. There are several interrelated dimensions to consider here.

The first dimension is that the analysis is anchored in some way by the teacher so as to give learners an initial entry point for reflection. Whether learners are engaging with textual material (authentic transcripts, textbook material, etc.) or audio-visual material (movies, YouTube clips, etc.), questions from teachers play a key role in shaping what is noticed (Kohler, 2015). A common entry point that was effective in this study was how the learners perceived the emotional states of the interactants, both generally and at specific points in the interaction. Relatively simple questions such as 'How do you think the speakers feel at the end of this interaction?' or 'How do you think Speaker A feels about this question?' can create an entry point for analysis which helps draw in the relational aspects of communication (learners focus on how speakers appear to feel about each other) as well as attention to the range of contextual elements, including who the speakers are, where they are, what they appear to be trying to do in their communication, and more. In this way, learners are encouraged to construct their own interpretations based on what they know about the sociocultural contexts in which the L2 is used and what they know about how communication occurs within relationships. This naturally foregrounds many assumptions that derive from the learners' L1, which can be brought into awareness through reflection (reflection-driven noticing) within classroom discussion. An alternative to initially anchoring the analysis in features of context is to draw learners' attention to features of the interaction. When dealing with pragmatics this can be done either at the level of the single utterance (What is speaker A doing in this sentence?) or through questions which encourage learners to take a discourse perspective on a given speech act or interactional routine (Where does the request begin and end? Why?).

The second dimension is that reflective tasks promote the voicing of diverse interpretations and thus consideration of meaning-making possibilities from multiple perspectives. This means creating the kind of interactional configurations and non-threatening environment in which a free range of interpretations can be generated by learners. However, whether this succeeds or not depends very much on the learners' own willingness to engage. While pair work and small-group work were effective within the context of this study, this was in large part due to the fact that the number of learners was so small, that they were close in age, and that they were all attending the course out of their own volition, based on their desire to study in the UK in the future. The learners who participated in this study were particularly cooperative from the beginning and it was not difficult to establish rapport. For teachers working with larger groups of learners, the process of building rapport and encouraging students to open up with their own views necessarily takes longer. The way that teachers need to engage with their learners is very much context dependent, but what can be said is that if the teacher hopes to promote a lot of exploratory discussion among learners, the teacher may need to do a lot of elicitation in the early stages to model the kinds of analysis that is sought. The role of teacher questioning is thus not only to elicit information but also to showcase analysis and thereby gradually socialize the learners into the practice of asking meaningful questions about language and culture (Liddicoat, 2008).

Scaffolding within interaction

It is important that language learners are encouraged to generate their own trajectories of analysis over time, but that does not mean that the teacher just sits back completely. Intermittent elicitation of interpretations and opinions by the teacher can help to expose convergences and divergences in interpretation, which then help give shape to the multi-layered processes of noticing, comparison and reflection. This means that the teacher makes active use of the learners' knowledge and interpretations to support the reflexive understanding of all classroom participants (Phipps & Gonzalez, 2004). The classroom context in which this study was based was particularly conducive to teacher scaffolding due to the small number of learners and the fact that all the learners shared Japanese as a first language and the teacher was also reasonably fluent in Japanese. In the case that there is a much larger number of students in one class, it will mean that the teacher cannot necessarily directly intervene in the learners' reflective discussions. When teaching in a classroom in which a larger number of learners are working in small groups, the teacher can orchestrate whole-class reflection through a process of eliciting interpretations from particular groups, relating those to interpretations which arise from other groups, and then leading learners to notice and further reflect on aspects of significance. In the process of eliciting from individual learners, the teacher can help these learners effectively articulate their ideas, presenting them on the board in the form of an idea map, or a variety of other techniques.

For the teacher, scaffolding the kind of reflection which helps learners articulate and problematize their taken-for-granted assumptions regarding language is particularly crucial to developing meta-pragmatic awareness and deriving affordances for intercultural learning. In first of all helping learners articulate their interpretations, reformulation was a common scaffolding strategy used in this study. This involves repeating part or all of a student's comment in a previous turn, either in the form of a statement or a question (Heritage, 1985; Nakamura, 2010), to consequently lead students to be able to articulate their interpretation with enhanced clarity. Beyond simply helping students articulate their ideas, the teacher also introduced meta-pragmatic concepts such as the name of speech acts and aspects of sociocultural context such as size of imposition, social distance and others, because tools for talking about interaction was seen to mediate the development of more elaborated accounts of students' interpretations as the students respond to them and actually utilize them in subsequent talk (van Compernolle, 2014).

Another important aspect of teacher scaffolding involves the use of students' L1 for checking the understandings behind students' use of L2 concepts, prompting comparison of the nature of concepts across cultures, and articulating more specifically the cultural assumptions that go along with particular concepts (Cook, 2010). In the case that the class is composed of students from a wide variety of linguistic and cultural backgrounds, this further enriches the potential for discovering and exploring the diverse ways in which learners make meta-pragmatic judgements about foreign language use and what the cultural basis of their judgements is. Such a classroom can potentially bring out a range of culture-specific concepts which underlie social norms, which can be used for reflection on how learners, as intercultural communicators, should make judgements about what is (in)appropriate and (im) polite and how this will affect the ways in which they use the target language. Holding up and contrasting culture-specific or culturally variable concepts used for meta-pragmatic judgements (such as politeness, for instance) drawn from multiple languages is an important part of intercultural language teaching, which both promotes decentring and helps learners develop a toolkit for ongoing intercultural learning (Liddicoat & Scarino, 2013).

In addition to the scaffolding work accomplished by the teacher, the ways in which learners scaffold learning for each other is crucial for intercultural learning to take place (Donato, 1994). One significant aspect of peer scaffolding is the ways learners prompt each other to elaborate on their interpretations of language and culture. Through the interaction, learners make requests for clarification, reformulate one another's utterances, and ask questions which help peers more fully reveal their perspectives and values. Furthermore, learners make use of the L1 for facilitating understanding of L2 input, for explaining the cultural significance of L1 interaction and for making intercultural comparisons (Kramsch, 1993). As the learners' interpretations come to be elaborated, the commentary from each student constitutes a potential communal learning resource as fellow learners and the teacher draw on it as a reference point for reflecting on their own knowledge. It is important to acknowledge that attempting to understand the perspective that another learner takes on an aspect of interaction is not a matter of 'comprehending' information; it requires an active attempt to view phenomena from a perspective that is potentially different to one's own (McConachy, 2013). Attempting to reconcile one's interpretation with the interpretation of others can lead not only to awareness of the nature of one's own knowledge, but to noticing of diverse ways of understanding cultural phenomena. Peer scaffolding for intercultural learning is thus constituted when learners' attention is drawn to the variable ways in which individuals interpret and evaluate language use and the nature of the cultural assumptions that inform such processes. It can be said that the contingencies of the interaction play a definitive role in the extent to which the interpretive architecture constituting each participant's meta-pragmatic awareness will be revealed and how this will be utilized for constructing insights into 'how language works to make the world meaningful' (Phipps & Gonzalez, 2004: 85) within and across cultures.

As was also an issue in this study, promoting interpretation of interactions (particularly intercultural interactions) can lead to the emergence of stereotypical views of other cultures. Stereotypical views can even be shared by learners from similar backgrounds due to drawing on ideologically shaped representations they have been exposed to in primary socialization or later in life through the media and education (Dervin, 2011). In the sense that a stereotype is a generalized picture of perceived reality, not all stereotypes are necessarily unrealistic or problematic (Hinton, 2015). However, what is important for the teacher is first to help elicit the logic behind learners' perceptions of languages and cultures and to encourage them to critically evaluate the conditions under which their views can be seen as realistic or unrealistic. Framed positively, the articulation of simplistic views of language, culture and cultural groups is one stage in development which the teacher can work with to prompt a more nuanced analysis by drawing attention to the contextual variability of behaviour and the value judgements that are associated with particular views of behaviour. However, there is also the danger, particularly in highly multicultural classes, that uninformed or stereotypical views voiced by particular learners may generate frustration or hostility in other learners. This is something that is always an issue when (perceived) cultural issues are broached, but is something for the teacher to deal with, primarily by allowing all voices to be heard, creating adequate space for scrutinizing all views while helping learners make their own criteria for evaluation as explicit as possible (Byram, 1997; Houghton, 2012).

This also raises the issue of how the teacher represents languages and cultures in the classroom, as the teacher also can be guilty of promoting excessively reductionist views of language – culture connections (Kramsch, 1993). What the teacher can and does say is very dependent on what the learners are perceived as being able to understand, and from that perspective it is sometimes necessary to present simplified accounts of language and culture in the beginning. This is one constraint within which teachers have to work. When bringing in personal accounts of intercultural experience or providing explanations about cultural phenomena, it is best if the teacher can give as much detail about the contexts in which the explanation may apply so as not to encourage the learners to generalize too far. This issue is particularly highlighted when the issue of language use in real-world contexts comes up, as the teacher is responsible for providing an informed perspective. Although learners in this study sometimes directly questioned the teacher regarding the nature of pragmatic norms and what would happen in particular interactional circumstances, the teacher tried to specify the context within which he considered his answer to be relevant. Additionally, the teacher made efforts to point to the inherent variability associated with language use. This is important because presenting a deterministic relationship between language use and context and absolutist notions of normativity will work against the development of learners' interpretive abilities and understanding of the negotiated nature of interaction (van Compernolle, 2014). A corollary of this is that the teacher has a responsibility to draw on his or her knowledge and experience to present a perspective on language use which the students can use as one reference point for developing their meta-pragmatic awareness (McConachy, 2013). In essence, the teacher's role in classroom interaction is to contribute his or her own meta-pragmatic awareness as a resource for the emerging analysis (Scarino, 2007) and, through meta-pragmatic talk, to make the tools used for intercultural work more salient for the learners.

Implications for Language Teacher Learning

The notion that the language classroom is not simply a place where learners develop linguistic skills but also become socialized into particular ways of looking at and working with languages has implications for language teacher learning. In order for language teachers to be able to help learners develop an intercultural perspective on language use, language teachers themselves need to be adept at reflecting on language use in insightful ways, while simultaneously being able to scaffold the development of learners' interpretive capacities. The teacher's own capacity for reflection and ability to scaffold reflection are, naturally, interdependent. They are also simultaneously dependent on how teachers conceptualize the nature of language, culture and learning (Liddicoat & Scarino, 2013).

As discussed in the Introduction, conceptualizations of language as code and of culture as something that resides primarily in language-external products, practices and perspectives are a fundamental barrier to intercultural language teaching (c.f. Crozet, 2003; Dervin & Liddicoat, 2013; Díaz, 2013; Kearney, 2016; Liddicoat & Scarino, 2013). Although communicative language teaching (CLT) has, for the most part, been successful in helping teachers conceptualize 'language' in terms of 'language use', this has not necessarily altered the orientation to language as code. In line with arguments made in Chapter 2, the tendency within CLT to treat language use as a matter of correctly applying itemized phrases for instantiating communicative functions still represents a code-based view of language. Moreover, the dominant trend within interlanguage pragmatics teaching and research towards the pragmalinguistic dimensions of language use and the operationalization of the sociopragmatic dimension of language use in terms of relatively narrow conceptions of 'appropriateness' have made it difficult for teachers themselves to conceptualize the cultural and intercultural dimensions of language use. It is by looking at language use as a form of behaviour whose social meanings are actively interpreted by individuals in interaction that teachers can begin to see that culture is a constituent part of language use – language use is a form of cultural behaviour (McConachy & Liddicoat, 2016). As such, teacher professional development for intercultural language teaching necessitates an interpretive engagement with pragmatic phenomena that tend to feature in the language curriculum, most notably conversational routines, speech acts, and other culturally variable forms of discourse such as narrative, meeting talk, and others.

It is highly beneficial for language teachers to make a habit of examining interactional transcripts, including those contained in textbooks or other learning resources, paying attention to their own personalized understandings of pragmatic phenomena. For example, when looking at a transcript of interaction, teachers can consider how speakers in a given interaction appear to make sense to each other on a turn-by-turn basis and, in particular, how speakers might derive impressions of others based on linguistic features. Teachers can also consider how speakers' linguistic decisions might be informed by aspects of sociocultural context and may also make relevant aspects of that context for others during the interaction (McConachy, 2009). Such analytical processes open up the possibility for teachers to gain insight into their own assumptions and how pragmatic features trigger certain impressions of others. When teachers are able to gain insight into the fact that communication is built around ongoing interpretation of self and other based on conscious and unconscious assumptions, it will be easier to recognize the complexity of language use as a form of social action and the need to help learners develop as active interpreters of communication, not just performers (Liddicoat & Scarino, 2013). Put simply, teachers can develop their own meta-pragmatic awareness and gain a sense for the areas of focus that can be taken up in the classroom. This, in turn, constitutes a foundation for the teachers' ability to construct analytical questions that will shape how learners engage with the samples of language use that they are exposed to inside and outside the classroom.

Throughout this book, I have highlighted the particularly important role of teachers' languaging practices in scaffolding learning in the classroom (Swain & Lapkin, 1995). Teachers scaffold learning not simply in the ways in which they overtly elicit learners' comments or prompt reflection;

the ways in which teachers talk about language use in relation to culture provide a model for learners (Liddicoat & Scarino, 2013; McConachy, 2013). As discussed above, when teachers begin to talk analytically about language, such as by drawing connections between language use and context or articulating alternative perspectives on an instance of communication, this constitutes a lens which helps socialize learners into more complex ways of looking at and working with languages. This is particularly the case when teachers engage in experience talk. Teacher experience talk, as co-constructed within classroom interactions, signals to students that the articulation of personal experience and one's interpretations of experience are a resource for learning itself rather than simply a collection of things that have occurred in the past. Particularly for teachers who have learnt the target language as a foreign language, the willingness and ability to share personalized knowledge and perspectives on L2 communication sends a potentially powerful message of encouragement to learners. It is an important implication of this study that teachers in training need to be supported in developing their abilities to articulate their own interpretations of interactions, including those derived from personal experience. When appropriate, teachers should be encouraged to draw on all the languages at their disposal to articulate their own perspectives, make cultural comparisons and justify judgements.

For teachers who wish to deepen their theoretical knowledge, empirical studies in cross-cultural, interpersonal and intercultural pragmatics can help them become familiar with some of the metalanguage in the area, some of the cultural variability in the construction of pragmatic acts, and the ways in which speakers from different cultural backgrounds construct and interpret messages and events. Empirical studies on interlanguage pragmatics can also be useful for developing awareness of variation in language learners' patterns of L2 language use and judgements of appropriateness (c.f. Ishihara & Cohen, 2010). Although much work in interlanguage pragmatics tends to regard learners' divergence from native-speaker norms as a deficiency, framed more positively, learners' variable evaluation of pragmatic appropriateness underscores both the cultural relativity of pragmatic norms and the fact that learners draw on and mediate between various understandings of the linguistically constructed social world within the process of language learning.

It is conceivable that moving away from a view of language as a tightly rule-governed system and engaging with language use as a form of culturally variable behaviour might present an initial challenge to teachers' deep-seated beliefs about language and how it should be taught (van Compernolle, 2014). In a sense, an interpretive engagement with language use represents a threat to cherished notions of stability, normativity and traditional views on authenticity in language teaching (van Lier, 1996). In an age in which languages are learned and used by individuals from diverse linguistic and cultural backgrounds for a range of purposes, challenging our taken-for-granted perceptions on what constitutes a language, what counts as appropriate language use – and according to whom and what criteria – and what it means to learn and teach a language for intercultural communication is an important activity and part of an increasingly interdisciplinary dialogue that needs to continue.

Conclusion

As established in the Introduction chapter of this book, the field of foreign language teaching is now beginning to take seriously the contention that language learning needs to be reconceptualized as an intercultural endeavour. While the notions of communicative competence and intercultural competence have different disciplinary origins and have tended to be treated separately, it is time to see intercultural competence as a central part of developing the ability to communicate in a foreign language. Intercultural competence is not something that you develop after you have enough foreign language competence; the development of foreign language competence itself is an intercultural engagement. Right from the beginning of learning, learners engage with the foreign language on the basis of their existing perspectives on the world – on people, relationships and actions – and engage in various levels of intercultural mediation throughout the learning process. The act of interpreting and constructing meanings constantly engages learners' knowledge, assumptions, values, and their sense of self and who they want to be. However, there is no guarantee that such constituents of what I have called interpretive architecture will rise to learners' consciousness without teacher support. The argument that I have presented in this book is that learners need to be actively encouraged to explore the intercultural dimensions of language learning, specifically to begin to look at language use as a form of culturally variable social action. Some teachers might think that such a goal is unattainable in a foreign language teaching context, particularly when access to authentic materials and opportunities to use the language outside the classroom cannot be guaranteed. My aim has been to show that such concerns are unfounded.

Of course, it would be unrealistic to claim that learners could develop an intercultural perspective on language use within one particular course, just as one would not claim that aspects of grammar, vocabulary or pragmatics could be mastered within one course. As with all forms of learning, the development of an intercultural perspective is an ongoing project, the seeds for which can be sown within the language classroom. Even without authentic materials on hand, language teachers can creatively utilize coursebook materials and aspects of learners' own knowledge and experience to begin to shift perspectives towards language use as a dynamic resource for them to own. Teachers can help learners come to interpret language use from a discourse perspective and develop insight into the potential impact of culturally derived knowledge, assumptions and values on the process of meaning making. Teachers, thus, help learners develop the meta-pragmatic awareness and interpretive capacities that can be further built upon throughout the learning endeavour.

References

Abdallah-Pretceille, M. (2006) Interculturalism as a paradigm for thinking about diversity. *Intercultural Education* 17 (5), 475–483.

Agar, M. (1994) *Language Shock: Understanding the Culture of Conversation*. New York: HarperCollins.

Agha, A. (1998) Stereotypes and registers of honorific language. *Language in Society* 27 (2), 151–193.

Alcón Soler, E. (2005) Does instruction work for learning pragmatics in the EFL context? *System* 33 (3), 417–435.

Alcón Soler, E. and Martínez-Flor, A. (2008) Pragmatics in foreign language contexts. In E. Alcón Soler and A. Martínez-Flor (eds) *Investigating Pragmatics in Foreign Language Learning, Teaching and Testing* (pp. 3–21). Bristol: Multilingual Matters.

Anderson, B. (1991) *Imagined Communities: Reflections on the Origin and Spread of Nationalism*. London: Verso.

Angouri, J. (2010) 'If we know about culture it will be easier to work with one another': Developing skills for handling corporate meetings with multinational participation. *Language and Intercultural Communication* 10 (3), 206–224.

Ashworth, P.D. (2004) Understanding as the transformation of what is already known. *Teaching in Higher Education* 9 (2), 147–158.

Arundale, R. (2006) Face as relational and interactional: A communication framework for research on face, facework, and politeness. *Journal of Politeness Research* 2 (2), 193–216.

Atkinson, J.M. and Heritage, J. (1984) *Structures of Social Action: Studies in Conversation Analysis*. Cambridge: Cambridge University Press.

Austin, J.L. (1962) *How to Do Things with Words* (2nd edn). Cambridge, MA: Harvard University Press.

Bachman, L.F. (1990) *Fundamental Considerations in Language Testing*. Oxford: Oxford University Press.

Baker, W. (2009) The cultures of English as a lingua franca. *TESOL Quarterly* 43 (4), 567–592.

Baker, W. (2011) Intercultural awareness: Modelling an understanding of cultures in intercultural communication through English as a lingua franca. *Language and Intercultural Communication* 11 (3), 197–214.

Baker, W. (2015) *Culture and Identity through English as a Lingua Franca: Rethinking Concepts and Goals in Intercultural Communication*. Berlin: Mouton de Gruyter.

Bardovi-Harlig, K. (1996) Pragmatics and language teaching: Bringing pragmatics and pedagogy together. In L. Bouton (ed.) *Pragmatics and Language Learning*. Monograph Series, Vol. 7 (pp. 21–39). Champaign, IL: Division of English as an International Language, University of Illinois at Urbana-Champaign.

Bardovi-Harlig, K. (2001) Evaluating the empirical evidence: Grounds for instruction in pragmatics? In K.R. Rose and G. Kasper (eds) *Pragmatics in Language Teaching* (pp. 13–32). New York: Cambridge University Press.

Bardovi-Harlig, K. and Dörnyei, Z. (1998) Do language learners recognize pragmatic violations? Pragmatic vs. grammatical awareness in instructed L2 learning. *TESOL Quarterly* 32 (2), 233–262.

Bardovi-Harlig, K. and Griffin, R. (2005) L2 pragmatic awareness: Evidence from the ESL classroom. *System* 33 (3), 401–415.

Bardovi-Harlig, K., Hartford, B.A.S., Mahan-Taylor, R., Morgan, M.J. and Reynolds, D.W. (1991) Developing pragmatic awareness: Closing the conversation. *ELT Journal* 45 (1), 4–15.

Barnlund, D.C. and Araki, S. (1985) Intercultural encounters: The management of compliments by Japanese and Americans. *Journal of Cross-Cultural Psychology* 16 (1), 9–26.

Barnlund, D.C. and Yoshioka, M. (1990) Apologies: Japanese and American styles. *International Journal of Intercultural Relations* 14 (2), 193–206.

Barraja-Rohan, A.M. (1999) Teaching conversation for intercultural competence. In J. Lo Bianco, A.J. Liddicoat and C. Crozet (eds) *Striving for the Third Place: Intercultural Competence through Language Education* (pp. 143–154). Melbourne: Language Australia.

Barraja-Rohan, A.M. (2003) How can we make Australian English meaningful for ESL learners? In J. Lo Bianco and C. Crozet (eds) *Teaching Invisible Culture* (pp. 101–118). Melbourne: Language Australia.

Barraja-Rohan, A.M. (2011) Using conversation analysis in the second language classroom to teach interactional competence. *Language Teaching Research* 15 (4), 479–507.

Barraja-Rohan, A.M. and Pritchard, R. (1997) *Beyond Talk: A Course in Communication and Conversation for Intermediate Adult Learners of English*. Melbourne: Western Melbourne Institute of TAFE.

Beacco, J.-C. (2004) Une proposition de référentiel pour les compétences culturelles dans les enseignements des langues [Suggested guidelines for intercultural competence in language teaching]. In J.-C. Beacco, S. Bouquet and R. Porquier (eds) *Niveau B2 pour le français: Textes et références* [*Level B2 for French: Texts and References*] (pp. 251–287). Paris: Didier.

Bennett, M. (1993) Towards ethnorelativism: A developmental model of intercultural sensitivity. In R.M. Paige (ed.) *Education for the Intercultural Experience* (pp. 21–72). Yarmouth, ME: Intercultural Press.

Bialystok, E. (1993) Symbolic representation and attentional control in pragmatic competence. In G. Kasper and S. Blum-Kulka (eds) *Interlanguage Pragmatics* (pp. 43–57). New York: Oxford University Press.

Billig, M. (1995) *Banal Nationalism*. London: SAGE.

Block, D. (2007) *Second Language Identities*. London: Continuum.

Blum-Kulka, S., House, J. and Kasper, G. (1989) *Cross-cultural Pragmatics: Requests and Apologies*. Norwood, NJ: Ablex.

Bou-Franch, P. and Garcés-Conejos, P. (2003) Teaching linguistic politeness: A methodological proposal. *International Review of Applied Linguistics* 41, 1–22.

Bourdieu, P. (1990) *The Logic of Practice*. Palo Alto, CA: Stanford University Press.

Breen, M.P. (1985) Authenticity in the language classroom. *Applied Linguistics* 6 (1), 60–70.

Brooks, F.B. and Donato, R. (1994) Vygotskian approaches to understanding foreign language learner discourse during communicative tasks. *Hispania* 77 (2), 262–274.

Brown, P. and Levinson, S. (1978) Universals in language use: Politeness phenomena. In E.N. Goody (ed.) *Questions and Politeness: Strategies in Social Interaction* (pp. 56–289). New York: Cambridge University Press.

Bucholtz, M. and Hall, K. (2010) Locating identity in language. In D. Watt and C. Llamas (eds) *Language and Identities* (pp. 18–28). Edinburgh: Edinburgh University Press.

Byram, M. (1991) Teaching culture and language: Towards an integrated model. In D. Buttjes and M. Byram (eds) *Mediating Languages and Cultures: Towards an Intercultural Theory of Foreign Language Education* (pp. 17–30). Clevedon: Multilingual Matters.

Byram, M. (1995) *Intercultural Competence and Mobility in Multinational Contexts: A European View*. Clevedon: Multilingual Matters.

Byram, M. (1997) *Teaching and Assessing Intercultural Communicative Competence*. Clevedon: Multilingual Matters.

Byram, M. (2003) On being 'bicultural' and 'intercultural'. In G. Alred, M. Byram and G. Fleming (eds) *Intercultural Experience and Education* (pp. 50–66). Clevedon: Multilingual Matters.

Byram, M. (2008) *From Foreign Language Education to Education for Intercultural Citizenship: Essays and Reflections*. Clevedon: Multilingual Matters.

Byram, M. (2009) The intercultural speaker and the pedagogy of foreign language education. In D.K. Deardorff (ed.) *The SAGE Handbook of Intercultural Competence* (pp. 321–332). Thousand Oaks, CA: SAGE.

Byram, M. and Zarate, G. (eds) (1997) *The Sociocultural and Intercultural Dimensions of Language Learning and Teaching*. Strasbourg: Council of Europe.

Byram, M., Nichols, A. and Stevens, D. (2001) Introduction. In M. Byram, A. Nichols and D. Stevens (eds) *Developing Intercultural Competence in Practice* (pp. 1–8). Clevedon: Multilingual Matters.

Byram, M., Barrett, M., Ipgrave, J., Jackson, R. and Méndez García, M.C. (2009) *Autobiography of Intercultural Encounters*. Strasbourg: Council of Europe. See http://www.coe.int/t/dg4/autobiography/source/aie_en/aie_autobiography_en.pdf.

Caffi, C. (1994) Metapragmatics. In R.E. Asher (ed.) *The Encyclopedia of Language and Linguistics* (pp. 2461–2466). Oxford: Pergamon Press.

Canagarajah, S. (2007) Lingua franca English, multilingual communities, and language acquisition. *Modern Language Journal* 91, Focus Issue, 923–939.

Canale, M. and Swain, M. (1980) Theoretical bases of communicative approaches to second language teaching and testing. *Applied Linguistics* 1 (1), 1–47.

Cardon, P.W. (2008) A critique of Hall's contexting model: A meta-analysis of literature on intercultural business and technical communication. *Journal of Business and Technical Communication* 22 (4), 399–428.

Cazden, C.B. (2001) *Classroom Discourse: The Language of Teaching and Learning* (2nd edn). Portsmouth, NH: Heinemann Educational.

Cheng, T. (2016) Authentic L2 interactions as material for a pragmatic awareness-raising activity. *Language Awareness* 25 (3), 159–178.

Cohen, A.D. and Ishihara, N. (2013) Pragmatics. In B. Tomlinson (ed.) *Applied Linguistics and Materials Development* (pp. 113–126). London: Bloomsbury.

Cohen, A.D. and Sykes, J.M. (2013) Strategy-based learning of pragmatics for intercultural education. In F. Dervin and A.J. Liddicoat (eds) *Linguistics for Intercultural Education* (pp. 87–111). Amsterdam: John Benjamins.

Cook, G. (2010) *Translation in Language Teaching: An Argument for Reassessment*. Oxford: Oxford University Press.

Cook, V.J. (2003) The changing L1 in the L2 user's mind. In V.J. Cook (ed.) *Effects of the Second Language on the First* (pp. 1–18). Clevedon: Multilingual Matters.

Corbett, J. (2003) *An Intercultural Approach to English Language Teaching*. Clevedon: Multilingual Matters.

Coulmas, F. (2013) *Sociolinguistics: The Study of Speakers' Choices* (2nd edn). Cambridge: Cambridge University Press.

Coupland, N. and Jaworski, A. (2004) Sociolinguistic perspectives on metalanguage. Reflexivity, evaluation and ideology. In A. Jaworski, N. Coupland and D. Galasinski (eds) *Metalanguage: Social and Ideological Perspectives* (pp. 15–51). Berlin: Mouton de Gruyter.

Crozet, C. (1996) Teaching verbal interaction and culture in the language classroom. *Australian Review of Applied Linguistics (ARAL)* 19 (2), 37–57.

Crozet, C. (2003) A conceptual framework to help teachers identify where culture is located in language use. In J. Lo Bianco and C. Crozet (eds) *Teaching Invisible Culture* (pp. 39–49). Melbourne: Language Australia.

Crozet, C. (2015) On language and interculturality: Teaching languages and cultures for a global world. In J.C.H. Lee (ed.) *Narratives of Globalization: Reflections on the Global Condition* (pp. 85–94). London: Rowman & Littlefield International.

Crozet, C. and Liddicoat, A.J. (1999) The challenge of intercultural language teaching: Engaging with culture in the classroom. In J. Lo Bianco, A.J. Liddicoat and C. Crozet (eds) *Striving for the Third Place: Intercultural Competence through Language Education* (pp. 113–125). Melbourne: Language Australia.

Crystal, D. (1997) *English as a Global Language.* Cambridge: Cambridge University Press.

Damen, L. (1987) *Culture Learning: The Fifth Dimension in the Language Classroom.* Reading: Addison-Wesley.

D'Andrade, R.G. (1984) Cultural meaning systems. In R.A. Shweder and R.A. LeVine (eds) *Culture Theory: Essays on Mind, Self, and Emotion* (pp. 88–119). Cambridge: Cambridge University Press.

Davies, C.E. (2004) Developing awareness of crosscultural pragmatics: The case of American/German sociable interaction. *Multilingua* 23 (3), 207–231.

Davis, J.M. (2007) Resistance to L2 pragmatics in the Australian ESL context. *Language Learning* 57 (4), 611–649.

Deardorff, D.K. (ed.) (2009) *The SAGE Handbook of Intercultural Competence.* Thousand Oaks, CA: SAGE.

Dervin, F. (2011) A plea for change in research on intercultural discourses: A 'liquid' approach to the study of the acculturation of Chinese students. *Journal of Multicultural Discourses* 6 (1), 37–52.

Dervin, F. and Gross, Z. (eds) (2016) *Intercultural Competence in Education: Alternative Approaches for Different Times.* London: Palgrave Macmillan.

Dervin, F. and Liddicoat, A.J. (2013) Linguistics for intercultural education. In F. Dervin and A.J. Liddicoat (eds) *Linguistics for Intercultural Education in Language Learning and Teaching* (pp. 1–25). Amsterdam: John Benjamins.

Deutscher I. (1973) *What We Say/What We Do, Sentiments and Acts.* Glenview, IL: Scott Foresman.

Dewaele, J.M. (2008) 'Appropriateness' in foreign language acquisition and use: Some theoretical, methodological and ethical considerations. *International Review of Applied Linguistics* 46 (3), 235–255.

Díaz, A.R. (2013) *Developing Critical Languaculture Pedagogies in Higher Education.* Bristol: Multilingual Matters.

Díaz, A.R. and Dasli, M. (2017) Tracing the 'critical' trajectory of language and intercultural communication pedagogy. In A.R. Díaz and M. Dasli (eds) *The Critical Turn in Language and Intercultural Communication Pedagogy* (pp. 3–21). New York: Routledge.

Donato, R. (1994) Collective scaffolding in second language learning. In J.P. Lantolf and G. Appel (eds) *Vygotskian Approaches to Second Language Research* (pp. 33–56). Norwood, NJ: Ablex.

Dufon, M.A. (2008) Language socialization theory and the acquisition of pragmatics in the foreign language classroom. In E. Alcón Soler and A. Martínez-Flor (eds)

Investigating Pragmatics in Foreign Language Learning, Teaching and Testing (pp. 25–44). Bristol: Multilingual Matters.

Duranti, A. (1997) *Linguistic Anthropology*. Cambridge: Cambridge University Press.

Eisenchlas, S.A. (2009) Conceptualizing 'communication' in second language acquisition. *Australian Journal of Linguistics* 29 (1), 45–58.

Eslami-Rasekh, Z. (2005) Raising the pragmatic awareness of language learners. *ELT Journal* 59 (3), 199–208.

Fairclough, N. (2015) *Language and Power* (3rd edn). Abingdon: Routledge.

Fantini, A.E. (1995) Introduction – language, culture and worldview: Exploring the nexus. *International Journal of Intercultural Relations* 19 (2), 143–153.

Ferguson, C. (1971) Absence of copula and the notion of simplicity: A study of normal speech, baby talk, foreigner talk and pidgins. In D. Hymes (ed.) *Pidginization and Creolization of Languages* (pp. 141–150). Cambridge: Cambridge University Press.

Firth, A. and Wagner, J. (1997) On discourse, communication, and (some) fundamental concepts in SLA research. *Modern Language Journal* 81 (3), 285–300.

Gadamer, H.-G. (2004) *Truth and Method* (trans. J. Weinsheimer and D.G. Marshall; 2nd edn). New York: Continuum.

Gass, S.M. and Houck, N. (1999) *Interlanguage Refusals: A Cross-cultural Study of Japanese-English*. Berlin: Mouton de Gruyter.

Geertz, C. (1973) *The Interpretation of Cultures*. New York: Basic Books.

Giddens, A. (1984) *The Constitution of Society: Outline of a Theory of Structuration*. Cambridge: Polity Press.

Giddens, A. (1991) *Modernity and Self-Identity: Self and Society in the Late Modern Age*. Palo Alto, CA: Stanford University Press.

Gilmore, A. (2007) Authentic materials and authenticity in foreign language learning. *Language Teaching* 40 (2), 97–118.

Goddard, C. (2012) Cultural scripts and communication style differences in three Anglo Englishes. In B. Kyrk-Kastovsky (ed.) Intercultural Miscommunication: Past and Present (pp. 101–120). Amsterdam: John Benjamins.

Goffman, E. (1959) *The Presentation of Self in Everyday Life*. New York: Anchor Books.

Goffman, E. (1981) *Forms of Talk*. Philadelphia, PA: University of Pennsylvania Press.

Gohard-Radenkovic, A., Lussier, D., Penz, H. and Zarate, G. (2004) La médiation culturelle en didactique des langues comme processus [Cultural mediation in language education as a process]. In G. Zarate, A. Gohard-Radenkovic, D. Lussier and H. Penz (eds) *La médiation culturelle et didactique des langues* [*Cultural Mediation and Language Education*] (pp. 225–238). Strasbourg: Council of Europe Publishing.

Golato, A. (2005) *Compliments and Compliment Responses: Grammatical Structure and Sequential Organization*. Amsterdam: John Benjamins.

Goodwin, C. and Duranti, A. (1992) Rethinking context: An introduction. In A. Duranti and C. Goodwin (eds) *Rethinking Context: Language as an Interactive Phenomenon* (pp. 1–42). Cambridge: Cambridge University Press.

Gudykunst, W.B. and Ting-Toomey, S. (1988) Verbal communication styles. In W.B. Gudykunst and S. Ting-Toomey (eds) *Culture and Interpersonal Communication* (pp. 99–115).

Gudykunst, W.B. and Nishida, T. (1999) The influence of culture and strength of cultural identity on individual values in Japan and the United States. *Intercultural Communication Studies* IX (1), 1–18.

Gumperz, J., Jupp, T. and Roberts, C. (1979) *Crosstalk*. Southall: National Council for Industrial Language Teaching.

Haidt, J. and Joseph, C. (2007) The moral mind: How five sets of innate intuitions guide the development of many culture-specific virtues, and perhaps even modules. In

P. Carruthers, S. Laurence and S. Stich (eds) *The Innate Mind* (3rd edn) (pp. 367–391). New York: Oxford University Press.

Haidt, J. and Kesebir, S. (2010) Morality. In S. Fiske, D. Gilbert and G. Lindzey (eds) *Handbook of Social Psychology* (5th edn) (pp. 797–852). Hoboken, NJ: John Wiley.

Hall, E.T. (1976) *Beyond Culture*. New York: Doubleday.

Hall, J.K. (1993) The role of oral practices in the accomplishment of our everyday lives: The sociocultural dimension for interaction with implications for the learning of another language. *Applied Linguistics* 14 (2), 145–166.

Halliday, M.A.K. (1978) *Language as Social Semiotic: The Social Interpretation of Language and Meaning*. London: Edward Arnold.

Hammersley, M. and Atkinson, P. (1995) *Ethnography* (2nd edn). London: Routledge.

Hanks, W.F. (1996) *Language and Communicative Practices*. Boulder, CO: Westview Press.

Hansen, K.P. (2000) *Kultur und Kulturwissenschaft*. Paderborn: UTB.

Harre, R. and van Langenhove, L. (1999) The dynamics of social episodes. In R. Harre and L. van Langenhove (eds) *Positioning Theory* (pp. 1–13). Oxford: Blackwell.

Haugh, M. (2003) Japanese and non-Japanese perceptions of Japanese communication. *New Zealand Journal of Asian Studies* 5 (1), 156–177.

Haugh, M. (2004) Revisiting the conceptualization of politeness in English and Japanese. *Multilingua* 23, 85–109.

Haugh, M. (2007) Emic conceptualizations of (im)politeness and face in Japanese: Implications for the discursive negotiation of second language learner identities. *Journal of Pragmatics* 39 (4), 657–680.

Haugh, M. (2010) Intercultural (im)politeness and the macro-micro issue. In A. Trosborg (ed.) *Handbook of Pragmatics. Vol. 7, Pragmatics across Languages and Cultures* (pp. 139–166). Berlin: Mouton de Gruyter.

Haugh, M. (2012) Conversational interaction. In K. Allan and K.M. Jazczolt (eds) *Cambridge Handbook of Pragmatics* (pp. 251–274). Cambridge: Cambridge University Press.

Haugh, M. and Chang, M. (2015) Understanding im/politeness across cultures: An interactional approach to raising sociopragmatic awareness. *International Review of Applied Linguistics in Language Teaching* 53 (4), 389–414.

Haugh, M. and Hinze, C. (2003) A metalinguistic approach to deconstructing the concepts of 'face' and 'politeness' in Chinese, English and Japanese. *Journal of Pragmatics* 35 (10–11), 1581–1611.

Hellermann, J. (2007) The development of practices for action in classroom dyadic interaction: Focus on task openings. *Modern Language Journal* 91 (1), 83–96.

Heritage, J. (1985) Analyzing news interviews: Aspects of the production of talk for an overhearing audience. In T. van Dijk (ed.) *Handbook of Discourse Analysis. Vol. 3, Discourse and Dialogue* (pp. 3, 95–119). London: Academic Press.

Hinkel, E. (1999) Introduction: Culture in research and second language pedagogy. In E. Hinkel (ed.) *Culture in Second Language Teaching and Learning* (pp. 1–7). New York: Cambridge University Press.

Hinton, P.R. (2015) *The Perception of People: Integrating Cognition and Culture*. London: Routledge.

Hirose, Y. and Hasegawa, Y. (2010) *Nihongo kara mita nihonjin: shutaisei no gengogaku*. Tokyo: Kaitakusha.

Hofstede, G. (1980) *Culture's Consequences: International Differences in Work-related Values*. Beverley Hills, CA: SAGE.

Holliday, A. (2009) The role of culture in English language education: Key challenges. *Language and Intercultural Communication* 9 (3), 144–155.

Holliday, A. (2010) Cultural descriptions as political acts: An exploration. *Language and Intercultural Communication* 10 (2), 259–272.

Holmes, P., Bavieri, L., Ganassin, S. and Murphy, J. (2016) Interculturality and the study abroad experience: Students' learning from the IEREST materials. *Language and Intercultural Communication* 16 (3), 452–469.

Houghton, S.A. (2012) *Intercultural Dialogue in Practice: Managing Value Judgment through Foreign Language Education*. Bristol: Multilingual Matters.

House, J. (2008) What is an 'intercultural speaker'? In E. Alcón Soler and M. Pilar Safont Jordá (eds) *Intercultural Language Use and Language Learning* (pp. 7–21). Berlin: Springer.

House-Edmonson, J. (1986) Cross-cultural pragmatics and foreign language teaching. In K.R. Bausch, F.G. Königs and R. Kogelheide (eds) *Probleme und Perspektiven der Sprachlehrforschung* (pp. 281–295). Frankfurt: Scriptor.

Huth, T. and Taleghani-Nikazm, C. (2006) How can insights from conversation analysis be directly applied to teaching L2 pragmatics? *Language Teaching Research* 10 (1), 53–79.

Hymes, D. (1972) On communicative competence. In J.B. Pride and J. Holmes (eds) *Sociolinguistics* (pp. 53–73). Harmondsworth: Penguin.

Hymes, D. (1974) *Foundations in Sociolinguistics: An Ethnographic Approach*. Philadelphia, PA: University of Pennsylvania Press.

Ifantidou, E. (2014) *Pragmatic Competence and Relevance*. Amsterdam: John Benjamins.

Ishihara, N. (2010) Maintaining an optimal distance: Nonnative speakers' pragmatic choice. In A. Mahboob (ed.) *The NNEST Lens: Nonnative English Speakers in TESOL, Vol. 1* (pp. 35–53). Newcastle upon Tyne: Cambridge Scholars Press.

Ishihara, N. and Cohen, A. (2010) *Teaching and Learning Pragmatics: Where Language and Culture Meet*. Harlow: Pearson.

Ishihara, N. and Tarone, E. (2009) Subjectivity and pragmatic choice in L2 Japanese: Emulating and resisting pragmatic norms. In N. Taguchi (ed.) *Pragmatic Competence in Japanese as a Second Language* (pp. 101–128). Berlin: Mouton de Gruyter.

Iwasaki, N. (2008) Style shifts among Japanese learners before and after study abroad in Japan: Becoming active social agents in Japanese. *Applied Linguistics* 31 (1), 45–71.

Jaworski, A, Coupland, N. and Galasinski, D (2004) Metalanguage: Why now? In A. Jaworski, N. Coupland and D. Galasinski (eds) *Metalanguage: Social and Ideological Perspectives* (pp. 3–13). Berlin: Mouton de Gruyter.

Judd, E.L. (1999) Some issues in the teaching of pragmatic competence. In E. Hinkel (ed.) *Culture in Second Language Teaching and Learning* (pp. 152–166). New York: Cambridge University Press.

Kádár, D.Z. and Bax, M.M.H. (2013) In-group ritual and relational work. *Journal of Pragmatics* 58, 73–86.

Kádár, D.Z. and Haugh, M. (2013) *Understanding Politeness*. Cambridge: Cambridge University Press.

Kasper, G. (1992) Pragmatic transfer. *Second Language Research* 8 (3), 203–231.

Kasper, G. (2006) Speech acts in action: Towards discursive pragmatics. In K. Bardovi-Harlig, C. Felix-Brasdefer and A.S. Omar (eds) *Pragmatics and Language Learning, Vol. 11* (pp. 283–316). Honolulu, HI: National Foreign Language Resource Centre/ University of Hawaii.

Kasper, G. and Dahl, M. (1991) Research methods in interlanguage pragmatics. *Studies in Second Language Acquisition* 13 (2), 215–247.

Kasper, G. and Rose, K.R. (1999) Pragmatics and SLA. *Annual Review of Applied Linguistics* 19, 81–104.

Kasper, G. and Rose, K.R. (2001) Pragmatics in language teaching. In K.R. Rose and G. Kasper (eds) *Pragmatics in Language Teaching* (pp. 1–9). Cambridge: Cambridge University Press.

Kasper, G. and Rose, K.R. (2002) *Pragmatic Development in a Second Language*. Oxford: Blackwell.

Kasper, G. and Schmidt, R. (1996) Developmental issues in interlanguage pragmatics. *Studies in Second Language Acquisition* 18 (2), 149–169.

Kearney, E. (2016) *Intercultural Learning in Modern Language Education: Expanding Meaning-Making Potentials*. Bristol: Multilingual Matters.

Kecskes, I. (2014) *Intercultural Pragmatics*. Oxford: Oxford University Press.

Kinginger, C. and Farrell, K. (2004) Assessing development of meta-pragmatic awareness in study abroad. *Frontiers: The Interdisciplinary Journal of Study Abroad* 10 (2), 19–42.

Kohler, M. (2015) *Teachers as Mediators in the Foreign Language Classroom*. Bristol: Multilingual Matters.

Kondo, S. (2008) Effects on pragmatic development through awareness-raising instruction: Refusals by Japanese EFL learners. In E. Alcón Soler and A. Martínez-Flor (eds) *Investigating Pragmatics in Foreign Language Learning, Teaching and Testing* (pp. 153–177). Bristol: Multilingual Matters.

Kramsch, C. (1993) *Context and Culture in Language Teaching*. Oxford: Oxford University Press.

Kramsch, C. (2003) Teaching along the cultural faultline. In D.L. Lange and R.M. Paige (eds) *Culture as the Core: Perspectives on Culture in Second Language Learning* (pp. 19–35). Greenwich: Information Age.

Kramsch, C. (2009) *The Multilingual Subject*. Oxford: Oxford University Press.

Lange, D.L. and Paige, R.M. (eds) (2003) *Culture as the Core: Perspectives on Culture in Second Language Learning*. Greenwich: Information Age.

Langer, E.J. (1989) *Mindfulness*. Cambridge, MA: Perseus Books.

Lantolf, J. and Thorne, S.L. (2007) Sociocultural theory and second language learning. In B. van Pattern and J. Williams (eds) *Theories in Second Language Acquisition* (pp. 201–224). Mahwah, NJ: Lawrence Erlbaum.

Leech, G. (1983) *Principles of Pragmatics*. London: Longman.

Liddicoat, A.J. (2002) Static and dynamic views of culture and intercultural language acquisition. *Babel* 36 (3), 4–11, 37.

Liddicoat, A.J. (2005) Teaching languages for intercultural communication. In D. Cunningham and A. Hatoss (eds) *An International Perspective on Language Policies, Practices and Proficiencies* (pp. 201–214). Belgrave: Fédération Internationale des Professeurs de Langues Vivantes (FIPLV).

Liddicoat, A.J. (2006) Learning the culture of interpersonal relationships: Students' understandings of personal address forms in French. *Intercultural Pragmatics* 3 (1), 55–80.

Liddicoat, A.J. (2007) *An Introduction to Conversation Analysis*. London: Continuum.

Liddicoat, A.J. (2008) Pedagogical practice for integrating the intercultural in language teaching and learning. *Japanese Studies* 28 (3), 277–290.

Liddicoat, A.J. (2014) Pragmatics and intercultural mediation in intercultural language learning. *Intercultural Pragmatics* 11 (2), 259–277.

Liddicoat, A.J. and Scarino, A. (2013) *Intercultural Language Teaching and Learning*. New York: Wiley-Blackwell.

Littlewood, W. (2001) Cultural awareness and the negotiation of meaning in intercultural communication. *Language Awareness* 10 (2–3), 189–199.

Liu, D. (1995) Sociocultural transfer and its effect on second language speakers' communication. *International Journal of Intercultural Relations* 19 (2), 253–265.

Livingstone, C. (1982) *Role Play in Language Learning*. New York: Longman.

Lo Castro, V. (2003) *An Introduction to Pragmatics: Social Action for Language Teachers*. Ann Arbor, MI: University of Michigan Press.

Lo Castro, V. (2012) *Pragmatics for Language Educators: A Sociolinguistic Perspective*. New York and Abingdon: Routledge.

Long, M.H. (1983) Native speaker/non-native speaker conversation and the negotiation of comprehensible input. *Applied Linguistics* 4 (2), 126–141.

Magnan, S.S. (2008) The unfulfilled promise of teaching for communicative competence: Insights from sociocultural theory. In J.P. Lantolf and M.E. Poehner (eds) *Sociocultural Theory and the Teaching of Second Languages* (pp. 349–379). London: Equinox.

Malinowski, B. (1923) The problem of meaning in primitive languages. In C.K. Ogden and I.A. Richards (eds) *The Meaning of Meaning* (pp. 296–336). New York: Harcourt Brace & World.

Martínez-Flor, A. and Usó-Juan, E. (2006) Developing communicative competence through listening. In E. Usó-Juan and A. Martínez-Flor (eds) *Current Trends in the Development and Teaching of the Four Language Skills* (pp. 29–47). Berlin: Mouton de Gruyter.

Martínez-Flor, A. and Usó-Juan, E. (2010) Pragmatics and speech act performance. In A. Martínez-Flor and E. Usó-Juan (eds) *Speech Act Performance: Theoretical, Empirical and Methodological Issues* (pp. 3–20). Amsterdam: John Benjamins.

Matsumoto, D. (2006) Culture and cultural worldviews: Do verbal descriptions about culture reflect anything other than verbal descriptions of culture? *Culture & Psychology* 12 (1), 33–62.

McConachy, T. (2008) Raising intercultural awareness through a focus on conversational routines. *Internet Journal of Language, Society and Culture* 24, 43–49.

McConachy, T. (2009) Raising sociocultural awareness through contextual analysis: Some tools for teachers. *ELT Journal* 63 (2), 116–125.

McConachy, T. (2013) Exploring the meta-pragmatic realm in English language teaching. *Language Awareness* 22 (2), 100–110.

McConachy, T. and Hata, K. (2013) Addressing textbook representations of pragmatics and culture. *ELT Journal* 67 (3), 294–301.

McConachy, T. and Liddicoat, A.J. (2016) Meta-pragmatic awareness and intercultural competence: The role of reflection and interpretation in intercultural mediation. In F. Dervin and Z. Gross (eds) *Intercultural Competence in Education: Alternative Approaches for Different Times* (pp. 13–30). London: Palgrave Macmillan.

McConachy, T. and Meldant, A. (2007) *Learning to Communicate in English: A Total Approach – Intermediate* (3rd edn). Tokyo: Lado International College Japan.

McConachy, T. and Spencer-Oatey, H. (forthcoming) Developing pragmatic awareness. In *Handbook of Clinical and Developmental Pragmatics*. Berlin: Mouton de Gruyter.

McKay, S. and Wong, S. (1996) Multiple discourses, multiple identities: Investment and agency in second language learning among Chinese adolescent immigrant students. *Harvard Educational Review* 66 (3), 577–608.

Meier, A.J. (1997) Teaching the universals of politeness. *ELT Journal* 51 (1), 21–28.

Meier, A.J. (1999) Identifying and teaching the underlying cultural themes of pragmatics: A case for explanatory pragmatics. In L.F. Bouton (ed.) *Pragmatics and Language Learning*. Monograph Series, Vol. 9 (pp. 113–127). Champaign, IL: Division of English as an International Language, University of Illinois at Urbana-Champaign.

Meier, A.J. (2003) Posting the banns: A marriage of pragmatics and culture in foreign and second language pedagogy and beyond. In A. Martínez-Flor, E. Usó Juan and A. Fernández Guerra (eds) *Pragmatic Competence and Foreign Language Teaching* (pp. 185–210). Castello: Universitat Jaume I.

Meier, A.J. (2010) Culture and its effect on speech act performance. In A. Martínez-Flor and E. Usó Juan (eds) *Speech Act Performance: Theoretical, Empirical and Methodological Issues* (pp. 75–90). Amsterdam: John Benjamins.

Meier, A.J. (2015) The role of noticing in developing intercultural communicative competence. *Eurasian Journal of Applied Linguistics* 1 (1), 25–38.

Miles, M. and Huberman, M. (1994) *Qualitative Data Analysis*. London: SAGE.

Moody, S.J. (2014) 'Well, I'm a *Gaijin*': Constructing identity through English and humor in the international workplace. *Journal of Pragmatics* 60, 75–88.

Moon, J.A. (2004) *A Handbook of Reflective and Experiential Learning: Theory and Practice*. London: Routledge Falmer.

Murray, N. (2010) Pragmatics, awareness raising, and the cooperative principle. *ELT Journal* 64 (3), 293–301.

Murray, N. (2012) English as a lingua franca and the development of pragmatic competence. *ELT Journal* 66 (3), 318–326.

Nakamura, I. (2010) Formulation as evidence of understanding in teacher–student talk. *ELT Journal* 64 (2), 125–134.

Neuendorf, K.A. (2002) *The Content Analysis Guidebook*. Thousand Oaks, CA: SAGE.

Nguyen, M.T.T. (2011) Learning to communicate in a globalized world: To what extent do school textbooks facilitate the development of intercultural pragmatic competence? *RELC Journal* 42 (1), 17–30.

Niedzielski, N. and Preston, D.R. (2009) Folk pragmatics. In G. Senft, J.O. Ostman and J. Verschueren (eds) *Culture and Language Use* (pp. 146–155). Amsterdam: John Benjamins.

Nikula, T. (2002) Teacher talk reflecting pragmatic awareness. A look at EFL and content-based classroom settings. *Pragmatics* 12 (4), 447–467.

Nishiyama, K. (2000) *Doing Business with Japan: Successful Strategies for Intercultural Communication*. Honolulu, HI: University of Hawaii Press.

Norton, B. (2013) *Identity and Language Learning*. Bristol: Multilingual Matters.

Ochs, E. and Schieffelin, B.B. (1984) Language acquisition and socialization: Three developmental stories. In R. Shweder and R. LeVine (eds) *Culture Theory: Essays on Mind, Self and Emotion* (pp. 276–320). New York: Cambridge University Press.

O'Dowd, R. (2007) *Online Intercultural Exchange: An Introduction for Language Teachers*. Clevedon: Multilingual Matters.

Ogiermann, E. (2009) *On Apologizing in Negative and Positive Politeness Cultures*. Amsterdam: John Benjamins.

Ohta, A.S. (2000) Re-thinking interaction in SLA: Developmentally appropriate assistance in the zone of proximal development and the acquisition of L2 grammar. In J.P Lantolf (ed.) *Sociocultural Theory and Second Language Learning* (pp. 51–78). Oxford: Oxford University Press.

Olshtain, E. and Cohen, A. (1983) Apology: A speech-act set. In N. Wolfson and E. Judd (eds) *Sociolinguistics and Language Acquisition* (pp. 18–35). Rowley, MA: Newbury House.

Padilla Cruz, M. (2013) Understanding and overcoming pragmatic failure in intercultural communication: From focus on speakers to focus on hearers. *International Review of Applied Linguistics in Language Teaching* 51 (1), 23–54.

Padilla Cruz, M. (2015) Fostering EF/SL learners' meta-pragmatic awareness of complaints and their interactive effects. *Language Awareness* 24 (2), 123–137.

Pennycook, A. (2007) *Global Englishes and Transcultural Flows*. London: Routledge.

Phipps, A. and Gonzalez, M. (2004) *Modern Languages: Learning and Teaching in an Intercultural Field*. London: SAGE.

Piller, I. (2011) *Intercultural Communication: A Critical Introduction*. Edinburgh: Edinburgh University Press.

Pizziconi, B. (2009) Stereotyping communicative styles in and out of the language classroom: Japanese indirectness, ambiguity and vagueness. In R. Moron, M. Cruz, M. Amaya and M. Lopez (eds) *Pragmatics Applied to Language Teaching and Learning* (pp. 221–253). Cambridge: Cambridge Scholars.

Rathje, S. (2007) Intercultural competence: The status and future of a controversial concept. *Language and Intercultural Communication* 7 (4), 254–266.

Ren, W. and Han, Z. (2016) The representation of pragmatic knowledge in recent ELT textbooks. *ELT Journal* 70 (4), 424–434.

Risager, K. (2006) *Language and Culture: Global Flows and Local Complexity*. Clevedon: Multilingual Matters.

Risager, K. (2007) *Language and Culture Pedagogy: From a National to a Transnational Paradigm*. Clevedon: Multilingual Matters.

Roberts, C. (1998) Awareness in intercultural communication. *Language Awareness* 7 (2–3), 109–127.

Roberts, C., Byram, M., Barro, A., Jordan, S. and Street, B. (2001) *Language Learners as Ethnographers*. Clevedon: Multilingual Matters.

Rose, K.R. (2005) On the effects of instruction in second language pragmatics. *System* 33 (3), 385–399.

Safont Jordá, M.P. (2003) Metapragmatic awareness and pragmatic production of third language learners of English: A focus on request acts realizations. *International Journal of Bilingualism* 7 (1), 43–68.

Sarangi, S. (1994) Intercultural or not? Beyond celebration of cultural differences in mis-communication analysis. *Pragmatics* 4 (3), 409–427.

Savignon, S.J. (1990) Communicative language teaching: Definitions and directions. In J.E. Alatis (ed.) *Georgetown University Round Table on Language and Linguistics* (pp. 207–217). Washington, DC: Georgetown University Press.

Saville-Troike, M. (2003) Extending communicative concepts in the second language curriculum: A sociolinguistic perspective. In D.L. Lange and R.M. Paige (eds) *Culture as the Core: Perspectives on Culture in Second Language Learning* (pp. 3–17). Greenwich: Information Age.

Scarino, A. (2007) Words, slogans and meanings. *Babel* 42 (1), 4–11.

Scarino, A. (2009) Assessing intercultural capability in learning languages: Some issues and considerations. *Language Teaching* 42 (1), 67–80.

Scarino, A. and Liddicoat, A.J. (2016) Reconceptualising learning in transdisciplinary languages education. *L2 Journal* 8 (4), 20–35.

Schegloff, E. (1996) Issues of relevance for discourse analysis: Contingency in action, interaction, and co-participant structure. In E. Hovy and D. Scott (eds) *Computation and Conversational Discourse: Burning Issues – An Interdisciplinary Account* (pp. 3–38). Heidelberg: Springer.

Schmidt, R. (1990) The role of consciousness in second language learning. *Applied Linguistics* 11 (2), 129–158.

Schmidt, R. (1993) Consciousness, learning and interlanguage pragmatics. In G. Kasper and S. Blum-Kulka (eds) *Interlanguage Pragmatics* (pp. 21–42). New York and Oxford: Oxford University Press.

Schmidt, R. (1995) Consciousness and foreign language learning: A tutorial on the role of attention and awareness in learning. In R. Schmidt (ed.) *Attention and Awareness in Foreign Language Learning*. Technical Report No. 9 (pp. 1–63). Honolulu, HI: University of Hawaii, Second Language Teaching and Curriculum Center.

Schmidt, R. (2010) Attention, awareness, and individual differences in language learning. In W.M. Chan, S. Chi, K.M. Cin, J. Istanto, M. Nagami, J.W. Sew, T. Suthiwan and I. Walker (eds) *Proceedings of CLaSIC 2010, Singapore, 2–4 December* (pp. 721–734). Singapore: National University of Singapore, Centre for Language Studies.

Schneider, K.P. and Barron, A. (2008) Where pragmatics and dialectology meet: Introducing variational pragmatics. In K.P. Schneider and A. Barron (eds) *Variational Pragmatics* (pp. 1–32). Amsterdam: John Benjamins.

Scollon, R. and Wong-Scollon, S. (2001) *Intercultural Communication* (2nd edn). Oxford: Blackwell.

Seargeant, P. (2009) *The Idea of English in Japan: Ideology and the Evolution of a Global Language*. Bristol: Multilingual Matters.

Searle, J.R. (1969) *Speech Acts: An Essay in the Philosophy of Language*. Cambridge: Cambridge University Press.

Selinker, L. (1972) Interlanguage. *International Review of Applied Linguistics* 10, 209–231.

Sewell, A. (2013) English as a lingua franca: Ontology and ideology. *ELT Journal* 67 (1), 3–10.

Siegal, M. (1996) The role of learner subjectivity in second language sociolinguistic competence: Western women learning Japanese. *Applied Linguistics* 17 (3), 356–382.

Snow, D. (2015) English teaching, intercultural competence, and critical incident exercises. *Language and Intercultural Communication* 15 (2), 285–299.

Soars, J. and Soars, L. (2002) *New Headway: Pre-Intermediate*. Oxford: Oxford University Press.

Spencer-Oatey, H. (1993) Conceptions of social relations and pragmatics relations. *Journal of Pragmatics* 20 (1), 27–47.

Spencer-Oatey, H. (1996) Reconsidering power and distance. *Journal of Pragmatics* 26 (1), 1–24.

Spencer-Oatey, H. (2008) Face, (im)politeness and rapport. In H. Spencer-Oatey (ed.) *Culturally Speaking: Culture, Communication and Politeness Theory* (pp. 11–47). London: Bloomsbury.

Spencer-Oatey, H. (2010) Intercultural competence and pragmatics research: Examining the interface through studies of intercultural business discourse. In A. Trosborg (ed.) *Pragmatics across Languages and Cultures* (pp. 189–216). Berlin and New York: Mouton de Gruyter.

Spencer-Oatey, H. (2013) Critical incidents: A compilation of quotations for the intercultural field. *GlobalPAD Core Concepts*. Coventry: GlobalPAD Open House. See http://www2.warwick.ac.uk/fac/soc/al/globalpad/openhouse/interculturalskills/

Spencer-Oatey, H. and Franklin, P. (2009) *Intercultural Interaction: A Multidisciplinary Approach to Intercultural Communication*. Basingstoke: Palgrave Macmillan.

Spencer-Oatey, H. and Kádár, D. (2016) The basis of (im)politeness evaluations: Culture, the moral order and the East–West divide. *East-Asian Pragmatics* 1 (1), 73–106.

Strauss, C. and Quinn, N. (1997) *A Cognitive Theory of Cultural Meaning*. Cambridge: Cambridge University Press.

Swain, M. and Lapkin, S. (2000) Task-based second language learning: The uses of the first language. *Language Teaching Research* 4 (3), 251–274.

Sugimoto, N. (1997) A Japan-U.S. comparison of apology styles. *Communication Research* 24 (4), 349–369.

Sugimoto, N. (1998) 'Sorry we apologize so much': Linguistic factors affecting Japanese and U.S. American styles of apology. *Intercultural Communication Studies* 8 (1), 71–78.

Swain, M. (1995) Three functions of output in second language learning. In G. Cook and B. Seidlhofer (eds) *Principle and Practice in Applied Linguistics: Studies in Honor of H.G. Widdowson* (pp. 125–144). Oxford: Oxford University Press.

Swain, M. (2006) Languaging, agency and collaboration in advanced second language proficiency. In H. Byrnes (ed.) *Advanced Language Learning: The Contribution of Halliday and Vygotsky* (pp. 95–108). London: Continuum.

Swain, M. and Lapkin, S. (1995) Problems in output and the cognitive processes they generate: A step towards second language learning. *ELT Journal* 16 (3), 371–391.

Swain, M. and Lapkin, S. (2010) Task-based second language learning: The uses of the first language. *Language Teaching Research* 4 (3), 251–274.

Taguchi, N. (2015) Instructed pragmatics at a glance: Where instructional studies were, are, and should be going. *Language Teaching* 48 (1), 1–50.

Takahashi, S. (2005) Noticing in task performance and learning outcomes: A qualitative analysis of instructional effects in interlanguage pragmatics. *System* 33 (3), 437–461.

Takimoto, M. (2012) Metapragmatic discussion in interlanguage pragmatics. *Journal of Pragmatics* 44, 1240–1253.

Thomas, J. (1983) Cross-cultural pragmatic failure. *Applied Linguistics* 4 (2), 91–112.

Tusting, K., Crawshaw, R. and Callen, B. (2002) 'I know, 'cos I was there': How residence abroad students use personal experience to legitimate cultural generalizations. *Discourse and Society* 13 (5), 651–672.

Usó-Juan, E. and Martínez-Flor, A. (2008) Teaching intercultural communicative competence through the four skills. *Revista Alicantina de Estudios Ingleses* 21, 157–170.

van Compernolle, R.A. (2010) Towards a sociolinguistically responsive pedagogy: Teaching second person address forms in French. *Canadian Modern Language Review* 66 (3), 445–463.

van Compernolle, R.A. (2011) Developing second language sociopragmatic knowledge through concept-based instruction: A microgenetic case study. *Journal of Pragmatics* 43 (13), 3267–3283.

van Compernolle, R.A. (2014) *Sociocultural Theory and L2 Instructional Pragmatics*. Bristol: Multilingual Matters.

van Compernolle, R.A. and Kinginger, C. (2013) Promoting metapragmatic development through assessment in the zone of proximal development. *Language Teaching Research* 17 (3), 282–302.

van Compernolle, R.A. and Williams, L. (2012) Reconceptualizing sociolinguistic competence as mediated action: Identity, meaning-making, agency. *Modern Language Journal* 96 (2), 234–250.

van Ek, J.A. and Alexander, L.G. (1975) *Threshold Level English*. Oxford: Pergamon Press.

van Lier, L. (1996) *Interaction in the Language Curriculum: Awareness, Autonomy, and Authenticity*. Harlow: Longman.

van Lier, L. (1998) The relationship between consciousness, interaction and language learning. *Language Awareness* 7 (2–3), 128–145.

Varonis, E.M. and Gass, S. (1985) Non-native/Non-native conversations: A model for negotiation of meaning. *Applied Linguistics* 6 (1), 71–79.

Verschueren, J. (2004) Notes on the role of metapragmatic awareness in language use. In A. Jaworski, N. Coupland and D. Galasinski (eds) *Metalanguage: Social and Ideological Perspectives* (pp. 53–73). Berlin: Mouton de Gruyter.

Vygotsky, L.S. (1978) *Mind in Society: The Development of Higher Psychological Processes*. Cambridge, Cambridge, MA: Harvard University Press.

Wang, Y. and Rendle-Short, J. (2013) Making the 'invisible' visible: A conversation analytic approach to intercultural teaching and learning in the Chinese Mandarin language classroom. In F. Dervin and A.J. Liddicoat (eds) *Linguistics for Intercultural Education* (pp. 113–136). Amsterdam: John Benjamins.

Warner, C. (2009) Hey, you! The Germans! Using literary pragmatics to teach language as culture. *Die Unterrichtspraxis/Teaching German* 42 (2), 162–168.

Warner, C. (2011) Rethinking the role of language study in internationalizing higher education. *L2 Journal* 3 (1), 1–21.

Wells, G. (1993) Reevaluating the IRF sequence: A proposal for the articulation of theories of activity and discourse for the analysis of teaching and learning in the classroom. *Linguistics and Education* 5, 1–37.

Wetherell, M. and Potter, J. (1988) Discourse analysis and the identification of interpretive repertoires. In C. Antaki (ed.) *Analysing Everyday Explanation: A Casebook of Methods* (pp. 168–183). London: SAGE.

Wierzbicka, A. (1985) Different languages, different cultures, different speech acts: Polish vs. English. *Journal of Pragmatics* 9 (2–3), 145–178.

Wierzbicka, A. (2006) *English: Meaning and Culture*. New York: Oxford University Press.

Wilkins, D.A. (1976) *Notional Syllabuses*. London: Oxford University Press.

Wilson, D. and Sperber, D. (2004) Relevance theory. In L. Horn and G. Ward (eds) *Handbook of Pragmatics* (pp. 249–290). Oxford: Blackwell.

Wittgenstein, L. (1958) *Philosophical Investigations* (3rd edn). New York: Macmillan.

Wolfson, N. (1981) Compliments in cross-cultural perspective. *TESOL Quarterly* 15 (2), 117–124.

Yashima, T. (2009) International posture and the ideal L2 self in the Japanese EFL context. In Z. Dörnyei and E. Ushioda (eds) *Motivation, Language Identity and the L2 Self* (pp. 144–163). Bristol: Multilingual Matters.

Zotzmann, K. (2017) Research on intercultural communication: A critical realist perspective. In A.R. Díaz and M. Dasli (eds) *The Critical Turn in Language and Intercultural Communication Pedagogy* (pp. 75–90). New York: Routledge.

Index